MARTIN HEIDEGGER ON THE WAY

For my favorite
philosophical team

Richard Hull

Spring 1997

VIBS

Volume 38

a volume in
Werkmeister Studies
WS
Richard T. Hull, Editor

MARTIN HEIDEGGER ON THE WAY

By

W.H. Werkmeister

Edited by

Richard T. Hull

Amsterdam - Atlanta, GA 1996

Cover design by Chris Kok based on a photograph, © 1984 by Robert Ginsberg, of statuary by Gustav Vigeland in the Frogner Park, Oslo, Norway.

Werkmeister Studies logo from a drawing by Wilhelm Werkmeister on the cover of his book of poetry, *Vorfrühling: Lieder eines Siebzehnjährigen*, published in 1919.

∞ The paper on which this book is printed meets the requirements of "ISO 9706:1994, Information and documentation - Paper for documents - Requirements for permanence".

ISBN: 90-5183-963-4 (bound)
ISBN: 90-5183-993-6 (paper)

Printed in The Netherlands

WERKMEISTER STUDIES

Contents

Editorial Foreword

The distinguished philosopher who signed his works W. H. Werkmeister was born Wilhelm Heinrich Gustav Werkmeister in 1901 in Germany. Moving to the United States in 1924, he was to become William Henry Werkmeister. To his colleagues and friends, he was Werkie.

Werkmeister was a towering figure on the American philosophical scene and an international figure of considerable note. He was a leader in the value inquiry movement. He played historical roles in the philosophy programs at the University of Nebraska, the University of Southern California, and Florida State University. He served as President of the American Philosophical Association, Pacific Division, and of the American Society for Value Inquiry. His publishing career, documented in the career bibliography of this volume, extended seventy-four years. In addition to his writings in English and German, his work has been published in Italian, Portuguese, Japanese, and Turkish. He was the editor of the unusual humanistic journal *The Personalist*, for which he reviewed 350 books.

A Werkmeister Chair has been established at the Florida State University, which also houses the Werkmeister Library. Within the Value Inquiry Book Series, Richard T. Hull, Werkmeister's literary executor, has designed the special series, Werkmeister Studies, to make available further works by the master, works by others dealing with his contributions, and works in value inquiry developed in conjunction with the programs of the Werkmeister Chair.

This book inaugurates the special series by offering Hull's definitive edition of Werkmeister's posthumous book on Martin Heidegger. It is a remarkably close study of major themes—and major shifts—in the thought of Heidegger. With a keen appreciation of the power and flexibility of the German language, Werkmeister works his way through the forest of Heidegger's daunting terminology. Werkmeister assesses the question of Heidegger and Nazism and reports on his meeting with the controversial thinker. The book is written with scholarly depth, independence of judgment, and clarity of style.

In the true spirit of collegiality, E. F. Kaelin, Werkmeister's long-time colleague in Florida, has contributed a substantial Guest Foreword that gives further help to the reader in dealing with Heideggerian language and Heideggerian controversy. Eva Hauel Cadwallader, a Hartmann scholar who closely followed Werkmeister's later work, has written a Guest Preface, characterizing Werkmeister's and Kaelin's very different readings of Heidegger as antinomy-like in character. Gwen A. Burda has joined Hull in compiling the astonishing record of

Werkmeister's publishing career as well as the useful list of works on Werkmeister, and in editing the manuscript into the work you now hold. This volume is thus both a record of Werkmeister's decades of reflection on Heidegger's thought and of the warm esteem in which he was held by his many friends.

Robert Ginsberg
Executive Editor

Editor's Preface

William Henry Werkmeister served as President of the American Society for Value Inquiry in 1974-1975. When Robert Ginsberg asked me to edit the Presidential Addresses of that society, I asked Werkie, as well as the other living past presidents, to prepare an autobiographical sketch that said something of how the presidency of that society and the interests that presidency of such a society bespoke were reflected in his intellectual life. He kindly produced a charming self-disclosure to which the reader is referred for additional details. In reviewing his comments and identifying the year of publication of the several books he mentioned having written, I noted a reference to his visit with Heidegger in the latter's home in Freiburg during the year 1936-1937 and to a work in which Werkmeister addressed the question of Heidegger's supposed sympathies with the Nazis: "See my *Martin Heidegger on the Way*." Unable to find any reference to it elsewhere, I planned in January of 1994 to visit him and ask about the work.

When I reached Tallahassee I learned quite by accident that Werkie had passed away the previous November. I called the Philosophy Department to see what I could learn of the manuscript and was put in touch with E. F. Kaelin. Kaelin suggested that I might want to visit Werkie's widow, Dr. Lucyle Thomas Werkmeister, and he arranged for my visit with her.

In the conversations that ensued, I learned that Werkie had been working on the Heidegger manuscript for some years but that he had decided not to publish it, because, in the discouragement of ill health and the waning days of his life, he had come to think it contained nothing new, and because interest in Heidegger was waning. I thought otherwise after reading the manuscript and talking with Kaelin and Lucyle Werkmeister, and I was able to interest the Value Inquiry Book Series in publishing the work posthumously.

In the following months, the wonderful legacy that the Werkmeisters had decided to leave to Florida State University came to light. Lucyle Werkmeister had asked me to be the executor of Werkie's literary estate, and, in thinking about how to make the Werkmeister Chair attractive to prominent scholars in value inquiry, the idea was born to dedicate a special series of VIBS to the chair and to further publications from Werkmeister's estate. Negotiations proceeded rapidly, and I was privileged to announce the creation of Werkmeister Studies at the public celebration of the creation of the Werkmeister Chair, on 9 August 1994, in Tallahassee.

I am not a Heidegger scholar, nor a student of Werkmeister in any of the usual senses of the term. So, readers might suspect arrogance, if not impropriety, in my being the editor of this work. To the extent that my naïveté has led to errors in the work, *mea culpa*. But I feel deeply privileged in being entrusted with the task of editing this book, and I have been moved to do so by the words of Werkmeister himself.

One of Werkmeister's essays that has become a favorite of mine is his "History and Human Destiny," published in 1957 in *The Personalist*. In it he sets out to answer a set of interrelated questions about the nature of human history and its sense and meaning. Being an empiricist, he quickly proceeds to questions about individual human beings and their capacities.

> The human is capable of pursuing and achieving ends whose realization he regards as desirable or as worthy of his efforts. He is a being, in other words, who not merely suffers and passively endures the events of his life as they occur, but whose desires, inclinations, and deliberate actions transcend any given moment, and who, in a measure at least, is actively engaged in determining and directing the course of his life and in pursuing goals which he projects into the future. (119)

The essay goes on to explore the "brute factualities of human existence":

> for the truth is that the harsh realities of this world tend to distort, to disrupt, and pervert our life-plans, and that often, all too often, they prevent us from realizing our goals; they lead to frustration. (120)

My sense was that through a remarkable series of coincidences and decisions, I had an opportunity to assist in the realization of a goal which Werkmeister had set but which the "brute factualities" of his human existence threatened to frustrate. Actively over a span of some 36 years (the period marked by the first and last publications listed by Kaelin in his Guest Foreword, below) Werkmeister had read, thought, and written about the issues of this book. For an additional 17 years, those musings had lain dormant, only to spring to active insistence in his ninetieth year. Despite failing health, he struggled to lay out this vision of Heidegger's Way, to articulate his conception and evidence of the actual order of Heidegger's work, and to come to a resolution of the question of Heidegger and German National Socialism.

Thus, with much the sense of a private who grabs the standard from the hand of a fallen superior on the battlefield, I have taken up the task of completing this last of William Henry Werkmeister's goals that, thanks to the willingness of the Editor and Publisher of the Value Inquiry Book Series, has been projected into the future beyond the limits set by the harsh realities of this world. The photo on the back cover of this book was selected to express the sense of triumph over such harsh realities occasioned by the posthumous publication of this, Werkmeister's last project.

Richard T. Hull
State University of New York at Buffalo
Amherst, New York

Acknowledgements

Bringing out a work posthumously, especially when the manuscript was not fully finished before the passing of its author, is a venture that requires the assistance of many who will ultimately not bear the responsibility for the final product. I am indebted to many for their aid in this project, as well as for the trust they have placed in me to shepherd it to completion.

First, I express my appreciation to Dr. Lucyle T. Werkmeister for her friendship, her trust, and her cooperation. Without them all, nothing like the final production here in the reader's hands could have been achieved. Her good sense, her unstinting loyalty to her husband, her friendship for E. F. Kaelin, her generosity to the Florida State University in establishing the William H. and Lucyle T. Werkmeister Eminent Scholar Chair in Philosophy, and her willingness to permit my examination of Werkmeister's papers and library were all essential to bringing this work, which he had decided not to publish, into the hands of scholars.

Second, an enormous expression of gratitude should be extended to the publisher, Editions Rodopi, and to the Executive Editor of the Value Inquiry Book Series (VIBS), Robert Ginsberg, for supporting the idea of a series dedicated to promulgating the unpublished and inaccessible work of Werkmeister and the scholarly production of occupants of the Werkmeister Chair. The commitment of the publisher to Werkmeister Studies as a special series in VIBS will help insure that the contributions of Werkmeister remain actively before the profession.

Third, I must express my admiration of and appreciation for the editorial skills of Gwen A. Burda. Her efforts at rendering Werkmeister's typescript into the word-processing language in which the final camera-ready copy was prepared and her careful checking of each of his citations were exceeded only by her painstaking efforts at assisting the reconstruction of Werkmeister's remarkable bibliography, for much of which she had to search painstakingly the pages of journals to which he was known or suspected to have contributed book reviews. Her work built upon the earlier work of Wallace Nethery and Larry Lustig, published in the 1981 *Festschrift, Man and Value: Essays in Honor of William H. Werkmeister,* edited by the Editorial Committee, Department of Philosophy, Florida State University, E. F. Kaelin, chairman, in honor of Werkmeister. Because this volume draws upon Werkmeister's published reviews of works by and about Heidegger, it seemed appropriate to supplement that earlier bibliography with a listing of his reviews and subsequent works, and that project grew into one with a life of its own.

Fourth, the fine scholarship shown by E. F. Kaelin, friend and colleague to

Werkmeister, in his Guest Foreword to the present volume illustrates his high standards, his intimate knowledge of the thought of Heidegger and Werkmeister, and his own independence of opinion about the matters addressed by this work. He has helped me avoid some embarrassing public errors, and he has shown unflagging support for this at times daunting project. I owe him a great debt for his efforts.

Fifth, a sincere and heartfelt appreciation to the other members of the Philosophy Department and of the Administration at the Florida State University, especially the Chair of the Department, Russell Dancy, and his wife Margaret Dancy, President Talbot D'Alamberte, and Vice President Robert Johnson, all of whom have shown me great courtesy and hospitality while providing the field of value inquiry great leadership in helping to establish the Werkmeister Chair and Library.

Many other individuals have contributed to this project in ways large and small. Just two others shall receive public acknowledgement: Eva Hauel Cadwallader of Westminster College, New Wilmington, Pennsylvania, has been instrumental in this project in many ways. From the interest in Nicolai Hartmann, expressed in her *Searchlight on Values: Nicolai Hartmann's Twentieth-Century Value Platonism* (1984), which she shared with Werkmeister, a friendship developed that, in turn, involved her in the work of the American Society for Value Inquiry. She involved me in that society and provided me with my introduction to Werkmeister. I found her insight into the underlying dispute between Werkmeister and Kaelin on whether Heidegger is an existentialist penetrating, and invited her to articulate it in the form of a Guest Preface. And Kah Kyung Cho, my colleague for many years and a noted Heidegger scholar in his own right, kindly read the proofs of this book as well and contributed invaluable suggestions, improvements, and insights. To them both I owe an enormous debt for the good qualities of this finished work; for the remaining flaws I must remain responsible.

The photograph on the back cover of this book was taken at the time of conferral of an Honorary Degree on Werkmeister in April 1978. It appears here courtesy of the Florida State University News Bureau.

Camera-ready copy was prepared on an IBM PS/Value Point 486DX computer and a Texas Instruments Microlaser Pro 600 printer provided by the generous support of the Office of the Dean of Social Sciences, State University of New York at Buffalo. Final editing was completed while I served as Visiting Scholar during a sabbatical leave at the Buffalo General Hospital in Buffalo, New York; to that fine organization I offer my appreciation for its support.

Guest Preface

1. Why This Book?

We pay a dear price for letting Heidegger's abstruse style mislead us either about what he was trying to do or what he actually accomplished. That price is underestimating the value of what has been regarded by many as one of the most important achievements in twentieth-century philosophy. Clearly W. H. Werkmeister must have so regarded Heidegger's work. Why else would he, in the very last year of his life, have devoted priceless days to his manuscript *Martin Heidegger on the Way?*

2. Heidegger's "Revolution"

Heidegger, taking a strong hint from Søren Kierkegaard (whom he never adequately acknowledged), and following the regrettably convoluted methodology of his teacher Husserl, did nothing less than redefine the philosophical meaning of "existence" as *human* existence. In so doing, he set the tone for Existentialism, the single-most important movement of the twentieth century in continental European philosophy. The Anglo-American "linguistic revolution" is usually seen by its practitioners as drastically different from, if not downright opposed to, the existentialist one. But from a broader historical perspective, these may actually express concurrence in complementary ways. Both constitute "revolutions in ontology" which relativize the philosophical enterprise to *human* ways of being.

The "linguistic mode" does this by relativizing ontology (or metaphysics) to human language(s). The "existentialist mode" (as it is rightly called) relativizes ontology to human feelings, moods, and attitudes. Their common stem is an emphatic agreement that Kant's second "Copernican revolution" is irreversible. Henceforth there can be no return to the carefree days of all those metaphysicians who from the pre-Socratics to Kant's pre-critical philosophy thought they could tell us what Being (or existence) *objectively is.* The twentieth-century majority agreement seems to be that reality as it really is in itself, apart from being experienced or described by us, is indeed unknowable, if it exists at all.

We must not allow Heidegger's failure to answer his question, "What is Being in general?" to confuse us. Although I believe that this ultimately confused *him.* He had already given his own lengthy and profound answer to that in his *Daseinanalytik* but did not realize this because—misled by his version of the

Husserlian program—he was never able to admit that he had in fact identified *Being* with *Being for us* from the very start. At times he seems to acknowledge this: for he treats *Dasein,* after all, as *human* being. However, I believe that he was misled by the fact that Husserl had always insisted that his own enterprise was an "objective" one, one that did not fall into "the trap of psychologizing," and one that was certainly not a form of *subjectivism.* Since, however, "a text belongs to its readers,"[1] we must judge both Husserl's and Heidegger's works in these respects by our own lights.

What was Heidegger doing when he asked about "the meaning of Being"?

3. Heidegger's Contributions

Heidegger thought that the Western world needed a *philosophical* account of Being, in addition to the scientific one permeating the twentieth century. Considering himself conversant enough in mathematics and physics to discuss the nature of time with Einstein, Heidegger believed that what was missing from the scientific account was the human dimension. He thought that because of this absent "spiritual" perspective, most people today feel "lost" in their world. (It is important not to confuse the term "spiritual" [*geistlich*] as Heidegger used it with either "moral" or "religious." He went out of his way to deny such connotations.)

Heidegger thus offered his "ontological" (philosophical) account of "Being" as opposed to the "ontic" or "factical" one posed by science and the unthinking ordinary mentality stemming from it in a technological era. He saw the "ontological" viewpoint as necessary for the possibility of living a genuinely *human life* as opposed to the mere biological and physical existence of a sapient humanoid among a world of things. Within this analysis of *human* existence (*Daseinanalytik*) Heidegger laid out in fascinating detail the possibilities for what he called "authentic" versus "inauthentic" existence. Here it was his genius to expand vastly some of Kierkegaard's major insights regarding *Angst* and the strong tendency to deny the inescapable reality of one's eventual death. Heidegger took what for Kierkegaard was deeply embedded in a nineteenth-century Christian context and transformed and elaborated it into the secular context of the twentieth century. The result included an exposition on the permutations of meaninglessness which contemporary Western people experience. This aspect of *Being and Time* can be breathtaking once the reader is able to sift through Heidegger's off-putting "hermeneutical" apparatus and vocabulary.

An equally powerful element in Heidegger's analysis of *human* being derives from Henri Bergson (although acknowledging his sources was not one of

Heidegger's strong suits). From Bergson, Heidegger learned that there is a fundamental ontological difference between scientific time and lived human time. Heidegger realized that most people live inauthentically because the quality of the moments making up their lives is not infused with an awareness of their "being-towards-death." Thus they lead empty lives frittered away in the meaningless pursuit of that "everydayness" that is dictated by the crowd. Killing time with "idle chatter" and the general refusal to see themselves as beings who can *choose* their lives are only two examples of what Karen Horney was later so aptly to call the "shallow living" of most people.[2] People refuse their own freedom and humanity in this way because they participate in the inauthenticity of their death-denying society. Heidegger is at his best, in my view, when he thus blends insights from Kierkegaard and Bergson into an original perspective on the spiritual bankruptcy of twentieth-century Western existence. *This* is his permanent contribution to philosophy. Whether it should be called "ontology," "phenomenology," or "existentialism" remains to be seen.

It is regrettable that Heidegger's penetrating observations about the meaning of *human being* (existence) are hidden behind the almost impenetrable thicket of words, arcane terminology, labyrinthine methodology, and unfulfilled expectations which make up *Being and Time.* The fact that his latter writings are also abstruse, although in somewhat different ways, is no help. Nor is the still steaming controversy over Heidegger's involvement with the Nazis and the extent to which this is relevant to history's assessment of his work. I think that all these factors, but especially the two problems to be discussed below, must have entered into Werkie's long delay in finishing *Martin Heidegger on the Way.* Only Heidegger's actual achievement despite these factors could account for the fact that Werkie chose the last days of his life to bring it to completion.

4. Was Heidegger an Existentialist?

The present manuscript, and E. F. Kaelin's "Guest Foreword," force us to address the question: Was Heidegger an existentialist? He himself adamantly rejected the label, insisting that he was an ontologist and not one of that ilk called "existentialist" (by then associated with Sartre). Werkmeister in *Martin Heidegger on the Way* defends this assessment by Heidegger of his own place in the history of philosophy. Kaelin, on the other hand, writes that, "according to one of the best of these readers [Thomas Langan][3], Heidegger produced an 'existential phenomenology' in writing *Being and Time*."[4] The opposition between Kaelin and Werkie on this point produces our first philosophical problem.

5. Does Heidegger's Involvement with National Socialism Discredit His Philosophy?

The issue here does *not* concern whether, or to what extent, Heidegger was a Nazi. The answer to that is depressingly clear to anyone who has open-mindedly studied the history and literature. Kaelin's comments on this are entirely apt. The problem for philosophers concerns the question whether we should base our final evaluation of Heidegger's philosophy on its author's political thought and actions. A troublingly convincing case can be made for either side of this argument. We thus find ourselves with two problems which are reminiscent of an ancient rabbi story.

> A rabbi was once consulted by two parties to a dispute. The first man presented his case, and the rabbi, nodding gravely, said, "You're right." The second man presented *his* case, which was in complete opposition to the first man's. Again the rabbi nodded gravely, saying "You're right." An exasperated observer then said to the rabbi, "But they both can't be right." The Rabbi answered, more gravely than ever, "You're RIGHT."

Do we find ourselves in the position of this rabbi with respect to our two Heidegger questions? To consider this, let us first reflect on the topics of ambiguity, gestalt shifts, and Kant's treatment of antinomies.

6. Ambiguity, Gestalt Shifts, and Antinomies

Spy and counterspy war movies are full of intriguing ambiguities and gestalt shifts. At first we think we know who our enemies and allies are. But as the story unfolds it is harder and harder to be sure. Friends turn out to be traitors, and enemies are suddenly on our side. The more shifts, the more fascinating the story. There is a difference, though, between such dramas and the ambiguities we are considering here. In most counter-espionage stories there is a final resolution of the plot, and we end with the satisfaction of knowing who was who and what was what. The difference in the Heidegger case is that we may be dealing with some genuine antinomies, concerning which—despite our most earnest efforts—it would be presumptuous to insist that we have achieved an indisputable resolution.

Nicolai Hartmann—Heidegger's contemporary on whose philosophy Werkie also wrote[5]—believed that some antinomies, especially those concerning value, are inherently irresolvable. Only these, he said, are genuine antinomies; "antinomies which can be resolved are not genuine."[6] We must examine the Heideggerian antinomies to see whether they are ultimately irresolvable because, as Hartmann believed regarding certain of our deepest value oppositions, the values themselves conflict. Or can they be resolved by following a hint from Kant?

7. Kant's Antinomies

Kant used two different approaches to resolving the antinomies of the transcendental dialectic in *The Critique of Pure Reason.* He said that in the case of the first two ("the mathematical"), both empiricists and rationalists were right in denying the dogmatic assertions of their opponents, but wrong in trying to prove their own counter-claims. In short, the theses of both parties to the dispute were false. In the case of the other two antinomies ("the dynamical"), however, Kant argued that the thesis of each might be true as soon as you made a critical distinction, that between "satisfying" the Understanding as regards the phenomena and Reason as regards the noumena.[7]

8. Existentialism Antinomy Outlined: Both Theses Are False

The resolution of our first Heideggerian antinomy will follow Kant's mathematical model. Each claim is true in what it denies but false in what it asserts.

Thesis: Heidegger was an existentialist, not a metaphysician.

The thesis is false. The thesis does contain some truth insofar as it agrees with Kaelin who rejects Heidegger's own insistence that he is not an "existentialist." But it need not follow from this that Heidegger was not also a metaphysician ("meditative thinker"). Thus, although the thesis is true when we examine the most important characteristics of "existentialism," it goes too far in claiming that Heidegger was an existentialist *only*, that is, an existentialist as distinct from a metaphysician. The thesis is therefore ultimately false.

Antithesis: Heidegger was a metaphysician, not an existentialist.

The antithesis is false. It is true insofar as Werkmeister is right in endorsing Heidegger's insistence that he was not an existentialist—given Heidegger's own understanding of the term. But the antithesis goes too far in claiming that Heidegger was not a part of the (secular) existentialist movement; he was perhaps its single most important founder. The thesis is thus ultimately false.

9. Nazism Antinomy Outlined: Both Theses Are True

Thesis: Heidegger was a Nazi, and this discredits his philosophy.

The thesis is true. A philosopher who teaches us about "the call of conscience to authenticity" and then commits such blatantly inauthentic acts as Heidegger's involvement with Nazism cancels out the validity of his writing by pragmatic inconsistency—incongruity of word and deed.

Antithesis: Heidegger was a Nazi, but this is irrelevant to the evaluation of his philosophy.

The antithesis is true. To evaluate Heidegger's work on the basis of his life is to commit "the genetic fallacy."

10. Existentialism Antinomy Discussed

Thesis discussed: Heidegger was an existentialist. The thesis is false. Support for the view that Heidegger should not be regarded as an existentialist consists of three main arguments. First, as is well known, Heidegger himself vehemently rejected that label. Second, Werkie endorsed Heidegger's disposition in this regard:

> When I visited Heidegger in 1937, knowing that Jean-Paul Sartre had been his student, I asked Heidegger about his relation to existentialism. His reply was an emphatic "My God, that I have never intended."[8]

We can only speculate on the full implications of Heidegger's rejection of the appellation "existentialist" insofar as it had become associated with Sartre, who was, among other things, a leftist activist. Be that as it may, as Kaelin points out, Heidegger did not want to be known as "the philosopher of nothingness" or as "the champion of meaninglessness."[9] Heidegger's indignation here can be understood if the term "existentialist" was taken by him to mean "nihilist" in the usual, purely destructive sense of the term. But, as Kaelin makes clear, even the author of *Sein und Zeit* would have been understandably angered at this term if hurled by critics in their failure to understand the *context* of his discussion of nothingness and meaninglessness and his *constructive purpose* in doing so.

The first two arguments against regarding Heidegger as an existentialist are historical and personal. The third is philosophically far more important. It involves identifying "the real" Heidegger as "Heidegger II" (Heidegger the meditative thinker) as opposed to "Heidegger I" (Heidegger "the existential phenomenologist"). This is Werkie's main philosophical argument. As Kaelin points out in the present Guest Foreword, Werkie thinks Heidegger should not be categorized as an existentialist because he has metamorphosed from "the fundamental ontologist" in *Being and Time* to "metaphysician" in later works.[10]

In order for Werkie to maintain that Heidegger should not be classified as an existentialist it appears that he might think that being an existentialist is fundamentally incompatible with being a metaphysician (meditative thinker). Whether or not even Heidegger I was an existentialist, in Werkie's view Heidegger II certainly was not. Heidegger II seems to be Werkie's "real Heidegger," a thinker who is an onto-theological believer in truth as *alethia*, in beauty as a form of truth, in language (rather than time) as the ultimate grounding of human Being, and in poetry not only as "original speech" (*Ursprache*) but as the supporting ground of history.[11, 12, 13] Heidegger II is so much further away from being a nihilist than Heidegger I that calling the latter "an existentialist"—if that is taken to imply nihilism in the popular sense—is ludicrous.

Since these three arguments lead plausibly to the conclusion that Heidegger was NOT an existentialist, the thesis has been shown false.

Antithesis discussed: Heidegger was not an existentialist. The antithesis is false, for it flies in the face of most informed opinion. For example, Thomas Langan writes, "Existentialist? Yes, but he develops a conception of existence that bursts through the bonds of what is often thought of in these terms."[14] Testimonials are not, however, arguments. We shall examine some of the most important arguments which can be made in support of the thesis. Each of these refers to what is generally regarded as a salient feature (if not defining characteristic) of existentialism and claims that Heidegger's work, at least as found in his magnum opus, *Sein und Zeit*, exhibits that feature. We shall then argue that Heidegger's *Being and Time* bears so many outstanding features associated with the "family resemblances" which other existentialists exhibit, that not regarding Heidegger as an existentialist is odd.

These features include: subjectivity; the correlativity of self and world; temporality; consciousness; freedom; the self as awareness of possibilities and projects; facticity; meaninglessness; focus on moods and feelings such as forlornness, loneliness, despair, alienation, angst, dread, guilt; the call of conscience to authenticity; responsibility for endowing your personal world with meaning and values; and resoluteness. True, Heidegger had little to say about that concept, "absurdity," which is popularly associated with existentialism as made famous by Sartre and Camus. But can we not earnestly wonder whether Sartre and Camus could have or would have written what they did without Heidegger's first having shown them the way? The reader is challenged to subtract from Sartre's *Being and Nothingness*, whose very title echoes *Being and Time*, all that was derived from the latter and see how much is left. No, to refuse to categorize Heidegger as an existentialist, probably as Ur-existentialist, is nothing less than—well, absurd. The antithesis has been shown false.

11. Resolution of the Existentialism Antinomy

An antinomy, or paradox, may be defined as consisting of a pair of theses, one of which is the direct denial of the other, such that each is the conclusion of an equally compelling argument. This is exactly what we seem to have here. However, if the thesis and antithesis are contraries rather than contradictories, both may be false. Thus this antinomy has been resolved by noticing that, although the assertion may be true in what it denies, it is false in what it *claims*. The crucial distinction making this possible is that between Heidegger I, who is indeed an existentialist, and Heidegger II, who, in having become a meditative thinker (metaphysician), is no longer such.

Let us now take a closer look at the second Heideggerian antinomy. Since no such tidy resolution will be possible there, it shall have to be dealt with in a different manner.

12. Nazism Antinomy Discussed

To repeat, the issue here is not whether or not Heidegger was a Nazi. I agree with Kaelin's remarks on this subject, and I can only try to understand why Werkie apparently felt moved to excuse Heidegger. Perhaps it was simply a fellow-feeling for a countryman of his own cohort. It is hard to imagine Werkie, the author of that marvelous logic text[15] on which I cut my logician's baby teeth, and from whom forty years of textbook writers have "borrowed," could have overlooked the simple point of logic to be discussed below.

Thesis discussed: Heidegger was a Nazi, and this discredits his philosophy. The thesis argues that Heidegger's actions invalidate his philosophy. Its advocates might include a long line of heroes who had the courage of their convictions, from Socrates to the present. Their final standard of evaluation would always be pragmatic consistency.

Existentialism, the argument goes, is not just any philosophy, and Heidegger is not just any philosopher. Existentialism is the movement which sought to bring about a *revolution* in Western philosophy. This revolution seeks to heal the disastrous split between mind and body introduced by Descartes, which led to a further split between thought and action, especially as this culminated in the Pyrrhonian skepticism of Hume. Heidegger is not just one swallow (that does not a summer make), but is rather like the dove sighted by Noah: unique, the harbinger of a whole new promising era. A would-be philosophy of authenticity collapses from within when inauthenticity is uncovered in its harbinger's personal and historical life. (An interesting case of the personal being political.) The argument leading to the thesis thus seems sound.

Antithesis discussed: Heidegger was a Nazi, but this is irrelevant to an evaluation of his philosophy. The argument that you commit the genetic fallacy (or at least a circumstantial ad hominem) in condemning Heidegger's work on the basis of his actions carries great force. After all, should Bertrand Russell's philanderings and marital history, Nietzsche's final madness, Schopenhauer's extreme misogyny, or innumerable other examples of human failings keep us from appreciating the philosophical works of their authors? The antithesis argues that they should not. For an intellectual product should always be evaluated on its own merits, never on the basis of its "originator," that is, its producer's character, actions, or life. The argument leading to the antithesis thus also seems sound.

Do we then have a genuine antinomy? Or is there, as before, a crucial distinction which resolves the issue? Now the suggestion might be made that what has been overlooked here is the difference between evaluating the man and his work. Thus the thesis and antithesis might both be true, with the former focussing on the man and the latter on his work. But unfortunately for this suggestion, this distinction has already been appealed to in the antithesis. Ignoring that distinction is the logical foundation of the genetic fallacy. Yet, it is still open to those siding with the thesis that, although in general we should not commit "the genetic fallacy," we must not here commit "the fallacy of accident" either. That fallacy consists of applying a rule which is a perfectly good rule "on the whole and for the most part" (as Aristotle would have said) to a particular case, where, because of unusual or even unique circumstances it should not be applied. Now it can be argued that the Heidegger case is just such a case. Philosophical works should in general be assessed on the basis of their own merits, not their author's actions. But in the case of a philosopher who makes authenticity one of his central themes, a gross inconsistency between that author's deeds and words is relevant to the evaluation of his work.

Must we not now admit that with this twist in the dialectic there can be no end to this discussion? We find only an endless loop of potential gestalt shifts—not unlike a Möbius strip. And this is because, in the end (which has no end), "the text belongs to the readers."

13. Peering into the Future

When the history of Western philosophy is written in the twenty-second century what will it say about Heidegger? Perhaps this is what Werkie was wondering when he decided to spend his last days completing *Martin Heidegger on the Way*.

My guess is he would have predicted that Heidegger's involvement with Nazism will be disposed of in a few sentences, or a footnote at most. The article might mention that in the twentieth century some thought the Nazi issue discredited Heidegger's philosophy, but that many more thought it irrelevant. It might even say that Heidegger had probably distinguished between the horrific political realities of National Socialism and some sort of *ideal* ideology he thought this expressed. That would leave each reader to decide to what extent Heidegger's attitudes and actions were naive, culpable, or "inauthentic."

I think that Werkie would have expected the question as to whether there were "two Heideggers" to have been settled long ago. Heidegger I was obviously the person who is widely regarded as the most important figure in the twentieth-century movement called "Existentialism." Although Heidegger himself had strongly rejected this appellation, the label seems accurate at least with respect to the "existential phenomenology" found in his magnum opus, *Being and Time*. Heidegger II was the man whose thinking is expressed in the essays after *Being and Time*, and who apparently changed his mind about the ultimate grounding of *human existence* from *time* to *language*. Thus Heidegger I was "the existentialist" without whose most famous work Sartre's *Being and Nothingness* could never have been written; and Heidegger II was "the meditative thinker" who wrote so abstrusely about "Being in General," the nature of truth as *aletheia*, and "Why is there something rather than nothing?"

Martin Heidegger on the Way implicitly raises the question: Which of these "Heideggers" is historically more important? Werkie's answer to this central question constitutes much of his special contribution to the Heidegger literature.

Werkie's unique contribution also consists in that illuminating assessment found in Chapter Three, which is from an ontologist's viewpoint the most valuable chapter in the book. Here Werkie provides a critique of *Being and Time* from an original standpoint, one which should retain its significance when the history of twentieth-century European philosophy is written two hundred years from now. Werkie, whose lifetime so nearly coincided with our century, was perhaps in an especially privileged position to write this critique. Having during his long career demonstrated both mastery of and sympathy for German philosophy, together with a decidedly empirical way of thinking more consonant with American modes of thought, he applies it *all* to his superlative critique of *Sein und Zeit*.

Who else but Werkie could have taken Heidegger to task for:

(1) having neglected the analysis of space along with time;

(2) having dodged scores upon scores of the most important ontological issues;

(3) having refused to admit that his ontology was, after all, a pragmatic one—as Peirce, James, or Dewey could have told him;

(4) having failed to acknowledge that his ontology was at its very core a process ontology, as any discerning student of Whitehead can tell;

(5) having deplorably failed to clarify "the value problem . . . essential to *Dasein*'s decision in resolving the problem of its own-most-possibility-to-be";[16]

(6) perhaps most significantly of all, having ignored the insights of his contemporary, Nicolai Hartmann, whose ontology supplies exactly the kind of analysis concerning both fact and value that Heidegger so blatantly neglected?

In the course of all this, Werkie continually clarifies not only what Heidegger actually said (or in some cases, what he meant to say) but also the many deeper and more far-reaching implications of those texts.

14. Martin Heidegger and Nicolai Hartmann

The last book Werkie published during his lifetime was *Nicolai Hartmann's New Ontology*. Werkie told me when we first met in 1968 that he was planning this book, the completion of which he postponed for twenty years. Upon learning that I was in the process of writing *Searchlight on Values: Nicolai Hartmann's Twentieth-Century Value Platonism*, which is a study of Hartmann's *Ethics*, Werkie told me that this delighted him. For it would enable him to omit that aspect of Hartmann's work from his own projected book.[17] About 1990 I asked him why he thought Nicolai Hartmann, who had so much to offer in ethics and ethical theory, is virtually unknown today. He answered that it was undoubtedly because of Heidegger; the sensation that Heidegger caused had completely eclipsed Hartmann. Werkie expressed deep regret at that.

It seems clear that Werkie considered Martin Heidegger and Nicolai Hartmann the two most important metaphysicians of twentieth-century continental philosophy. He had given some thought to comparing and contrasting them. They shared a common starting point from Husserl early in their careers. The two had turned away from classical metaphysics in the Hegelian mode, and both had turned their backs on "the old ontology." Werkie writes that what is wrong with the "old ontology" in Hartmann's case is that it "becomes essentially teleological and deductive."[18] Hartmann also disliked "the Kantian subjectivism" of his teachers Hermann Cohen and Paul Natorp and moved away from it by claiming a position "this side of idealism and realism."[19] Heidegger also had thought of his own work as non-subjectivist and "non-psychologistic." This seems inexplicable except in terms of its historical origin in Husserl's assessment of his own position (which assessment is challenged by critics).

Heidegger intended *Sein und Zeit* to be an introduction to *ontology*, but Werkie writes that "although Heidegger thus turns away from Husserl's phenomenological reductionism, the method of ontological investigation which he means to employ is still 'a phenomenological construction' and is not concerned with the manifold forms of the *Seienden* but with the abstract understanding of Being(30)."[20]

Werkie's preference for Hartmann over Heidegger thus gradually emerges. For one thing, he writes that Hartmann "took the first real step beyond Hegel" in his new ontology.[21] Then, too, Werkie clearly prefers Hartmann to Heidegger because Hartmann was more empirical than Heidegger; Hartmann did the hard work of articulating the specific details of the numerous "strata" of Being which Heidegger neglected. But, most importantly, Werkie observes that Hartmann rejected phenomenology because ". . . it provides no criterion for distinguishing between appearance and reality."[22]

Might it not be an interesting challenge, after a careful reading of Werkie's last two books in close succession, to consider first, whether Werkie thought Heidegger or Hartmann had produced the more enduring philosophy, and then, more importantly, which man's work is *in fact* the more significant? The present posthumous publication provides the means for us to decide. As Kaelin so ably reminds us, the texts, after all, belong to each of us, the readers.

Eva Hauel Cadwallader
Westminster College
New Wilmington, Pennsylvania

Guest Foreword

The year was 1937. W. H. Werkmeister was enjoying the last year that an American professor had been appointed Director Pro-tempore of the Institute for American Culture at the University of Berlin. While he was holding that position during the academic year of 1936-1937, he was called upon to lecture at various German universities, including the University of Münster, where he had begun his academic career. Asked to lecture in English by his German hosts, Werkie responded to an overflow crowd, some of which were students. The others were army officers, SS Corps members, and even some Gestapo, there to keep surveillance over the event. Two sets of verbatim notes were produced of the lecture, one by the Gestapo members and the other by agents of the American Consular Service, there to protect the visiting exchange professor from any unjust charges that might have been fomented by the wily Germans. General of the Army Karl Rudolf von Rundstedt was called to Berlin on urgent matters of state, and so had to miss the widely advertised lecture. Werkmeister was given an apology in his name, and the incident was closed. No charges were made; the apology was accepted. Some years later, in 1949, the content of that lecture was to be found in Werkie's *A History of Philosophical Ideas in America,* published by the Ronald Press—a book which has since become a classic for scholars interested in the history of American thought.

During that same exchangeship, Werkmeister was to call upon Martin Heidegger, then a professor at the Albert-Ludwigs-Universität at Freiburg-im-Breisgau, which through the efforts of Edmund Husserl had become the world center for Phenomenological inquiry. Although he began his university studies at Freiburg, Heidegger had already spent some time at Marburg, where he was the colleague of Nicolai Hartmann, with whom he continued to struggle against the regnant post-Kantianism of that university's faculty. When Heidegger was invited to join the faculty at Freiburg, needing a publication to do so, Husserl agreed with complacence to publish Heidegger's *Sein und Zeit* in his own *Jahrbuch für Philosophie und phänomenologische Forschung* (vol. 7, 1927).

That same year the work was published as an independent treatise with its dedication to Husserl intact; it was inscribed on 8 April 1926. Heidegger's inaugural lecture at Freiburg, entitled "Was ist Metaphysik?," was delivered on 24 July 1929; it was published by Friedrich Cohen, in Bonn, that same year.

At the time of his meeting with Werkmeister, Heidegger had already gone through two public humiliations. First, he had joined the Nazi party on 1 May

1933, very shortly after having been elected by his colleagues on 21 April as Rector of Freiburg University. During his tenure as rector Heidegger was known for having attempted to establish the *Führer-Prinzip* into German academic politics. After a year of attempting to elicit the cooperation of students in the growing war effort of Nazi Germany, Heidegger felt it the better part of discretion to resign his post (because, he has said, of interference by leading Nazi officials) and to take up again the practice of philosophy.

He resigned his position as rector after a year, but did not resign from the Nazi Party until after Germany's defeat in 1945. Consequent upon a political screening by the French (who occupied that area of Germany), Heidegger was declared unfit to lecture publicly in a German University. He continued to lecture privately, and to live, almost as a hermit, in the surrounding hills of the Black Forest.

Werkmeister takes a stand on the issue of Heidegger, the politician, in the final chapter of this text. Of this, more later.

The second humiliation of Heidegger was perhaps of greater consequence. His inaugural lecture at Freiburg contained reference to *das Nichts* as the phenomenological basis for all negation. Human subjects become aware of the objective correlate of their own subjective *Angst,* of their own felt nothingness, in an attempt to veer out of the subjective boredom caused by their relationship to the wholeness of the extant universe, the *Seiende-im-Ganzen.* Although Heidegger was driven to both these concepts in order to challenge the supremacy of logic as the final court of decision on the topic of meaning, he quickly became known as "the philosopher of nothingness" and "the champion of meaningless-ness" within the purview of philosophical discourse. What had really happened was a change in philosophical position from ontology (as a recognized study of things that might be said to exist) to metaphysics, the study of Being itself which was somehow possessed by everything that exists. The metaphysician's purpose was to discuss this "somehow."

This change in scholarly purpose announced the arrival of Heidegger, the meditative thinker, as opposed to Heidegger, the hermeneutical phenomenologist who had written *Sein und Zeit.* Critics of the man have ever since referred to "Heidegger I" and "Heidegger II" as the person who played the role of fundamental ontologist in his first phase only to assume the role of meditative thinker in the second. That thought usually was directed to the concept of Being itself, and so, as he himself has said, is primarily metaphysical.

At this stage in his career, Heidegger had already begun to show the effects of his vaunted destruction of traditional ontology; but, to pull off the feat, there had to be created an as yet nontraditional view of metaphysics founded upon the notion of truth as *"a-letheia,"* the uncoveredness of the Being of things. No longer relying upon truth as the correspondence between our words and objective fact, his plan was to show how the meaning of the Being of things, even when these are taken as a whole, actually reveals itself.

In *Being and Time,* the entity used for this revelation was *Dasein* itself. One of the properties of human beings was their capacity to comprehend their own being, and so at least to understand vaguely Being itself. But from now on Heidegger's attention was brought to the whole of the existent world and the Being it exhibited. Heidegger I was to become the infamous Heidegger II. Yet it was the same man who merely chose to follow a different path through the woods.

More on the changing of paths as a conception for a change in philosophical method is to follow.

Heidegger's resentment of his reception was expressed in his total refusal to accept the appraisal of his work as that coming from a philosopher of nothingness. Not that European nihilism was a non-topic. He had devoted years to the study of that phenomenon, especially as it concerned the reputation of the German philosopher, Friedrich Nietzsche. Heidegger produced a two volume interpretation of Nietzsche as metaphysician in 1961 (Pfullingen: Günther Neske), when he published the studies begun during his political ostracism from the German university system. What riled him most was the general refusal to recognize that "*das Nichts*" and "*das Seiende-im-Ganzen*" were correlative terms, and that consequently an understanding of the one implied an equal understanding of the other. Concerning *Being and Time,* the missing second half of the treatise was supposedly in the top drawer of Heidegger's working desk, upon which he furiously pounded to emphasize his point to Werkmeister. Under the circumstances, what could a misunderstood philosopher do? Read the poets, enter into dialogue with dead thinkers, publish his findings, think, and read, and wait, if for nothing other than a return of the gods; Hölderlin himself had heralded their departure, and Nietzsche made a serious point of the fact that the Christian God had died, the very idea of Him having left the minds and behavior of contemporaneous Christians.

And for this idea to recover its past efficacy humankind itself had to undergo a change that would permit the transvaluation of contemporary values. The philosopher had only to wait, all the while continuing to shepherd Being, or plying the trail that led on the way to the language that encapsulated Being. The God would return with the renewed Spirit of men.

The two impressions stuck in the visitor's mind. Werkmeister, believing his interlocutor, accepted the appearance of Heidegger's *Kant and das Problem der Metaphysik* (Frankfurt am Main: Klostermann, 1929), which was first delivered as a set of lectures at Marburg during the winter semester of 1925-1926, and *Grundprobleme der Phänomenologie,* vol. 24, *Heidegger Gesamtsausgabe* (Frankfurt: Klostermann, 1975) as the missing second half of the originally conceived *Being and Time.* Until the preparation of his *Gesamtsausgabe* Heidegger had refused publication of the latter text. In the meantime, *Zeit und Sein,* the missing third part of the first half of *Sein und Zeit,* had been published both as a lecture (including a recorded version) and a written text, translated by Joan Stambaugh as *On Time and Being* (New York: Harper and Row, 1972). This lecture heralded the "end of philosophy" and "the beginning of [meditative] thought," the infamous "turn" in the path of Heidegger's own thinking process. From this time on, there was clearly a "Heidegger II."

Altogether the indicated texts completed the plan of the original *Sein and Zeit.* But the Kant and metaphysics volume appeared two years after that treatise; the reversal theme, found in *On Time and Being,* three and a half decades later than the treatise; and the actual destruction of the history of ontology found in the *Basic Problems* volume, almost a half-century later. All this work, except for the reversal theme, had already been prepared while Heidegger was still at Marburg; as a lecture, *Zeit und Sein* was first delivered in its entirety at Freiburg in 1962. It took an act of faith to accept the fact that the original manuscript was already complete in 1937. Except for the missing third part of the first half, reversing time and being, however, the statement was apparently true. Werkie lifted the Kantian volume to serve as an introduction to the discussion of *Sein and Zeit;* see his Chapter I, below.

Heidegger's claim that the world was not yet ready for the publication of the missing parts of the original treatise may be taken as further disappointment at the reception of the first half, and of Heidegger's consequent efforts, as in *Was ist Metaphysik?,* to adumbrate on its significance. What mystery, then, that such a philosopher should have been misunderstood?

Some interpreters will continue to associate the work of Heidegger I with the dominating existentialist movement, while others will indicate the further developments of the philosopher who refused to be so categorized, and who sketched out a career that led still others to refer to Heidegger II.

The current volume, by Werkmeister, is posthumous, and is of the latter sort. He was working at the time of his death on his final evaluation of the phenomenon the philosophical world has known as Martin Heidegger. A secretary, Cathy

Butler of FSU's Department of Philosophy, was working on a diskette version of the Werkmeister manuscript found herein below. Had not Richard T. Hull appeared on campus to inquire of any unpublished work of his former colleague (both were past presidents of the American Society for Value Inquiry), and had Mrs. Werkmeister not indicated her approval that this final text be prepared for publication, the story would have ended there, with Werkie's final judgment, characteristically but all too modestly, that his manuscript contained nothing the scholarly world did not already understand.

That judgment too indicates more about the judge than about the truth of what was said. Werkie was already approaching his ninety-third year, and his strength was waning. His attempts to refurbish his manuscript were both slow and painstaking; moreover, he felt that the work was unfinished, and that he would never be strong enough to perfect his project. And for those reasons, he tended to lose sight of his manuscript's ultimate worth.

For the record, let the values to be found in his text be stated here: in *Martin Heidegger on the Way*, (i) the author attempts to justify textually the actual path followed in Heidegger's philosophical development as indicated in his own "My Way to Phenomenology" (see Stambaugh, *On Time and Being*, pp. 74-82); (ii) the manuscript sets out the centrality of *Being and Time* in that development, giving a lucid account of Heidegger's principal text; (iii) with that centrality established, the author follows Heidegger to establish the conditions of his philosophical turning (from Kant as an introductory figure to Heidegger's own destruction of ontology, as explained in the *Basic Problems*); (iv) Heidegger II is seen as fundamental ontologist metamorphosed into metaphysician, but who leaves the question of space and spatiality hanging in a Cartesian and Galilean limbo of three dimensionality unconnected with the fourth dimension of time and temporality, and who consequently lacks the means for showing the structures of beings as they go to make up *das Seiende-im-Ganzen*, where these unifying structures are already apparent in the ontological thought of Nicolai Hartmann; (v) also explained are the roles art, poetry, and technology have played in Heidegger's thought; (vi) nihilism—both ideal (philosophical, as per Nietzsche) and real (the valueless views of reigning political systems)—is given its hearing; and, finally, (vii) the subject of Heidegger and Nazism is treated in the light of all the themes preceding this last.

The seven reasons found for salvaging Werkmeister's commentary on Heidegger correspond to his seven chapters explicating the path this philosopher has followed to point out the way others must follow to achieve wisdom as one of the prevailing values of life. Neither the original way or ways, nor the commentary upon the person having chosen to follow them, has been without some concern.

Werkmeister had long been aware of Heidegger and his putative significance. After their meeting in 1937 Werkie had published a number of pieces indicating his continuing fascination with Heidegger, his philosophy, and his scholarly reception; see, for example,

"An Introduction to Heidegger's Existential Philosophy," *Philosophy and Phenomenological Research* 2 (September 1941): 79-87;

"On 'Describing a World'," *Philosophy and Phenomenological Research* 11 (March 1951): 124-131;

Review of Thomas Langan, *The Meaning of Heidegger* (New York: Columbia University Press, 1959), *The Personalist* 41 (Autumn, October 1960): 515;

Review of Martin Heidegger, *Being and Time*, trans. John Macquarrie and Edward Robinson (New York: Harper & Brothers, 1962), *The Personalist* 4 (Spring, April 1963): 244;

Review of Martin Heidegger, *Discourse On Thinking*, trans. John M. Anderson and E. Hans Freund (New York: Harper & Row, 1966), *The Personalist* 47 (Fall, October 1966): 559-560;

"Grundzüger der menschlichen Existenz," in *Menschliche Existenz und moderne Welt*, vol. 2, ed. Richard Schwartz (Berlin: Walter de Gruyter, 1967), 150-156;

"Hegel and Heidegger," in *New Studies in Hegel's Philosophy*, ed. Warren E. Steinkraus (New York: Holt, Rhinehart and Winston, 1971), 142-155;

"Heidegger and the Poets," *The Personalist* 52 (Winter 1971): 5-22;

Review of Charles M. Sherover, *Heidegger, Kant and Time* (Bloomington: The Indiana University Press, 1971), *Journal of the History of Philosophy* 15 (January 1977): 119-123.

Such were the texts that prepared this volume.

The difficulties experienced by anyone working in the field were mostly the effect of Heidegger's determination to make German speak Greek; under the circumstances, when is it proper to cite Heidegger's German into a readable English? "Being" might do for "*Sein*" and "a being" for "*ein Seiendes*." But what we to do with "*Dasein*"? It might be left untranslated, as is mostly the case; but surely we must understand that this ontological term differs from the common, even banal, meaning of "existence." Werkmeister leaves the term untranslated, but indicates the specific use of the term introduced by Hegel to mean a distinctive manner of being. Heidegger used the term in the same technical sense.

Those translators of the term who had opted for "human being" were perhaps seduced by Heidegger's own suggestion that "*Dasein*" is the distinctive form of being human, i.e., projected into a world as being both here and there, and consequently as being a possibility to exist in a certain way. As far as we know, only human beings have that form of being; so "*Dasein*" becomes "human being"; concretely, "a human being."

"Being there," or more literally "There-being," neglects the ambiguity of "da," which means both "here" and "there." And the ambiguity is useful to describe the opening or "clearing" within Being effectuated by the here-there projection of a human being. Only the *da* of *Da-sein* makes this clearing an existential possibility. Here translators merely opt for what makes sense to them, and pass the difficulty on to those who know no German.

Take the concept of "*ein Seiendes*"; everything depends upon an understanding of the idea. "*Sein*," in lower case, of course, is the infinitive of the verb "to be," and "*seiend*" is a participle being clearly enough "being," also in English a participle. But what happens when this participle is made into a gerund (a verbal noun substantive)? In German, you merely capitalize the "s"; so we have the stem "*Seiend*," which needs both an ending and a gender denoting article. In the singular, the stem becomes a neuter substantive: "*ein Seiendes*"; in the plural, "*die Seiende*." But there is no gender in the plural, although if you were to be a stickler on the matter, the plural of all German neuter nouns would be noted to take the feminine article, except for the dative, which is nondifferentiating. We would translate these terms first, in the singular, as "a being," "an entity," or "some existent thing"; and, in the plural as "beings," "entities," and so on, except that the definite form of the expression "*das Seiende*" may be considered either a singular or a plural, as explained below.

There is no problem here: in *Sein und Zeit* there are only two kinds and three classes of entities mentioned. Beings are either *Dasein*-like *(daseinsmassig)* or not-*Dasein*-like *(nichtdaseinsmassig),* and the second of these kinds are either tools (whatever is at hand ready for use) or things (everything perceptible or extant in a human subject's world). *Dasein* itself is the investigator, the self-projection into its world; it is a human being.

Asking the question about the Being of these entities in *Sein und Zeit* is a simple matter: a thing, as an ontic entity, has the being of presence-at-hand; a tool, of readiness-to-hand. *Dasein* itself, as an entity, knows itself ontologically as care (because it concerns itself with the other entities that surround it), and the meaning of this Being is temporality. In the major treatise, therefore, although the study began with an inquiry into the meaning of Being, the published version of the text allowed for the description of various beings, their Being, and the meaning of that Being. It was the discovery of temporality as the meaning of the being of care that necessitated Heidegger's reconsideration of the notion of time, and his corresponding destruction of the history of ontology based upon that notion.

A different problem arose when Heidegger posed the question of the meaning of the Being of *"das Seiende-im-Ganzen."* Here is another concept virtually left untouched until that fateful lecture on metaphysics, "Was ist Metaphysik?"

This new concept is grammatically singular, but as a conglomerate or collection of individual entities; hence, possibly plural as well. What is to be made of this new concept?

In an attempt to make myself clear, I begin by declining the entire expression, which grammatically can only be singular:

Nominative, *das Seiende-im-Ganzen*;
Genitive, *des Seienden-im-Ganzen;*
Dative, *dem Seienden-im-Ganzen;*
Accusative, *das Seiende-im-Ganzen.*

To what are these terms being used to refer? Answer: to the world, to everything that might be spoken of, to nature, to *"physis,"* the term preferred by Heidegger, or, alternatively, to everything found in the world, or Nature, or to everything that extends itself outward into a permanent substance. Note, however, where the article has the strong ending, the gerund itself has the weak endings of German declension. The expression itself is of a mixed declension, and has no plural, since it needs none.

As a singular term, the declension of the simple expression runs

Nominative, *ein Seiendes;*
Genitive, *eines Seienden* (this gerund looks, to an English reader, like a plural, but it is not);
Dative, *einem Seienden* (same remark);
Accusative, *ein Seiendes*;

and there is no ontologically proper sense of the term in the plural. For that idea Heidegger was driven to other particles or to the ambiguously singular or plural interpretation of "*das Seiende*." Sometimes, however, he emphasizes the possible plurality of this notion by adding the expression "*-im-Ganzen*" to this seemingly singular term.

Citing these terms without respect to their case declension—which is perhaps the best ploy to exercise—or ignoring the play of the weak and the strong declension endings, or, even, associating the gerund's ending with a corresponding English article read as if it were German, could result in confusion. The first of these alternatives seems to me to have the least lethal consequences, but Werkmeister—perhaps because German was his native tongue—chose the last of these alternatives. As a result of that decision I have adopted the following recourse.

In order to avoid any confusion of German and English terms, I have ever so ungrammatically translated the singular term for a concrete entity as "*ein Seiendes*," irrespective of the case, whenever the corresponding English article is indefinite (an "a" or an "an"). But when the definite article "the" is used in translation, the German will always read "*das Seiende*," even though there will be a resulting ambiguity between the concrete (always singular) and the collective sense of the term, whose own ambiguity (either as a singular, collective term or a plural, distributive one) may be interpreted contextually whenever the reader is not forewarned by the "*-im-Ganzen*" of Heidegger himself. I can see no alternative to such contextual definition of this term.

For the collective term, "*das Seiende-im-Ganzen*," sometimes lengthened by Heidegger to be "*das Seiende-als-solches-im-Ganzen*," we usually translate as "whatever exists, taken as a whole." When stretched, the term should read "whatever exists considered as such taken as a whole," or, if it is any plainer, "whatever exists, considered as existent, and taken as a whole." I can therefore avoid talking about the world as a collective term as if it were an "essent."[1]

The important thing to remember is that "*das Seiende-im-Ganzen*" is a collective term that may be considered either as a collection (the world) or a distribution, covering the entities found in the world. Heidegger thought that this concept was definitive of all metaphysics. What he lacked, according to Werkmeister, was an idea corresponding to the relativity of the things within the world, such as that defined by Whitehead out of Einstein. The world is a four-dimensional continuum where individual entities are related in such a way as to elicit a process from God, as an originating source, to God, the consequent nature of the universe. Aristotle's *Physik*, it is claimed, fails to describe the facts of concretion.

The Greeks had no equivalent for the Western concept of space and had to make do with the notion of place (*der Ort*). Change, force, and the emergence of concrete objects took place under the four types of causality that guided all physical changes of "motion."[2]

It was here, Werkmeister thought, that we could profit most from a reading of Nicolai Hartmann, whose doctrine of stratification within the phenomenological formulation of objects permitted us to understand how such objects came to be what they are. But that was another ontological exercise, one which Heidegger neglected to acknowledge. He was content to differentiate ontic entities from their ontological "existentials"—those essential structures whose togetherness or concretion was sufficient to explain the meaning of the Being of entities—and so to separate everyday reality from a state of existential possibility or necessity. Of the relations between the things of the world nothing was said outside of the obvious, that they constituted the things found in the world itself.

The further confusion of Heidegger's terms "*existentiel*" and "*existenzial*" merely avoids two prominent clues of interpretation: the ontic-ontological distinction, and a corresponding similarity in the distinction between the German terms "*reell*" and "*real*" or "*ideell*" and "*ideal*." What is real (*reell*) or ideal (*ideell*) is of the nature of the thing (the reality of a fact or the reality of a thought's occurrence), but what is real (*real*) or ideal (*ideal*) is a part of the concept of a thing or of the nature of a thought qua thought. Abiding by these two clues makes translation of the two original terms an easy matter. Without the distinction noted, as is usual in English, however, the corresponding German terms cannot be translated.

What is "*existenziel*" is the set of conditions under which a human being undergoes some experience. He or she is born and dies, and everything else that happens in between will be an event of the real world—an object of some concern, no doubt, but only ontic in significance, as would be such things as the world, signification, space, time, and even history. Philosophers have always used "categories" to describe such events.

The word "*existenzial*" was coined by Heidegger to apply to all those "existentials" *(Existenzial, Existenzialieri)* by which the possibility of necessity of human existentiality may appropriately be described. They are structures and form the basis of Heidegger's famous *Daseinsanalytik.* Here, instead of the "categories" mentioned above, we employ such "existentials" as worldhood, significance, spatiality, temporality, and historicality. But if we keep the models of the coinage in mind, and continue to focus upon the ontic-ontological distinction, these words are no more mysterious than those already mentioned.

The problem becomes more pressing, however, when Heidegger uses the terms "*Seiendes*" and "*Nichts*" without an appropriate article. His *Einführung in die Metaphysik* (Tübingen: Max Niemeyer, 1958) was the publication of a lecture course delivered at Freiburg in the Summer of 1935. Besides characterizing both the grammar and the etymology of his terms in a second chapter, the master began his lecture with a quotation rendered into German from the work of the Freiherr von Leibniz. We read, "*Warum is überhaupt Seiendes und nicht vielmehr Nichts?*" (Leibniz's question, expressed in French as "Pourquoi y a-t-il quelque chose plutôt que rien?" was erected into a title of a dissertation by A.-T. Tymieniecka, "Why is there Something rather than Nothing?")[3]

I have given two translations of the Heideggerian formulation of the thought to emphasize the change from "*Seiendes*" to "*quelque chose*" and "something" and from "*nichts*" to "*rien*" and "nothing." Gone is the pretention that *ein Seiendes* is a concrete entity even of the whole of the universe; the term is used without the specification of an article, and so is understood as clearly expressing the idea conveyed by the French and English. But "something" *(aliquid)* is clearly a term medievals preferred to call one of the transcendentals, all five of which ("one," "thing," "something," "true," and "good") could be used convertibly with "Being." So it should come as no surprise that Heidegger called into question the philosophical question *par excellence,* or, if you prefer, the question of all questions.

But the question raised in the mind of this interpreter is "Whatever has happened to the common pronomial German terms for *quelque chose* and *rien?*" To use the indefinite pronouns "*etwas*" and "*nichts*" (even though "*nichts*" was originally the genitive of a noun) might have been a clear statement of what Leibniz had in mind. Both terms have an obvious transcendental use, and neither needs the capitalization required of German nouns.

Heidegger's worrying over the metaphysical question, however, may remind us of his treatment of *der Satz vom Grund*, expressed by Leibniz in the Latin *Nihil est sine ratione.* In his work of that German title,[4] Heidegger points out the double negative of the statement, and straightens that out into a single affirmative statement, that every existent thing possesses a ground. The trick is to conceive of reasons as grounds for being.

The German version of the principle changes meaning, Heidegger claimed, if the emphasis on his German translation changes from "Nichts *ist* ohne *Grund*" to "*Nichts* ist *ohne* Grund." The same expression intoned in one way refers to entities and in another to *das Sein.* That precisely was the movement from ontology to metaphysics, as Heidegger understood them, and following out that movement produced a change from Heidegger I to Heidegger II. In this way, the famous ontic-ontological distinction of his earlier work was replaced by the metaphysical drive of the later. "*Seiendes*" became the name for anything that exists, whether it is a real thing (or concrete entity), an idea, or the totality of such things. And what was originally a concrete and relative term became by this metaphysical transmutation something that is both abstract and absolute.

Is all this to say that Heidegger is nothing but a linguistic philosopher? Merely posing the question may give some hints for a defensible interpretation of the matter. We remember that his earlier period was described as the shepherding of Being; but when Being has been discovered within the use of language—when language itself is interpreted as the house of Being, a place where philosophers habitually dwell—we might say that the philosopher is *On the Way to Language,* as Heidegger informed us in his *Unterwegs zur Sprache.*[5] At the time of this writing, Heidegger had begun his colloquy with the poets and deepened his dialogues with the ancient Greek philosophers.

The case was no different when he translated the Greek *hodos* as *Weg* (or "way"). Pursuing a method of inquiry, whether it be phenomenological or merely posing and answering questions, using whatever language occurs to one, is to choose a way. In this sense, all philosophical inquiry, whether phenomenological or linguistic, whether methodical or mystical, follows a path from a here to a there. For this reason, Heidegger entitled a series of articles that led him from his first to his second philosophical period *Wegmarken,* that is, signposts marking out the direction of a path. For an understanding of Werkmeister's argument, we could do worse than familiarize ourself with these essays. The philosopher, like any other normal human individual, is always on the way—to language, which is the house of Being, or to truth, whose principal function is to uncover Being.

Hans-Georg Gadamer has recently referred to the "ways" that have defined Heidegger's path. That such ways should be more than a simple division into the two of Heidegger I and II should surprise no one. Gadamer's text, translated as *Heidegger's Ways,*[6] includes references to Heidegger the theologian, the Marburg professor, the existentialist, the nonrepentent politician, the thinker, the metaphysician, and so forth—all ways that have been summed up into a philosopher's career. That career veered off from phenomenology[7] to meditative thinking, but the first way followed the signs leading to the second. Whether he was to be found in the first, or within the second, Heidegger was always on the way, as three scholars have attested: Richardson, Gadamer, and now Werkmeister.

As for the political involvement of Heidegger with the affairs of the German state, a number of attitudes have been adopted. Werkmeister objected to Victor Farias's *Heidegger and Nazism*[8] as too prosecutorial. Rather than excusing Heidegger's actions, as Werkmeister seems to do, an anxious reader might follow the lead of Gadamer, and refer to that episode in Heidegger's life as the blunder it was. It is far preferable to let the documents speak for themselves, as Guido Schneeberger had done in his *Nachlese zu Heidegger,*[9] even though that author was forced to print his work privately, as even no Swiss publisher would undertake the task, even at that late date. The fact remains that Heidegger joined the Nazi Party and did not resign from it until after Germany's defeat. Heidegger even acceded to the Nazi demand that the dedication of *Sein und Zeit* be removed if the Party's *imprimatur* were to be given, a book originally dedicated to a Jew who happened to be his former teacher. The "authenticity" of this move may forever be up in the air.

Heidegger's various explanations of his rectorship and of his political stand have all raised as much criticism and condemnation as awareness and quiet approval. To understand how the approval is justified, the best plan of action is to read the published version of *Sein und Zeit* to see what in that volume betokened a fashion of thinking that would be useful to the political directors of Germany's war effort, or for Heidegger's thinking that he himself might be useful to them.

Failing such a study, those people who have found it profitable to reject Heidegger for his politics will face only a philosopher's respect for creativity for the work of a country's poets, philosophers, and political leaders. Surely it was no error to perceive political leadership as creative of a renewed human destiny; Heidegger's error was to perceive *der Führer* and his henchmen as actively creative statesmen. A victim of an ideal (National Socialism as it was thought), he could not perceive the evil of the real governmental apparatus headed by Adolph Hitler. He was working, he claimed, in the name of the ideal, and it took a lengthy period of psychotherapy to convince him of the difference between his understanding of the ideal and the reality that tended to destroy his credibility. After all, creativity leads the thoughtful person to the discovery of some value, whether that be truth, beauty, or social justice in any particular real situation. But whether something gets uncovered in a reading of Heidegger only a reader can decide.

Werkmeister's discussion of *Martin Heidegger on the Way* ends with a consideration of his author's politics. The time has come to follow that discussion—in the hope of finding Heidegger himself somewhere on his way.

E. F. Kaelin
The Florida State University
Tallahassee, Florida

Abbreviations

All translations from the works listed below are Werkmeister's own. For each work, it is indicated whether Werkmeister's citations are to the German, an English translation, or both. When both the German and an English translation of a work are cited, the German pagination is followed by the English pagination, the two being separated by a slash (/).

Works by Martin Heidegger

B/E *Vom Wesen der Wahrheit* (Frankfurt am Main: Vittorio Klostermann, 1943).

(B) "On the Essence of Truth," trans. John Sallis, in *Martin Heidegger: Basic Writings*, ed. David Farrell Krell (New York: Harper & Row, 1977), pp. 117-141.

(E) "On the Essence of Truth," trans. R. F. C. Hull and Alan Crick, in *Existence and Being* (Chicago: Henry Regnery, 1949), pp. 317-351.

Page references are to the two English translations.

BH "Brief über den Humanismus," in *Wegmarken* (Frankfurt am Main: Vittorio Klostermann, 1967), pp. 145-194. [Originally published in 1947 by A. Francke Verlag, Bern.]

"Letter on Humanism," trans. Frank A. Capuzzi, in *Martin Heidegger: Basic Writings*, ed. David Farrell Krell (New York: Harper & Row, 1977), pp. 193-242.

Page references are to the Capuzzi translation.

DS "*Der Spiegel* Interview with Martin Heidegger," trans. Lisa Harries, in *Martin Heidegger and National Socialism*, eds. Günther Neske and Emil Kettering (New York: Paragon House, 1990), pp. 41-66.

[A previous translation by Maria Alter and John D. Caputo was published in *Philosophy Today* 20 (Winter 1976): 276-284.]

EM *Einführung in die Metaphysik* (Tübingen: Max Niemeyer, 1953).

An Introduction to Metaphysics, trans. Ralph Manheim (New Haven: Yale University Press, 1959).

Page references are to the Manheim translation.

EN "Der europäische Nihilismus," in *Nietzsche*, 2 (Pfullingen: Günther Neske, 1961), pp. 31-256.

FT "Die Frage nach der Technik," in *Vorträge und Aufsätze* (Pfullingen: Günther Neske, 1954), pp. 13-44.

"The Question Concerning Technology," trans. William Lovitt, in *The Question Concerning Technology, and Other Essays* (New York: Garland Publishing, 1977), pp. 3-35.

Page references are to the Lovitt translation.

G *Gelassenheit* (Pfullingen: Günther Neske, 1959).

Discourse on Thinking, trans. John M. Anderson and E. Hans Freund (New York: Harper & Row, 1966).

Page references are to the Anderson and Freund translation.

GP *Die Grundprobleme der Phänomenologie*, vol. 24 of the Heidegger *Gesamtausgabe* (Frankfurt am Main: Vittorio Klostermann, 1977).

The Basic Problems of Phenomenology, trans. Albert Hofstadter (Bloomington, Ind.: Indiana University Press, 1982, rev. ed. 1988).

Page references are to the German and the Hofstadter translation.

HWD *Hölderlin und das Wesen der Dichtung* (Frankfurt am Main: Vittorio Klostermann, 1951).

"Hölderlin and the Essence of Poetry," trans. Douglas Scott, in *Existence and Being* (Chicago: Henry Regnery, 1949), pp. 293-315.

Page references are to the German and the Scott translation.

KPM *Kant und das Problem der Metaphysik* (Frankfurt am Main: Vittorio Klostermann, 1951).

Kant and the Problem of Metaphysics, trans. James S. Churchill (Bloomington, Ind.: Indiana University Press, 1962).

Page references are to the German and the Churchill translation.

NW "Nietzsches Wort 'Gott ist tot,'" in *Holzwege* (Frankfurt am Main: Vittorio Klostermann, 1950), pp. 193-247.

"The Word of Nietzsche: 'God Is Dead,'" trans. William Lovitt, in *The Question Concerning Technology, and Other Essays* (New York: Garland Publishing, 1977), pp. 53-112.

Page references are to the German.

PMD ". . . Poetically Man Dwells . . . ," trans. Albert Hofstadter, in *Poetry, Language, Thought* (New York: Harper & Row, 1971), pp. 213-229.

SZ *Sein und Zeit*, in Edmund Husserl's *Jahrbuch für Philosophie und phänomenologische Forschung*, Band 8, 1927.

Being and Time, trans. John Macquarrie and Edward Robinson (New York: Harper & Row, 1962).

Page references are to the Jahrbuch edition and the Macquarrie and Robinson translation.

UK "Der Ursprung des Kunstwerkes," in *Holzwege* (Frankfurt am Main: Vittorio Klostermann, 1950), pp. 7-68.

"The Origin of the Work of Art," trans. Albert Hofstadter, in *Martin Heidegger: Basic Writings*, ed. David Farrell Krell (New York: Harper & Row, 1977), pp. 149-187.

Page references are to the German and the Hofstadter translation.

WD "Wozu Dichter?" in *Holzwege* (Frankfurt am Main: Vittorio Klostermann, 1950), pp. 248-295.

"What Are Poets For?" trans. Albert Hofstadter, in *Poetry, Language, Thought* (New York: Harper & Row, 1971), pp. 91-142.

Page references are to the Hofstadter translation.

WMK "Der Wille zur Macht als Kunst," in *Nietzsche*, 1 (Pfullingen: Günther Neske, 1961), pp. 11-254.

Other Works

A/B/NKS Immanuel Kant, *Critique of Pure Reason*, trans. Norman Kemp-Smith (New York: St. Martin's Press, 1961).

Page references preceded by "A" and "B" are to the first and second German editions, respectively, and those preceded by "NKS" are to the Kemp-Smith translation.

WL Georg Wilhelm Friedrich Hegel, *Wissenschaft der Logik*, vol. 56 of *Philosophische Bibliothek* (Leipzig: Georg Lasson, 1932).

Hegel's Science of Logic, vol. 1, trans. W. H. Johnston and L. G. Strutters (New York: Macmillan, 1929).

Hegel's Science of Logic, trans. A. V. Miller (New York: Humanities Press, 1969).

Page references are to the German.

One

INTRODUCTION

> I have forsaken an earlier position, not to exchange it for another, but because even the former position was only a pause on the way. What lasts in thinking is the way.
>
> Martin Heidegger[1]

This quotation explains the title of my book and defines its content thesis.

Let us face it: Heidegger's fame—or is it notoriety[2]—rests primarily upon the fragment—"Erste Hälfte"—of one book, *Sein und Zeit*, published in 1927 in Husserl's *Jahrbuch für Philosophie und phänomenologische Forschung*, volume eight. It was meant to open up a new approach to ontology.

Six years earlier, in 1921, Nicolai Hartmann's *Grundzüge einer Metaphysik der Erkenntnis* also opened up a new approach to ontology.[3] In some respects, Hartmann anticipated Heidegger's basic orientation. In most respects, however, the two thinkers were poles apart; and the question is: Who has contributed the truly lasting version of the new ontology?

The work of both thinkers must be seen in relation to Husserl's *Phenomenology*, according to which "the principle of all principles" in philosophy, and in science generally, asserts that "an absolute beginning" must be an intuitive one. But none other than Hegel had already emphasized this theme. Consider his argument in the opening sections of his *Wissenschaft der Logik*. Let me quote rather extensively:

> It has only recently been felt that there is a difficulty in finding a beginning in philosophy, and the reason for this difficulty, as also the possibility of solving it, has been much discussed. The beginning of philosophy must be either something *mediated* or something *immediate*, and it is easy to show that it can be neither (WL51).
>
> If no presupposition is to be made, and the beginning itself is to be taken immediately, it determines itself by being the beginning of thinking as such.

> Only the resolve (which in itself can be seen as arbitrary) to contemplate thinking as such is present. This beginning must be absolute . . . and must *presuppose nothing*. It must be something immediate or, rather, *the immediate itself* (WL59). This beginning is not pure Nothing, but is a Nothing from which Something is to proceed: that is, Being is already contained in the Beginning (WL63).
>
> An original beginning of philosophy has recently become famous and cannot be passed over without mention, namely that which begins with the *I* (WL66).

The reference is, of course, to Descartes and his opening statement "I think, and therefore I am." But, Hegel finds, even if the *I* as intellectual intuition could be asserted to be the beginning of philosophy, the crucial point is "the *Dasein* . . . (i.e.) the determinateness which what is intrinsic in thinking has in *Dasein*" (WL68). As Hegel put it:

> *Dasein* is *determinate* Being; its determinateness is an existent determination . . . . It is *variable* and *finite* . . . . That is *Dasein* appears as something primary from which a beginning ought to be made. . . . *Dasein* (i.e., determinate Being) is such that the connection of space does not belong to it. As far as its becoming is concerned, *Dasein* is Being in general with a non-Being so that the latter is taken up into a simple unity with Being in such a way that the concrete whole in the form of Being, of immediacy, constitutes *determinateness* as such . . . . But the determinateness of *Dasein* itself is the one that is posited and also is implied in the expression *Dasein* (Determinate Being). . . .*Dasein* is a determinate Being, a concrete Being. Various determinations and distinct relations of its moment disclose themselves (WL106-108).

Hegel discussed *Dasein* for several more pages. But enough has been said to show where Heidegger got his conception of *Dasein* as the proper beginning of philosophy.

Hegel, of course, made *Dasein* the basis of his dialectical disclosure of the categories of Being, and Heidegger is right in accusing him of "looking in the same direction as does ancient ontology, except that he no longer pays heed to Aristotle's problem of the unity of Being as over against the multiplicity of 'categories' that are applicable to things" (SZ3/22f). Still, Heidegger obviously accepts Hegel's basic assertion that *Dasein*—the "*Seiende das ich selbst bin*" (SZ114f/150)—"the entity which in each case is I myself"—is the proper beginning for philosophy.

But if Dasein—our own personal "*being-there*"—is the basic fact which is the legitimate beginning of philosophy, it is also legitimate to ask: What does the "*Da*" in "*Dasein*" refer to? What is meant by the "*there*"? To this question Heidegger has replied that *Dasein* is "*in-der-Welt-sein*"—that it is "being-in-the-world" (SZ65/93).

And now the question is: What is the world? Heidegger's answer is: "It is that 'wherein' a factual *Dasein* 'lives' as this particular one . . . . World is the 'public' we-world or one's 'specific' (*eigene*) and nearest (domestic) *Umwelt* (environment)" (*ibid.*).

This *Umwelt*—this *Lebenswelt*—Husserl regarded as the starting point of phenomenology. The *Seiende* within that world consists of the things of nature, of human beings, and of the things "invested with values." It is the world which our sciences investigate as "Nature," and which Nicolai Hartmann interpreted in great detail in the categorial analysis of *his* new ontology.[4]

We are born into this world but do not remember the event. To us it is as if we had been "thrown" into the world (SZ175-180/219-224). However, once we are in the world we cannot doubt its, or our own, existence. As Descartes put it:

> It is manifestly impossible to doubt . . . that I am in this place, seated by the fire, clothed in a winter dressing-gown, that I hold in my hands this piece of paper, with other intimations of the same nature. But how could I deny that I possess these hands and this body, and with all escape being classed with persons in a state of insanity . . . . I must here consider that I am a man, and that, consequently, I am in the habit of sleeping . . . . At the present moment, however, I certainly look upon this paper with eyes wide awake . . . . I extend this hand consciously and with express purpose. . . . It must be admitted at least . . . that eyes, a head, hands and an entire body . . . really exist . . . . We are absolutely necessitated to admit this reality of at least some other objects . . . . To this class of objects seem to belong corporeal nature in general and its extensions: the figures of extended things, their quantity or magnitude, and their number, as also the place in, and the time during, which they exist.[5]

Heidegger could not have put it better. *Dasein* finds itself in an environing world of ordinary things in space and time. But Heidegger insists that "the meaning of *Dasein* is temporality" (SZ331/380). And *Sein und Zeit* is devoted to an elucidation and vindication of this assertion. The Being of *Dasein* as such "is an issue" (SZ12/32).

However, *Sein und Zeit* is deficient in several respects.

To begin with, it is only a fragment, and is clearly marked so in the German edition as "Erste Hälfte." More importantly, however, Heidegger himself has stated that in the publication of *Sein und Zeit* the third division of the first part was held back. "We shall carry our analysis no further until we have clarified our interpretation of worldhood by a case of the opposite extreme" (SZ85/122)—that is, by *Time and Being*. And in his "Brief über den Humanismus" ("Letter on Humanism") Heidegger wrote: "in the publication of *Sein und Zeit* the third division of the first part, 'Time and Being,' was held back . . . . Here everything is reversed. The section . . . was held back because thinking failed in the adequate saying of this turning (*Kehre*) and did not succeed with the help of the language of metaphysics" (BH207f). And in the essay "Vom Wesen der Wahrheit" ("On the Essence of Truth") Heidegger wrote: "The crucial question (viz. my *Sein und Zeit*, 1927) regarding the 'meaning' . . . that is, . . . the truth of Being [*Sein*] and not merely of 'what-is' [*das Seiende*] has been deliberately left undeveloped" (B140/E351).

Sein und Zeit is obviously only a transitional work. And anyone who has read the whole of Heidegger's *opus* knows that Heidegger is not a system thinker—although there is a change in his thinking that might be interpreted as progress. It is therefore difficult to give a straightforward account of his philosophical position as a whole. His most famous work, *Sein und Zeit*, is by no means indicative of his final position.

I find still other difficulties with that work. Since Being is here presumably interpreted in terms of time, we would expect to find in *Being and Time* a clear-cut definition—or at least an explanation—of the very essence of time; but there is none. We have to turn to the posthumously published *Grundprobleme der Phänomenologie* to find a full-scale discussion of the meaning of time and temporality (GP322-452/227-318).

We must realize, however, that between 1929 and 1935 a "turn" occurred in Heidegger's approach to the basic problems of philosophy. Although this *Kehre* did not mean a radical change in his ultimate position, it certainly added new aspects to that position; and some of these aspects are crucial for an understanding of Heidegger's position as a whole. The *Kehre* implies at least a shift in accent which will become evident as we study all of Heidegger's publications—including his various lecture courses as published in his two volume *Nietzsche*.

Two

HEIDEGGER AND KANT

In 1924, when Heidegger was an instructor at the University of Marburg, his colleague, Nicolai Hartmann, raised the question, "How is Critical Ontology possible at all?" He regarded the task of finding an answer to this question to be twofold: (1) to return to the problems faced by traditional ontology; and (2) to avoid the speculative metaphysical approach which had obscured the problem in the past. "What separates us for ever" from the old ontology, Hartmann wrote, is the Kantian re-orientation in epistemology. The *Critique of Pure Reason*, in so far as it is at all concerned with ontology, was directed against ontology's speculative and *a priori* presuppositions that have become traditional in metaphysics.[1]

Heidegger also saw in Kant's *Critique of Pure Reason* "what separates us for ever" from the ontology of philosophical tradition, and, like Hartmann, he was convinced that a new ontology must come to terms with Kant. Two of Heidegger's works are in this respect of special significance. One consists of his *Vorlesung* (lecture course) of the summer of 1927, included as Chapter One and parts of Chapter Two of the *Grundprobleme der Phänomenologie*; the other is Heidegger's book *Kant und das Problem der Metaphysik*. I shall deal with the *Grundprobleme* but briefly.

In a footnote to the first page of the *Einleitung* to this work Heidegger states that the *Vorlesung* of 1927 is "a new elaboration (*Ausarbeitung*) of the third section of Part I of *Sein und Zeit*"; and he bluntly states: "We assert: *Being* is the proper and sole theme of philosophy." Or, stated negatively, "philosophy is not a science of *Seiendes* (of something extant) but of *Sein* (Being) or, as the Greeks expressed it, it is ontology" (GP15/11).

It is in the spirit of this assertion that we must understand at least the first phase of Heidegger's philosophy. And it is in this perspective that we must see his reaction to Kant.

Kant had argued that Being is not a real predicate, and he had done so twice: (1) in his essay "Der einzig mögliche Beweisgrund zu einer Demonstration des Daseins Gottes" (1763); and (2) in the *Critique of Pure Reason*: "*Von der Unmöglichkeit eines ontologischen Beweises vom Dasein Gottes*." (Let it be noted that Kant uses the term "*Dasein*" [*existentia*] in both cases. But what Kant called

Dasein is what is generally understood by "*extant*," that is, what Heidegger called *vorhanden*." In stating his own position, Heidegger uses the term "*Dasein*" in the Hegelian sense with reference to the mode of Being of the human subject. And in this sense he identifies it terminologically with existence rather than with extantness or *Vorhandenheit*.)

The ontological argument is, of course, part of the philosophical tradition. Anselm of Canterbury (1033-1109) is generally regarded as the first to have employed it. Thomas Aquinas challenged its validity. But, as Heidegger points out, "the Kantian repudiation of the possibility of the ontological proof for the existence of God is much more radical and more fundamental than that which Thomas provides" (GP41f/31f).

In the *Grundprobleme* Heidegger discusses the Kantian thesis that "Being is not a predicate" with respect to three theses: (1) the thesis of the Scholastics as derived from Aristotle; (2) the thesis of modern ontology according to which the basic modes of Being are the Being of nature (*res extensa*) and the Being of the mind (*res cogitans*); and (3) the thesis of logic which, in effect, identifies Being with the meaning of the copula in a judgement. Heidegger thus extends the Kantian argument by pointing out that, if Being is not a predicate, "it is not a predicate of anything at all" (GP47/36).

The Kantian thesis rests, of course, on Kant's interpretation of the categories which determine our thinking. He derives them from the "Table of Judgements." This implies that categories are the possible forms of unity as combinations in judgement, that they represent the idea of unity in a judgement. Reality and existence, however, belong to entirely different classes of categories. As Heidegger points out, "reality belongs among the categories of quality" whereas "existence or actuality belongs among the categories of modality" (GP48/36). Kant himself had seen this difference; for he pointed out in the *Critique* that, "as regards reality, we obviously cannot think *in concreto* without calling experience to our aid. For reality is bound up with sensation, the matter of experience" (A223/B270/NKS 241).

We must note, however, that what interests Heidegger is not the ontological argument as such but Kant's explication that *Being* is "but the positing of a thing, as expressed in the copula of a judgement," whereas *Dasein* is an "absolute positing" (A598/B626/NKS504). And Heidegger asks: Does this distinction still leave us face to face with an obscurity? (GP57/43) We speak of things as *Seiendes*, as something that is extant, that has Being. The problem of the ontological argument thus turns into the problem of an interpretation of Being and becomes a problem of positing. And now the question is, How is the Kantian distinction between "positing" and "absolute positing" to be understood?

In his attempt to answer this question Heidegger develops a phenomenological analysis of Kant's explanation of the concepts "Being" and "*Dasein*."

In his discussion of "the postulates of empirical thought in general" Kant argued that

> the categories of modality (possibility, reality, necessity) have the peculiarity that, in determining an object, they do not in the least enlarge the concept to which they are attached as predicates. They only express the relation of the concept to the faculty of knowledge. (A219/B266/NKS239)

And he had argued further that

> in the *mere concept* of a thing no trace of its existence can be found . . . . The perception which supplies the content of the concept is the sole mark of reality and our knowledge of the existence of things reaches only so far as perception and its advance according to empirical laws can extend. (A225f/B272f/NKS243)

It is in perception that what is extant reveals its reality.

And now Heidegger asks: How does Kant dare to say that perception and *Dasein* are the only characteristics of reality? After all, existence *as such*, that is, in itself, is not a perception. To be sure, perception is "something real in a real subject" (GP64/47); but the reality of the object is not the reality of its perception, and perception *as a perceiving* is not the reality of the object but only a mode of approach to it. Even when we take perception in the sense of *what is being perceived* the question still is: Can existence be equated with what is being perceived *as perceived*? Kant's discussion of *Dasein*, of existence and of reality *as perception* is at best unclear.

In his "Beweisgrund" essay of 1763, Kant stated that "the concept 'position' is one and the same as that of Being in general" (GP60/45). But this statement is ambiguous. Does "position" (*Setzung*) mean an attitude of the subject—that is, a positing? Or does it mean "that which has been posited"—that is, the object? On this point Kant leaves us in the dark.

Let us assume that by "position" (*Setzung*) Kant meant to identify "being perceived" with *extantness*. The question then is: Is something extant *because* it is being perceived? This can hardly be so. A tree does not come into existence because I perceive it. On the contrary, I perceive it *if* and *because* it exists.

Perception is at most a mode of coming to know something that is extant or that exists. "Position" (*Setzung*) in the sense of positing (*setzen*) is not the Being of a *Seiendes* but is at best only the "*How*" *of comprehending* what is extant.

According to Kant, all positing is an "I think." But as Heidegger points out, Kant is here still limited by "a very crude psychology." If he had had the possibility, which is available today, of investigating with precision something like perception, "he might have obtained a different insight into the essence of *Dasein* and existence" (GP 69/50).

However, Kant's thesis that Being is not a real predicate cannot be repudiated in its negative sense; for Being is not a *Seiendes*. What is and remains obscure in the Kantian position as interpreted in the *Grundprobleme* is the *Seinsverfassung*—the ontological character—of perception. And this is so, Heidegger maintains, because "the explicit ontology appropriate to *Dasein*, to the *Seiende* which we ourselves are, is in disarray (*liegt im Argen*)" (GP 77/55f). A new approach is needed; and Heidegger intended to provide it by coming to terms with Kant. He did so in *Kant und das Problem der Metaphysik.*

When this book was published, readers, misunderstanding by and large Heidegger's intention, denounced the work as a fine example of Heidegger's distortion of the views of other thinkers, and dismissed it as "bad Kant," or ignored its thesis altogether. A notable exception was Charles M. Sherover; but even he did not see its true relation to *Sein und Zeit.*

In the book's second edition (1950) Heidegger responded to the criticisms. "My critics," he wrote, "have constantly reproached me for the violence of my interpretations, and the grounds for this reproach can easily be found in the work . . . . But I refrain from making it a patchwork through the addition of supplements and postscripts" (KPMxvii/xxv).

Heidegger was right, I believe, in making this decision; for what he intended to do in *Kant und das Problem der Metaphysik* was "to bring out what Kant 'intended to say'" (KPM193/206).

Within this perspective Heidegger defines his task as that of "explicating Kant's *Critique of Pure Reason* as a laying of the foundation of metaphysics in order thus to bring before us the 'problem of metaphysics' as the problem of a fundamental ontology" (KPM194/208); and he is convinced that, in the end, the solution of this problem can be found only by way of an ontological analysis of what is meant by "to be a human being." It is this idea that is the basic theme underlying the whole of Heidegger's early philosophy. And it is this fact, incidentally, which underlies my conviction that, although *Kant und das Problem der Metaphysik* was first published in 1934, or seven years after *Sein und Zeit*, it may well be read as an introduction to that work. This suggestion finds support in the lecture course entitled "Phänomenologische Interpretation von Kants Kritik der reinen Vernunft" which Heidegger gave at the University of Freiburg during the winter semester of 1927-28. And we must remember that at German universities a lecture course is indeed a *Vorlesung*. It means that the professor *actually reads* a text which he has written. And so it is not only possible but a fact that *Kant und das Problem der Metaphysik* was actually written prior to the publishing of *Sein und Zeit*, and not as a mere afterthought, and may therefore well serve as an introduction to *Sein und Zeit*.

In the opening statement of *Kant und das Problem der Metaphysik* Heidegger makes it clear that "the task of the following investigation is to explicate Kant's *Critique of Pure Reason* as a laying of the foundations of metaphysics in order thus to bring before us the 'problem of metaphysics' as that of a *fundamental ontology*"—"of human *Dasein*." It is, therefore, an analytic which "asks the concrete question: 'What is man?'" (KPM1/3f).

It is essential for our understanding of *Kant und das Problem der Metaphysik* to keep Heidegger's introductory statement in mind as we follow his argument.

As far as Kant is concerned, transcendental philosophy (or metaphysics in itself) is not a science but only "the idea of a science for which the critique of pure reason has to lay down the complete architectonic plan. It has to guarantee, as following from principles, the completeness and certainty of the structure in all its parts. It is the system of all principles of reason" (A13/B27/NKS60); or, as Heidegger puts it: "The disclosure of the possibility of ontological knowledge must become an elucidation of the essence of pure reason" (KPM13/19), and "laying the foundation of metaphysics as disclosure of the essence of ontology *is* critique of pure reason" (KPM14/19).

We must keep in mind, however, that the human reason is finite and that this is crucial for the problematic which arises from the fact that "besides the two sources of knowledge (sensibility and understanding) we have no other" (A294/B350/NKS298), and that "only because they combine can knowledge (*Erkenntnis*) arise" (A51/B75f/NKS93). "Through sensibility objects are given to us; through the understanding they are thought" (A15/B29/NKS61f). Kant himself said that he carried out his work in the *Critique of Pure Reason* by "beginning at the point at which the common root of our faculty of knowledge—a root unknown to us—divides" (A835/B863/NKS655).

Heidegger is thus justified in maintaining that "the Kantian laying of the foundation of metaphysics . . . does not lead to the clear and absolute evidence of a first principle but points deliberately (*bewusst*) to the unknown"

(KPM34/41f). And reacting to this fact, Heidegger wonders "how a finite being (man), delivered up to the status of a *Seiendes* and dependent upon perceiving it, can have knowledge of—can intuit—the *Seiende* before it is given, without being its 'creator'?" Put otherwise, "How must this finite being (man) be constituted in order that, without the aid of experience, the bringing forth of the constitution of Being (*die Seinverfassung*) of the *Seiende*—that is, an ontological synthesis—be possible?" (KPM35/43). The question is particularly pertinent in the case of cognition *a priori.*

In laying the foundation of scientific knowledge reason depends for its content on sensory intuition. As Kant put it: "Objects are given us by means of sensibility, and it alone gives us *intuitions*; they are *thought* through the understanding" (A19/B33/NKS65), which provides *a priori* principles—such as the principle of causality. But it is sensory intuition which relates all cognition to objects. Knowledge, therefore, consists of sensory data and specific concepts. But, so Heidegger observes, since intuition is essentially receptive, being induced by an object, it is "just as little creative" as it is infinite; and whatsoever is knowable "must show itself by itself." Hence, Heidegger continues, "what finite knowledge is able to make manifest must be a *Seiendes*—something extant—which shows itself as something which appears—an appearance" (KPM26/35).

The distinction between things themselves and appearances corresponds to the two ways in which things can stand in relation to finite and infinite cognition: the *Seiende im Ent-stand*—that is, a *Seiendes* outside the cognitive relation—and *the same Seiendes* as object (KPM29/37). Kant is quite clear on this point. In the *Opus postumum* he stated: "The difference of the conceptions 'thing-in-itself' and 'appearance' is not objectively real but is merely subjective." That is, the "thing-in-itself" is but "a different aspect (*respectus*) of the representation with regard to *the same object.*"[2]

But let us note also that Kant referred to his *Critique of Pure Reason* as a "study of our inner nature," which "to the philosopher is a matter of duty" (A703/B731/NKS570). The question is—and this is the question basic to *Sein und Zeit*—"How must the finite *Seiendes* which we call *man* be constituted in its innermost essence in order to be open to the *Seiendes* which he himself is not (and) which therefore must be able to reveal itself by itself?" (KPM39/47)

It is well known, of course, that Kant regarded space and time as pure intuitions which make possible our experience of objects and their interrelations. Space, however, cannot be a characteristic of our innermost nature. It is constitutive neither of consciousness nor of reason. As far as time is concerned,

Kant wrote that it is "but the form of inner sense"; that "it has to do neither with shape or position but with the relation of representations (*Vorstellungen*) in our inner state" (A33/B49f/NKS77). But—and here Heidegger gets his clue for the basic theme of *Sein und Zeit*—Kant also asserted that "time is the formal *a priori* condition of all appearances whatsoever" (A34/B50/NKS77). Heidegger takes this Kantian statement as implying that "time has superiority (*Vorrang*) over space," and that, "as universal pure intuition, it must become the *leading* and *supporting* essential factor (*das Wesenselement*) of that pure cognition which constitutes transcendence" (KPM44/54).

Here we have Heidegger's justification for making *time* the basic factor in his own ontology.

Kant, of course, had made the intuition of space and spatial relations equally important with time and temporal relations. On this point Heidegger differs radically with Kant, and rightly so. The objects we intuit and their relations are objects of our outer senses and are by no means internal constituents of the experiencing subject. But "*as states of representing* all representations fall immediately in time, (and) that which is *represented* in representing belongs *as such* in time" (KPM45/55). And if this is so, then it follows that "*the more time is subjective, the more original and extensive is the liberation from limitations (die Entschränkung) of the subject*" (KPM45/54, Heidegger's emphasis).

In his discussion of the schematism of the pure concepts of the understanding (A137-47/B176-87/NNKS180-87), Kant had argued that, in cognition, sensory intuitions are being unified in concepts, and that this unity of concepts can be seen and held in advance of all determinative statements concerning the many. Kant put it this way: Every determinative statement concerning man—in other words, every determination of something *as* something (that is, every judgement)—contains "the unity of the act of bringing various representations under one common representation" (A68/B93/NKS105); and this is an act of judgement.

However, the reflection which leads to a judgement is already "the precursory (*vorgängige*) act of representing a unity," and the unities thus represented are the content of our concepts—that is, of the categories—"which in advance (*im vorhinein*) belong to the essential structure of the reflection" (KPM49/57f). This implies that in the categories the understanding provides the pure unities of possible unifications. And this, in turn, means that "in pure understanding lies hidden a *systematic whole* of the multiplicity of the pure concepts"—that is, of the categories. What is thus revealed as "the essential unity of a first principle" is "a multiform (*vielgestaltige*) action" (KPM59/68).

But we may well ask: Who does the acting? Here Heidegger faces the problem which led Hegel to the conception of *Dasein* as the proper starting point in philosophy. Kant, of course, did not see it quite that way. But even he wondered: "How, then, is the *subsumption* of intuitions under pure concepts, that is, how is the *application* of a category to appearance, possible?" (A138/B177/ NKS180). The answer to this question Kant gives in his interpretation of the *transcendental schema.*

It is his conviction that "*time*, as the formal condition of the manifold of the inner sense, and therefore of the connection of all representations, contains an *a priori* manifold in pure intuition"; that "time is contained in every empirical representation of the manifold," and that "thus an application of the category to appearance becomes possible by means of the transcendental determination of time which, as the schema of the concepts of understanding, mediates the subsumption of the appearances under categories" (A138f/B177f/NKS181). In order for this to be possible, the "pure *a priori* concepts" or categories "must contain *a priori* formal conditions of sensibility, namely, those of the inner sense" (A140/B179/ NKS182). This "schema of concepts" is in itself always "a product of the imagination." The schema of a triangle, for example, is "a rule of synthesis of the imagination . . . [and] the concept 'dog' signifies a rule according to which my imagination can delineate the figure of a four-legged animal in a general manner, without limitation to any single determinate figure such as experience actually presents" (A141/B18o/NKS182f). This formation of "schemata," Kant added, is the "sensibilization (*Versinnlichung*) of concepts"— "an action concealed in the depth of the human soul."

When we now read in the *Critique of Pure Reason* that "the pure image of all objects of the senses in general is *time*" (A142/B182/NKS183) and keep in mind what Kant said about the basis of human knowledge in general, we cannot doubt that Heidegger derived his basic concept of experience as developed in *Sein und Zeit* from Kant's *Critique of Pure Reason.* It is in this sense that I regard his book *Kant und das Problem der Metaphysik* as an introduction to *Sein und Zeit*, and not as a mere afterthought.

But let me elaborate.

In the second edition of the *Critique of Pure Reason* Kant eliminated two passages which specifically present the imagination as a third fundamental faculty in addition to sensibility and the understanding (A94/NKS127 and A115/NKS141). He stated instead:

> That which, as representation, can be antecedent to any and every act of thinking anything, is intuition; and if it contains nothing but relations, it is

> the form of intuition. Since this form does not represent anything save in so far as something is posited in the mind, it can be nothing but the mode in which the mind is affected through its own activity (namely, through this positing of its representation), and so is affected by itself; in other words, it is nothing but an inner sense in respect of the form of that sense (B67f/NKS87f).

That is, the "inner sense" receives nothing from the outside, only from itself. "Pure self-affection provides the transcendental primordial structure (*Urstruktur*) of the finite self as such" (KPM182f/196). It is neither "on hand" nor "outside us" as things are, but is "pure intuition in so far as out of itself and without the aid of experience it performs the aspect of succession" (KPM180/194). This pure intuition, together with what is intuited in it, pertains only to itself, and does so without the aid of experience. That is, "in its very essence, time is pure affection of itself" (KPM180f/194). Still, as "pure self-affection, time constitutes the essential structure of subjectivity" (*ibid.*). In this respect it becomes clear that "time necessarily affects the concept of the representations of objects" (KPM181/195). That is, "time belongs to the inner sensibility of letting something stand as an object," and in this sense "time originally forms finite selfhood, and does so in such a way that the self can be something like self-consciousness" (*ibid.*).

In positing itself, the finite self not only relates itself to something else, but relates that something else to itself also. This "from-it-self-to . . . and back-to-itself" first constitutes the "mental character of the mind as a finite self" (KPM183/196). And this Heidegger insists, "makes obvious at once (*mit einem Schlage*) that, as pure self-affection, time does not exist 'in the mind' side by side with pure apperception, but that *the ground for the possibility* of selfhood rests already in pure apperception, and does so in such a way that it makes mind into mind" (KPM183/197).

This implies that "the pure finite self has in itself a temporal character." As Kant put it: "The abiding (*bleibend*) and unchanging 'I' (of pure apperception) forms the correlate of all our representations in so far as it is to be possible that we should become conscious of them" (A123/NKS146). As pure self-affection time is thus nothing "besides" pure apperception, but "is already included in pure apperception and (actually) constitutes the mind-character of mind (*Gemütscharakter des Gemüts*) as a finite self" (KPM183/196). As Heidegger sees it, this means that "*as basis of the possibility of selfhood*, time is already included in pure apperception and thus makes mind first possible as mind" (KPM183/197).

But this means that "the pure finite self has in itself the character of time." "Time and the 'I think' are no longer irreconcilable and unlike, but are the same" (*ibid*). As Kant put it: "The abiding and unchanging 'I' (of pure apperception) forms the correlate of all our representations" (A123/NKS146). And in the chapter on schematism Kant said of time that it is "unchanging (*unwandelbar*) and abiding" (A143/B183/NKS184). "The time in which all change of appearances has to be thought, remains and does not change" (A182/B224f/NKS213).

But since the "I" is also "abiding and unchanging" does this not mean that the "I" is "so temporal that it is time itself and that only as time is 'I' possible in its ownmost essence?" (KPM184/198). And in the primordially forming time this "abiding and unchanging I" lets "stand both the object and its horizons" (KPM185/199). In other words, "the interpretation of the transcendental imagination as root—that is, the illumination of how the pure synthesis lets the two stems grow out of itself and leads into the intimate interrelation (*Verwurzelung*) of this root: primordial time" (KPM187/201). That is, pure apprehension, pure reproduction, and pure recognition are distinct not because they are related to the three elements of pure cognition, but because they are originally unified as time-forming (*zeitbildend*). They are the "temporalization (*Zeitigung*) of time itself" (KPM188/201) and only because the transcendental imagination is rooted in time can it at all be "the root of transcendence" (KPM188/202).

The Kantian interpretation thus leads to the central position of time. That is, as far as Kant is concerned, the laying of the foundation of metaphysics is based upon time, and "the question as to Being, the fundamental question concerning a foundation of metaphysics, is the problem of *Sein und Zeit*" (KPM194/208).

As far as Heidegger is concerned, this Kantian laying of the foundation of the unity of the human mind (*des menschlichen Gemüts*) leads to the question concerning the existence of the human being. That is, it leads to anthropology.

In the *Critique of Pure Reason* Kant stated that "all temporal interests of my reason, speculative as well as practical, combine in the three following questions:

1. What can I know?
2. What ought I to do?
3. What may I hope?

"The first question is merely speculative . . . . The second is purely practical . . . . And the third is at once practical and theoretical" (A805/B833/NKS635f).

In his *Logik,* Kant is quoted to have said what seems to be quite obvious: that, "basically, all three aspects can be classified as anthropology."[3]

To be sure, following Aristotle, Kant speaks in the *Critique of Pure Reason* of the "physiology of pure reason" (A845/B873/NKS662). But physiology does not provide an understanding of man's existence as the subject of all experience—as the key to all *Seiendes* and to the Being of every *Seiendes*. And, as Heidegger points out, the comprehension of Being must actually precede that of a *Seiendes as seiend*, as of man's existence as well.

The question concerning the possibility and essence of Being is thus entailed in man's preconceptual realization of his own existence.

To be sure, "our own *Dasein* is manifest to us. We have, therefore, an understanding of Being—of our own Being, of our *being there*—even though the concept (of Being) is lacking" (KPM217/234). If this elementary comprehension of our own "being-there" were not a fact, man would never be the *Seiende* he is, "no matter how wonderful his faculties are." But, in fact, "man is a *Seiendes* in the midst of others in such a way that the *Seiende* which he is and the *Seiende* which he is not are always already manifest to him" in his being-in-the-world. "With the existence of man there comes an eruption (*Einbruch*) into the totality of the *Seiende* such that only now does the *Seiende* become manifest in itself in always different expansion (*Weite*) and different degrees of clarity and certainty" (KPM218/235).

But we must note also that "there is and must already be something like (*der gleichen wie*) Being where finitude (*Endlichkeit*) has become extant" (KPM 219/236)—as it is in the case of man in his *Dasein*. And so Heidegger can, and does, assert that "the laying of the foundations of metaphysics is based on a metaphysics of *Dasein*" (KPM220/238). The first stage of this metaphysics of *Dasein* is fundamental ontology—the subject matter of *Sein und Zeit*.

But, Heidegger now points out, we receive no really informative disclosure of the Being of *Dasein* from the "I" as a moral person. And in the Kantian interpretation of the *personalitas transcendentalis* we also seek in vain for an answer to the question "What is Being?" (KPM221f/242). Although as ground of the possibility of the "I think" the "I" is also "the ground and condition of the possibility of the forms of combination"—that is, of the categories—these forms cannot be applied to the "I" itself. "The pure 'I' is never given to me as something determinable—that is, for an explication in terms of the categories . . . . The only thing that can be said is: the 'I' is an 'I-am-acting'" (KPM223/243). As Kant put it in a Note: "The 'I think' expresses the act of determining my *Dasein* (that is, my extantness). The *Dasein* is thereby already given, but the mode in which I am to determine it, that is, the manifold pertaining to it, is not thereby given. In order that it be given, self-intuition is required; and such intuition is conditioned by a given *a priori* form, namely, time, which is sensible and belongs to the receptivity of the determinable [in me]" (B158/NKS169).

Since there is no basis for an application of the categories to the "I," Kant was right when he declared the categories or fundamental concepts (*Grundbegriffe*) to be unsuitable for a determination of the "I." The interpretation which he gives to the *Ichheit*—to the nature of the "I"—as "spontaneous intelligence" is in effect the same as that of traditional metaphysics. But Heidegger now interprets metaphysics in a new way as *fundamental ontology* according to which *Dasein* is to be constituted in its finitude and with a view of the inner possibility of an understanding of Being—the topic of *Sein und Zeit*.

Three

THE PROBLEMATIC OF *SEIN UND ZEIT*

The title *Sein und Zeit* suggests that Being and Time are interrelated in a way that implies that each is definable in terms of the other. To be sure, Heidegger concedes at once that "Being," although "the most universal concept," is also the most obscure. It is undefinable but "self-evident." Everyone understands statements such as "The sky is blue" and "I am happy." Any inquiry into the meaning of "Being" is thus already "guided beforehand" by "a vague understanding of Being" (SZ5/25). But the question is: What is "the Being that determines what exists as a *Seiendes*," as what is actual? "What is a *Seiendes* in itself?" (SZ6/25)

Before turning to the argument presented in *Sein und Zeit* let us note that the book actually consists of two divisions, identified as "Erster Abschnitt" (SZ41-230/65-273) and "Zweiter Abschnitt" (SZ231-438/274-488). The two divisions are interrelated in such a way that they must be read together as supplementary arguments.

The argument as a whole is preceded by an Introduction (SZ2-40/21-64) in which Heidegger attempts to clarify the question concerning the meaning of Being. After all, he points out, "'Being' is the most general and the emptiest concept; as such it resists every attempt at definition" (SZ2/22). But this does not mean that it is the "clearest" concept. It is rather "the darkest of all" (SZ3/23), and is essentially "indefinable" (SZ4/23).

What is at issue is the Being of a *Seiendes*—that is, the Being of something that exists, that is extant. And Being as such is not a *Seiendes*—not something that exists. But as I have shown in the Introduction to the present book, Heidegger followed Hegel in taking our own *Dasein* as the proper starting point for his inquiry. He affirms now that the exemplary *Seiende* with which our inquiry can begin is our own personal *Dasein* (SZ7/27). As Heidegger puts it later: "*Dasein* exists as a *Seiendes* for which Being is itself an issue" (SZ406/ 458). But, as he makes clear also, *Dasein* exists only as "being-in-the-world"; and in being-in-the-world, it "has always expressed *itself*." Moreover, as being alongside the *Seiende* encountered in that world, *Dasein* constantly "addresses itself to the very object of its concerns, and discusses it" (SZ406/458). In doing so, it expresses also a "now here," a "then when," and an "at that time" (*ibid.*). *Dasein* does so, Heidegger believes, because "Temporality constitutes ecstatico-horizontally the clarification (*Gelichtetheit*) of the *Da*, and therefore is primarily interpretable in the *Da*, and therefore is known to us" (SZ408/460). In this perspective, any reference to "formerly," "now," and "then when" "refers to the ecstatical constitution of Temporality and *therefore* is essential to time itself" (SZ408/461).

The question is: "Does *Zeit* as such manifest itself as the horizon of Being?" (SZ438/488); and—more importantly—does *Sein und Zeit* give us a satisfactory answer to this question?

In the Preface to the seventh edition of *Sein und Zeit* Heidegger himself states that "should I have finished what I intended to do [in *Sein und Zeit*], what I actually finished would have to be changed."[1] And as a matter of fact, his answer to the question of *Sein und Zeit* Heidegger gives us in the posthumously published *Grundprobleme der Phänomenologie*, which is the subject matter of the next chapter. We are here concerned with *Sein und Zeit* only.

In the opening chapter of that book Heidegger makes it quite clear that the *Seiende* which is to be analyzed is in each case *my own* (*das je meinige*) (SZ41/67). Its analysis is guided anticipatorily by the assumption of *Dasein*'s "existence" (SZ231/274). Its "essence lies in its to be" (SZ42/67).

Of this *Dasein* two aspects are characteristic: (1) Its "mode of Being" is either *authentic* or it is *inauthentic*; and (2) it "determines itself as a *Seiendes* by virtue of its possibilities of being this or that." That is, *Dasein* determines itself as a *Seiendes* in the light of possibilities which it itself *is*, and which it somehow understands (SZ43/69).

We must realize that "the person is not a thing, not a substance, not an object," but is "a performer of intentional acts that are bound together by the unity of meaning" (SZ48/73). Moreover, as Heidegger sees it, "*Dasein* is a *Seiendes*" which, in its Being, "takes an attitude toward that Being understandingly" (SZ53/78).

Moreover, this *Dasein* is grounded in what Heidegger calls "*In-der-Welt-sein*"—*Dasein*'s "being-in-the-world" (SZ53/78). In fact, as Heidegger tells us, "in saying 'I,' *Dasein* expresses itself as being-in-the-world" (SZ321/368). What does this mean? Heidegger devotes three chapters to this problem.

He begins by asking what is meant by "being-in"—by "*In-Sein*." Ordinarily it means that a particular *Seiendes* is "present within" some other *Seiendes*—as water is in a glass. Heidegger calls this the "categorical" *Insein*, and points out that it is not *Dasein*'s mode of being-in-the-world, which he calls "existential" (SZ54/79) and identifies with "the formal existential expression of the Being of

Dasein" (SZ54/80).[2] As such the existential *Insein* must not be confused with *Dasein*'s "being with" other *Seiende*. It but characterizes a "horizon" of *to do, to affect, to provide for* (SZ57/83f). And this essential aspect of *Dasein*'s constitution (*Seinsverfassung*) is "somehow always already known" (SZ58/85) —"having its ontic foundation in the constitution of Being as such" (SZ61/88).

Fundamental to *Dasein*'s being-in-the-world is thus the fact that *Dasein* is always "outside" next to other entities encountered in the world (SZ62/89) and is capable of describing them—of fixating them conceptually-categorically as "things—things of nature, and things related to values" (SZ63/91). We must realize, however, that "nature as such is a *Seiendes* encountered within the world, and which in various ways and at various levels is discoverable by *Dasein*" (SZ63/92).

The world closest to our own everyday *Dasein* is, of course, our *Umwelt*—our environing world (SZ66/94). Our *Dasein* always finds itself already in this world. The world is the object of all our concerns (SZ67/95).

The ontological explication of this *Umwelt* leads progressively to such characteristics of Being as "substantiality, materiality, expansiveness, side-by-sideness." But what we thus encounter in our daily concerns is at first conceived pre-ontologically. Heidegger calls it *Zeug*—"that which is useful" (SZ68/97). Strictly speaking, a *Zeug* never simply "*is*." It is essentially always "something in order to" and can best be understood only as such.

However, any particular useful thing—a *Zeug*—may be related to something else that also is useful. Thus, something for writing—a pen, for example, is related to "inkstand, pen, ink, paper, blotting pad, table, lamp, furniture, windows, doors room" (SZ68/97)—all of which are things "useful for . . ." and are understood as such.

The mode of Being of that which is directly available for use Heidegger calls "*Zuhandenheit*"—at-handness. Tools are, however, by no means the first with which our daily activities are concerned. Our first concern is "that which is to be achieved—the work" (SZ69/99)—"the *Wozu*" for which the tools are needed (SZ70/99). And the tools—hammers, pliers, nails, and so forth—consist of steel, wood, stones—that is, of materials encountered in Nature. And so, in the use of tools, "Nature" is discovered—"Nature" in the light of the products of Nature (SZ70/100).

But more is involved. The work reveals not only "*Seiende* which are at hand" but also *Seiende* of the mode of Being of that *Dasein* for whom in its concerns that which has been made (*das Hergestellte*) is at hand (SZ71/100). This is especially evident when we consider the public character of our environing world: streets, bridges, buildings, and so on. And in this environing world we note the changes of days and nights.

But the world as a whole does not consist merely of what is at hand (SZ75/106). To be sure, *Dasein*'s concern always is the way it is on the basis of familiarity with the world (SZ76/107); but this familiarity is not the whole story. In its concerns with the environing world the human subject encounters "usable objects"—such as signs which "indicate" the "right way." And there is "the hammering of the hammer." But neither "indicating" nor "hammering" are *entities*; and neither are they properties. Their character can best be defined in terms of their appropriateness (SZ83/114f).

Insofar as *Dasein is*, it encounters *Seiende* as *Zuhandene*—as what are at hand; and this encounter "in the mode of Being" is *Dasein*'s involvement in the *phenomenon "world."* The structure of that to which *Dasein* relates is what constitutes the "worldness of the world—*die Weltlichkeit der Welt*" (SZ86/119). In its familiarity with significance *Dasein* is thus the ontic condition of the possibility of discovering *Seiende* encountered in the world, which manifest themselves in their *In-itselfness* (SZ87/120). In its very Being *Dasein* is thus already essentially (*wesenhaft*) found within the context of what is at-hand—and thus is dependent upon the presence of that world (SZ87/121).[3]

If Being-in-the-world is the basic constitution of *Dasein*, "then it must always be ontically possible for *Dasein* to come to know itself. It would be completely unintelligible if the *Dasein* which responds to its environing world would remain in total ignorance about itself" (SZ59/86) or about its world. Any "objective character" of such a statement provides the means for a "circumspect-ive interpretation" of the world as well as of *Dasein* (SZ156f/198ff). That is, comprehending (*Erkennen*) has "its ontic foundation as a mode of *Dasein*'s being-in-the-world" (SZ61/88). That is, it is "anticipatorily grounded" (*vorgängig gegründet*) in this "being-with" which from the very beginning is not "a mere gaping (*Begaffen*) at something present in the world" (*ibid.*), but is a matter of *Dasein*'s concerns. If knowledge, as contemplative determination of what is present, is to be possible, then there must first be the experience of a deficiency in the concernful dealings with "the world." "In refraining from all constructing, manipulation, and the like, concern must put itself into the sole remaining mode of being-in—into merely tarrying (*verweilen*) with . . ." (*ibid.*).

On the basis of this mode of Being relative to the world, that which is encountered in the world is "pure appearance" (*pures Aussehen*), but it makes possible an explicit examination of that which is encountered (*ibid.*). In directing itself toward and comprehending what is encountered *Dasein* is in its "primary mode of Being" always already "outside" (*draussen*) itself by "objects encountered in the already discovered world" (SZ62/89). Still, in cognition (*im Erkennen*) *Dasein* attains a new relation to the already discovered world (*zu der je schon entdeckten Welt*) (*ibid.*).

To describe that world "phenomenologically" means to exhibit the *Seiende* encountered [in] it and "to solidify (*fixieren*) it conceptually-categorially (*begrifflich-kategorial*)" (SZ63/91). The *Seiende* in the world are then recognized as "things—things of nature and things having value (*wertbehaftet*)." But insofar as the latter are based on the Being of things of nature, nature as such becomes the "primary theme." The question is: "What constitutes their ontological meaning?" (SZ63/92)

As Heidegger sees it, "'World' is ontologically no fixation (*Bestimmung*) of that *Seiende* which *Dasein is not*; it is rather a characteristic of *Dasein* itself" (SZ64/92). That is, it is "'wherein' a factual (*faktisches*) *Dasein* as such 'lives'" (SZ65/93). The term "world" has thus for Heidegger "a pre-ontological existential significance"—and in this sense "world" means "the 'public' We-world or one's 'Own' nearest (domestic) environment (*Umwelt*)" (SZ65/93). Being in this *Umwelt* is characterized by such "exemplary phenomena" as "using, handling, making what is at hand"—the Being of "what belongs to the every-day needs" of any *Dasein* (SZ352/403).

The first mode of dealing with such things is the "handling (*hantierend*), using concern which has its own kind of 'cognition' (*Erkenntnis*)" (SZ67/95). *Dasein* finds itself always already in this every-day situation. "Opening the door [for example] I already make use of the latch" (SZ67/96).

Calling a *Seiendes*, such as a latch, a "*thing*" entails an unexpressed anticipatory reference to an ontological characteristic which, progressively, entails characteristics such as "substantiality, materiality, extension, side-by-sideness" (SZ68/96). But more than this: "one characterizes such 'things' also as 'invested with values' (*wertbehaftet*)" (*ibid.*). They are the things with which we are concerned in our daily life. We call them "*Zeuge*"—that is, that which is useful in our daily concerns. We thus speak of "*Schreibzeug*"—what is useful for writing; "*Nähzeug*"—what is useful for sewing; "*Fahrzeug*"—what is useful for traveling; "*Masszeug*"—what is useful for measuring. However, strictly speaking, a *Zeug*—that which is useful—never simply *is*. It is essentially always "something in order to . . . " and it is always interrelated with something else that is useful. Thus we find this: "Inkstand, pen, ink, paper, blotting pad, table, lamp, furniture, windows, doors, room" (SZ68/97). Such things are at first encountered more or less individually; but in their interrelations as real things they fill a "room"; and beyond this, they fill our immediate environment as such.

However, the *use* of tools is not a *comprehending* of things as such. Heidegger is thus justified in distinguishing between the *Seinsart*—the "mode of Being" of *Zeuge* and that of *things as such.* The former he calls *Zuhandenheit*—at-handness; the latter he calls *Vorhandenheit*—extantness. And we must realize that in our daily concerns are, at first, not the tools but the *das Werk*—"the work" to be accomplished—that is, that for which the tools are to be used (SZ69f/99). But this "for which" also has the mode of Being (*die Seinsart*) of a tool. Making a watch, for example, is but the making of a means for determining the lapse of time.

However, through the use of tools "Nature" is discovered—"Nature" as revealed in its products—*Naturprodukte* (SZ70/100). And what is being made by the use of tools not only indicates what the object that is made is to be used for, it also refers to the "bearer and user" of what has been made. And so that which has been made reveals "not only a *Seiendes* which is at hand but also a *Seiendes* of *Dasein*'s kind of Being" (SZ71/100). It thus entails a "public world" which is accessible to everyone—a world including "streets, bridges, buildings" (*ibid.*).

Being-in-the-world, beginning with what is at hand, thus advances to "the ontological-categorial determination of a *Seiendes* as it is 'in itself'" (SZ71/101). That is, what is at hand as useful leads to what is in itself extant.

It is true, of course, that what in *Dasein*'s concerns is most readily available is actually usable for the purpose intended or it is not part of what is at hand. And it is also possible that what is at hand is not only unsuitable for the purpose intended "but actually is an obstacle to it" (SZ73/103). Meaningful and effective concern is thus possible only on the basis of "a familiarity (*Vertrautheit*) with the world" (SZ76/107) that makes possible the selection of the appropriate useable object.

Of all useful things, "signs" play a special role in *Dasein*'s dealings with the world. As Heidegger sees it, a sign is not just a thing. It is "a thing which explicitly raises a whole complex of relations." That is, "a sign is something that is ontically at hand as this particular thing but at the same time it is something that indicates the ontological structure of at-handness, of reference-totality (*Verweisungsganzheit*) and worldhood" (SZ82/114).

What is at hand (*zuhanden*) is within the world. Its Being stands therefore in some kind (*irgendeinem*) of ontological relation to world and worldhood (*Weltlichkeit*). And this means that "in all of that which is at hand the world is always already there" (SZ83/114). And this implies that "it is ontologically impossible" that there is only *one* useful object—only one *Zeug* (SZ353/404). In the disclosedness of the world is grounded the discovery of all that is at hand or is at least extant (SZ297/344). And with the "in order to," public time—"world-time" (*Weltzeit*)—also reveals itself (SZ414/467).

But it was Descartes who laid the foundation for the ontological characteristic of that inner-worldly *Seiende* which is directly available and is the foundation of our knowledge of all other *Seiende*—including "material nature" (SZ98/131). [See Descartes's "First Meditation."]

This Cartesian analysis of the "world," Heidegger asserts, makes possible the "secure structure" of what at first is available to us only as phenomena. But once we acknowledge these phenomena in their availableness (*Vorhandenheit*) we can and do attribute value to them. This addition of value predicates does not give us a new insight into the Being of "goods" but presupposes the mode of Being of things. That is, "values are actual determinations of things" and have their ontological origin exclusively in the antecedent reality of things as the basic stratum (*Fundamentalschicht*) of all there is (SZ99/132).

We must remember, however, that *Dasein*, being in the world, is surrounded by other *Seiende*; and this means that both *Dasein* and what surrounds it are present in space (SZ101/134). It follows that what is at hand in our daily concerns has "the character of *nearness* in various degrees" (SZ102/135). A tool, for example, has its specific place. It is "here" or "there" or "in some place else" (SZ104/138). Such orientation in the manifold places of our surrounding world is characteristic of our daily endeavors. It creates "a spatiality (*Räumlichkeit*) on the basis of which existence always determines its 'place.'" But it is a spatiality "grounded in the constitution of the being-in-the-world" (SZ299/346).

To be sure, "*Dasein* has an essential tendency toward nearness" (SZ105/-140); but this does not impose upon it limits in its endeavors to reach out. "The objective distances of inner-worldly things are not 'nearness' and 'distance'"; for things simply *are* where and what they are. It is *Dasein* which, in existing, "distances itself" from other *Seiende*—a fact which entails spatial "directionality." In other words, insofar as *Dasein is*, "it already has a directing-distancing (*ausrichtend-entfernendes*) of its own discovered region" of near and far (SZ108/143). In this "spatialization" *Dasein*'s "bodily nature" (*Leiblichkeit*) is also characterized. Right and left are in this situation not something subjective but are directions of *Dasein*'s orientation within an always present world. That is, "I necessarily orientate myself within, and with respect to, a world that is familiar to me" (SZ109/144). [See Descartes's "First Meditation."]

The space thus disclosed lacks as yet "the pure multiplicity of three dimensions" (SZ110/145). We must note, however, that the space thus disclosed is not in the subject nor is the world in it. As Heidegger sees it, the space is rather in the world insofar as the being-in-the-world which is constitutive of the subject discloses space. "The 'subject'—*Dasein*—properly understood, is spatial" (SZ111/146), and spatiality is discoverable only as co-constitutive of the world (SZ113/148).

Within the world, "*Dasein* is that *Seiendes* which I myself am. Its Being is always my own (*das je meinige*)" (SZ114/150). In this sense, and without having to say so, *Dasein* is conceived as something actual. "Nothing is as indubitable as is the givenness of the I" (SZ115/151). (Shades of Hegel!) But if the "I" is an essential determination of *Dasein*, it must be existentially interpreted (SZ117/152).

The world in which *Dasein* finds itself includes not only "things" but "other" *Dasein* as well. That is, "the world of *Dasein* is a shared world (*eine Mitwelt*)" and "the being-in is a being-in-with-others" (SZ118/154). One's own Being is a "being-with and an encountering of others. It is a *Mitdasein*" (SZ121/157); and *Mitdasein* is first and often exclusively based on what is a matter of common concerns. But it is not exclusively so. There are also conflicts. And between the two extremes of "positive solicitude" and "open hostility" there are varying degrees of each and mixtures of both (SZ122/159). An understanding of *Dasein* thus includes already "an understanding of others." And this understanding of others is "a basic existential mode of Being which, prior to anything else, makes cognition (*Erkennen*) and knowledge (*Kenntnis*) possible" (SZ123f/161).

What is here ontologically important is that the subject-character of one's own *Dasein* and that of others is existentially determined by their inner-worldly comportment. "They *are* what they *are doing*" (SZ126/163).

Our task now is to develop a "thematic analysis of the Being-in (*das Insein*)." That is, we are now concerned with the existential constitution of the *Da* of *Dasein*. As Heidegger sees it, the key here is the fact that *Dasein* is a state of mind which we experience in "the undisturbed equanimity as well as in the restrained ill-humor of our every-day concerns" (SZ134/173). Moods obviously make manifest "how one is and becomes," and thus bring our Being into our environment in our various *concerns*.

In these concerns *Dasein* encounters other *Dasein* in a general way. Anyone can represent them all. They are "the faceless mass"—the *They*. In the *They* individual differences fade out. "Everyone is the other and no one is himself" (SZ126/164). Even one's own *Dasein* becomes absorbed in the mode of Being of "the Other." We take pleasure in what *They* find pleasurable. "We read, see, and judge about literature and the arts as *They* see and judge" (SZ126f/164).

In this obliteration of individual differences "the *They* discloses its real dictatorship," for it prescribes the mode of Being that typifies "ordinary averageness." The *They* determines what is permissible and what is not. Everything which is in any sense exceptional is silently suppressed or disregarded. What is new and original is glossed over as something already well known. "Public opinion" determines what is acceptable as an explication of *Dasein* and of the world. It claims to be "always right," and does so not on the basis of some special insight but because it does not concern itself with the facts. It is "insensitive to all differences of levels and degrees of genuineness" (SZ127/165). The *They* can always be invoked as "authority" and can readily be made answerable for anything. It is so easy to say: It was *They*. And saying this really means "it was 'nobody'" (*ibid.*). Absorbed in the *They*, every *Dasein* is absorbed in its every-day-ness.

And yet, the particular *Dasein* which is *I*—the authentic I-myself—is simply *there* as a primordial phenomenon that is not derivable from anything else. Heidegger calls this fact *Dasein*'s *Geworfenheit*—*Dasein*'s "thrownness." *Dasein* is simply *there* as being-in-the-world (SZ135/174). Its moods reveal that it *is*; but the "whence" and the "whither" (*das Woher und Wohin*) remain obscure (SZ134/173).

The question is: How is this empirical Self, this particular *Dasein* which I myself am, to be interpreted? We must keep in mind, of course, that Heidegger's intention is to develop a *fundamental ontology*, not a psychological analysis of the Self (SZ134/172f).

Dasein is a "primary phenomenon" which is simply there—a ghost of Hegel's theme—and is not derivable from anything else. But this fact does not preclude that a manifoldness of equally primordial characteristics is constitutive of *Dasein*. As Heidegger sees it, there are two "equally primordial constitutive modes of *being-there*": (1) State-of-mind or Mood (*Befindlichkeit*) and (2) Comprehending (*Verstehen*). Both are "equipotentially determined through discourse"; and both are "essentially modes of Being" rather than mere properties of something that is simply present-at-hand (SZ133/171f).

Heidegger's analysis now concentrates on the *Da* of *Dasein*—on being-*there*—(1) as a state-of-mind or mood and (2) as an understanding, that is, as an explication in language and discourse (SZ133/171f).

What Heidegger means by Mood (*Befindlichkeit*) is the most familiar kind of experience in our everyday concerns—the state of mind in which we find ourselves here and now. "The Mood reveals 'how one feels and is getting along'; and in this 'how one feels' our *being-there* manifests itself . . . . But the 'from where' and the 'where to' remain in darkness" (SZ134/173). That is, the Mood simply "brings *Dasein* face to face with the thrownness of its 'being-there' (*dass-es-da-ist*)" (SZ265/310). This Mood reveals itself primarily when it no longer prevails. That is, it reveals itself *"primarily* in its 'having been' (*primär in der Gewesenheit*)" (SZ340/390), but it discloses *Dasein*'s dependence upon a world in which *Dasein* encounters things and events that matter to it (SZ137f/177).

This existential situation must now be analyzed from a phenomenological point of view.

However, Heidegger's intellectualistic version of phenomenology will not do. Heidegger himself refers in one sentence to St. Augustine, Pascal, and Max Scheler (SZ139/178). Brief as it is, this reference is crucial to any understanding of Heidegger's whole approach to ontology.[4] Let me therefore expand the reference briefly.

We have seen in Division One, Chapter One of *Sein und Zeit* that in the *Jahrbuch für Philosophie und phänomenologische Forschung* of 1913/14—the same *Jahrbuch* in which *Sein und Zeit* was first published—Max Scheler had published his "new attempt at finding a basis for an ethical personalism": *Der Formalismus in der Ethik und die materiale Wertethik* (SZ47/73). The work was intended to be and is a constructive alternative to Kant's "formalistic" ethics. It is keyed to the idea of a cognitive significance of "feeling-states" (*Gefühlszustände*).

Throughout the history of philosophy, so Scheler points out, feelings and desires have been regarded as essentially non-cognitive. Very few thinkers have held a different view. With special reference to Pascal's famous statement that "the heart has its reason of which our intellect knows nothing," Scheler argued that it would be a mistake to take Pascal's thesis to mean merely that, after reason has reached its conclusion, our "heart"—our feelings—may also affect our experience. What Scheler takes Pascal to mean is that there is a mode of experiencing whose objects are inaccessible to reason but which, nevertheless, gives us genuine knowledge. Its laws are as understandable as are the laws of logic. In particular, it reveals our having been thrown into a world which is not of our own making.

In this spirit of an "amended" or modified phenomenology, but not precisely with Scheler's meaning, Heidegger now argues that "a state-of-mind (*Gefühlszustand*) not only discloses *Dasein* in its having-been-thrown into, and being dependent upon, a world which is opened up together with *Dasein*'s own Being," but that "the State-of-mind as such is the existential mode of Being in which *Dasein* surrenders itself constantly to the world in such a way that in a specific sense it evades itself" (SZ139/178).

The fundamental State-of-mind here in evidence Heidegger calls *Furcht—Fear* (SZ140/179). He begins his analysis by "disclosing Temporality as *fear*" (SZ341/391).

Fear involves three aspects: (1) the *object* of fear—that which is being feared; (2) the *fearing* as such; and (3) the *why* of the fear—the reason for fearing what is being feared (SZ140/179).

1. What we fear is the "fearsome"—something which we encounter in our being-in-the-world. It has the character of something which threatens and may threaten in various ways. "*As threatening* it is as yet not in controllable nearness but is approaching . . . . It may strike us, and yet it may not" (SZ140/179f). This uncertainty, however, merely enhances its fearsomeness.

2. *Fearing* as such is an immediate State-of-mind. It does not first identify a "future evil" and then fear it. Nor does it first try to understand what it is that is approaching. It simply discloses directly whatever is feared in its fearsomeness. Looking at the fearsome more closely, fear can "make clear to itself" what it is that makes what is feared fearsome; but the fear is there first (SZ141/180).

3. The Why? of fear is the very Being which is afraid—*Dasein* as such. Only someone who is concerned about his own Being can be afraid; for fearing discloses his *Dasein* as endangered, as being abandoned unto itself. Fear thus always discloses primordially some *Seiendes* in the world as threatening or as being threatened. In this general sense fear transcends the individual *Dasein* and includes other persons as well. "We fear for them." In any case fear is a State-of-mind which discloses the being-*there* of *Dasein* (SZ141f/180f).

We must note, however, that the constitutive elements of the total phenomenon of fear may vary. There are different modes of fearing. If what is threatening appears suddenly, fear changes into *alarm.* The suddenness thus changes the fear. If what is threatening is something completely unfamiliar, fear turns into *dread.* But if what threatens has the character of dread and also appears suddenly, fear becomes *terror.* As states-of-mind all of these modifications of fear reveal most forcefully to any *Dasein* its own existence—its being-in-the-world (SZ142/182).

But we can and do fear also for others. We fear for them especially when they do not fear for themselves but foolhardily challenge what threatens them (SZ141/181). This fearing for others is obviously a "being-with"—*ein Mitsein*—with others of whom we might be deprived (SZ142/181).

A *Mood* is but one of the existential aspects of *Dasein*'s Being. Equally basic is *Understanding—Verstehen*—which has its own Moods. That is, in its basic mode of Being *Dasein* is "a *Seiendes* which, in its Being-in-the-world, is an issue unto itself." It always *is* the possibilities-to-be which it realizes (SZ143/183). And these possibilities are revealed to *Dasein* in its Moods (SZ148/188). Comprehending them discloses them as existentially essential to the very nature of *Dasein*. That is, *Dasein* now comprehends what it actually *is* and what it *can be*. It comprehends that it *is* its own possibilities of Being and that it is at stake in them.

Comprehension encompasses, of course, the whole structure of being-in-the-world. It discloses in particular what is ready-to-hand as the useful and the destructible. The totality of what is ready-to-hand is thus disclosed to *Dasein* as a context of possibilities. This is so, Heidegger maintains, because, in itself and essentially, comprehension has the character of a *projection*. It projects with equal primordiality the "for-the-sake-of-which" of what is present-to-hand and of its "significance" as the "world-ness" of *Dasein*'s actual world as a *There* of possibilities-for-Being (SZ145/185).

But a projection must not be mistaken for a plan that has been thought out and in accordance with which *Dasein* arranges its Being. It is a projection of possibilities only. But so long as *Dasein is*, it understands itself, and continues to understand itself, in terms of projected possibilities of Being. *Dasein*'s actual mode of existence is thus that of its comprehended possibilities—of possibilities, however, that are limited by *Dasein*'s having been thrown into the world and that can be actualized only as a Being-in-the-world (SZ148/188).

Still, in the projections of its own possibilities *Dasein* is always "more" than what it *factually* is. That is, projectively *Dasein* is what it is not in actuality. It can therefore say to itself "Become what you are"—and can say so with comprehension.

But this projection of *Dasein*'s own possibilities of development requires an explication—a clarification and elaboration of the projected possibilities (SZ148/188). Such an explication, however, is never without presuppositions; for it involves "the articulation of what is comprehended"; and this is "grounded in intention, foresight, and preconception" (SZ150/191). In and through it, a *Seiendes* is disclosed in its possibilities and is projected into a totality of meaning—that is, into "reference-relations—(*Verweisungsbezüge*)"—in which, from its very beginning, Concern is deeply involved with *Seiendem*. Because of *Dasein*'s being-in-the-world, it could not be otherwise. Meaning—characterized by intention, foresight, and preconception—is therefore that at which *Dasein*'s projection aims and in terms of which something becomes comprehensible *as something*. *Dasein* itself has meaning insofar as its being-in-the-world "can be fulfilled" by the disclosedness of discoverable *Seiende* within that world. Since

Dasein alone experiences this disclosure, "it alone can be meaningful (*sinnvoll*) or meaningless (*sinnlos*)" (SZ151/193).

As the disclosure of the *there*, comprehension is always concerned with the whole of *Dasein*'s being-in-the-world and includes a comprehension of existence. Every explication which is to yield comprehension must in some way already have "understood" what is to be explicated (SZ152/194). This "circle in comprehension" is rooted in *Dasein*'s existential constitution. That is to say, to every *Dasein* for which its own Being is an issue as a Being-in-the-world belongs ontologically the "structure of a circle (*Zirkelstruktur*)" (SZ153/195).

In this sense the present is rooted in its having-been and in its future. This fact entails that what has been projected in circumspective understanding can be brought closer to reality by *Dasein*'s conforming itself to what is encountered in maintaining and awaiting—in the "ecstatico-horizontal unity of Temporality" (SZ360/411).

"All explication is grounded in comprehension" (SZ153/195). What comprehension provides and is articulated is an explanation expressed in an assertion or judgment. And it is here that the *problem of truth* arises; for the primary function of an assertion or judgment is "to show-forth or exhibit (*aufzeigen*) what is given." It is to let a *Seiendes* "be seen from itself" (SZ154/196). In the assertion "This hammer is too heavy," for example, there is disclosed not just a meaning but a *Seiendes*—this hammer—in the mode of its "being-ready-at-hand." That is, the assertion is the disclosure of the *Seiende* as such and not a mere idea (*Vorstellung*) of it. And to say that the assertion is true means that the *Seiende* referred to actually *is* as asserted. This, of course, is the traditional "correspondence meaning" of truth. When there is no such correspondence between the assertion or judgment and what is "given" the judgment is false.

However, an assertion may also be a *predication.* That is, it may attribute a "predicate" to a "subject." We may thus speak of "true joy," of "actual gold," and so on. In all such cases of attribution the object is characterized in a specific way. Such characterization, however, delimits the basic referent to a *Seiendes* in some specific way. It does not negate the *Seiende* as such.

Finally—and this is most significant for Heidegger's analysis of the Being of *Dasein*—an assertion is also a means of communication (*Mitteilung*). What the assertion refers to in its first and second functions can be communicated and thus can be shared (*kann weitergesagt werden*) (SZ155/197). Of course, what was disclosed in the original assertion may become veiled again in the re-telling. Even then, however, that which is being told and heard—Heidegger calls it the "hearsay"—still refers to being-in-the-world and to the Being of that which is being told and heard.

All in all, then, "an assertion is a communicative and determinative exhibition (*Aufzeigung*) of something" (SZ156/199). It involves comprehension and explication and manifests itself in language.

> The existential-ontological foundation of language is *Gerede*. (SZ160/ 203)

Here we encounter a difficulty in translating Heidegger's key term—*Gerede*. W. J. Richardson has translated it as "loquacity." But Heidegger's use of the term has nothing to do with talkativeness or garrulity. Macquarrie and Robinson render *Gerede* as "idle talk." But the Anglo-Saxon origin of "idle"—vain, useless—suggests a meaning of "idle talk" that is completely foreign to Heidegger's intention. I shall here stress his intention by translating *Gerede* simply as *Talk* (capitalized)—the employment of words for the sake of communication in general. [Ed. note: Macquarrie and Robinson first speak of "*Rede*," not "*Gerede*," and translate it as "talk" or "discourse," not "idle talk" (see Macquarrie and Robinson's translation, p. 203). They later (p. 211) speak of "*Gerede*" which they do translate as "idle talk." In the *Jahrbuch* edition of *Sein und Zeit* (p. 160), Heidegger uses "*Rede*," not "*Gerede*."] It is in particular the *Talk* of the undifferentiated *They*—of the many—in their every-day-ness. Talk so understood "signifies a positive phenomenon which constitutes the core of comprehension and explication on the part of any every-day *Dasein*" (SZ167/211).

In this sense *Talk* is a discourse and, as ingredients of it, assertions or statements provide not only the possibility of explication but also the possibility of accepting what is understood. Language thus takes on an existential-ontological significance (SZ160/203), for discourse belongs essentially to *Dasein*'s disclosedness (SZ223/266). The use of language in discourse is thus existentially primordial along with "state-of-mind" and comprehension, and is therefore also "constitutive of *Dasein*'s existence" (SZ161/204). In discourse *Dasein's being-with* is "explicitly shared" (SZ162/205).

But "sharing," being a mode of communication, involves also a listener or "hearer" who is constitutive of *Dasein*'s authentic openness to Others. In being-in-the-world with Others who understand, *Dasein* is, in its own hearing, "enslaved" to a *Dasein-with* as well as to itself. "It is itself enslaved and part of the enslavement" (SZ163/206). This enslavement to others—in particular to the *They*— is a crucial point in Heidegger's interpretation of *Dasein*.

The German language provides Heidegger with an easy transition from "hearing" the *Talk* of the *They* to an "enslavement to the *They*"—a transition which depends on the cognates of *hören* (to hear), *hörig* (belonging to), *Hörigkeit* (bondage, enslavement). The transition is linguistically not possible in English; but Heidegger's meaning is clear: By listening to what *They* are saying we fall into bondage to *Them*.

To say it more fully: When we listen as *They* are engaged in *Talk*, we do not necessarily attain a true comprehension of whatever it is that is being talked about; we merely understands what is being said. The participants in the discourse all mean *the same* because they all understand *in the same averageness* what is being said. Communication is here not a sharing of the primary experiential relation to what is actually the case; it consists simply in talking-with-one-another—either in direct discourse or in written communication. The concern is with what is being said rather than with things. In this context of *Talk* "things are such and so *because one says they are*" (SZ168/212).

To be sure, *Talk* is not a mode of deliberate deception. It provides, however, the possibility of understanding everything without prior examination of the facts, and without any special reference to them. That is, "*Talk*, which anyone can pick up, not only frees from the task of genuine comprehension but develops an indifferent intelligibility for which nothing is any longer hidden" (SZ169/213). Although this talk of the *They* is not a deliberate covering-up of anything, and although in fact it provides all our knowledge in early life, a *Dasein* which does not transcend it is and remains cut off from the primary and genuine relation to the world and remains suspended in an uncertainty with respect to the world, with respect to Others, and with respect even to itself (SZ170/214)—and all of this despite our being-in-the-world.

However, intrinsic to *Dasein*'s every-day-ness there is also a tendency toward wanting to "see" or to "understand" what really is the case. Aristotle referred to it when he wrote that "by nature all men desire to know." Heidegger calls it *Neugier*—curiosity—in the sense of "being desirous to learn," not in the sense of "meddlesomeness." This desire to know is essential to the Being of man and is a way of his being-in-the-world, disclosing a new Mode of *Dasein*'s Being (SZ172f/216f).

Curiosity, to which nothing is closed, and *Talk*, in which nothing is understood, disclose a basic *ambiguity* in *Dasein*'s every-day-ness. If in its being-with-others *Dasein* encounters something that is accessible to everyone, and about which everyone can say anything, then it becomes impossible to decide what is genuine understanding and what is not. This ambiguity extends even to the very Being of *Dasein* itself. Everything looks as if it were understood and comprehended, but actually it is not (SZ173/217).

This ambiguity pertains not only to the way in which we deal with what is accessible for use or enjoyment; it is present also in the comprehension of our own possibilities, and thus is "the most insidious way in which ambiguity presents alleged possibilities of *Dasein* in order to suffocate them at the same time" (SZ173/218). That is, insofar as *Dasein* adopts the projection of its own possibilities from the *They*, it constantly misconceives its genuine possibilities-for-Being (SZ174/218).

This ambiguity pertains also to *Dasein*'s comprehension of Others. "The 'Other' is 'there' insofar as one has heard about him" (SZ174/219). *Talk* thus intrudes from the very beginning into the primordial relation of "being-with-one-another." It changes the indifferent side-by-sideness into "a strained and ambiguous watching-one-another, into a secret listening-in-on-one-another" (SZ174f/219). Under the mask of the "for-one-another" there is an "against-one-another" at work.

This ambiguity is not the result of some deliberate disguising or distorting of the relationship with others but is inherent in the being-with-others as all of us are *thrown into the world.* Along with our everyday *Talk*, this ambiguity forms the context which constitutes the basic mode of the Being of every-day-ness which Heidegger calls *Verfall*—the deterioration—of *Dasein.* He characterizes it as "the absorption in being-with-one-another insofar as this being-with is guided by *Talk*, by the desire to know, and by ambiguity" (SZ175/220). This deterioration of *Dasein* into a "not-being-itself," into the every-day-ness of the *They*, functions as one of the possibilities of the existential mode of being-in-the-world (SZ176/220f).

However, with the realization that this is so, the phenomenological basis is given for "a comprehensive interpretation of the Being of *Dasein* as *Concern*—as *Sorge*" (SZ180/224).

Division One, Chapter Six of *Sein und Zeit* is entitled "Die Sorge als Sein des Daseins"—"Concern as the Being of *Dasein*." The problem which Heidegger here faces involves the "primordial wholeness of the structure of *Dasein* in its totality" (SZ180/225). Just what does Heidegger mean here?

As he sees it, being-in-the-world is "primarily and permanently one unitary whole," and the problem is how to comprehend this whole in its essential structure (SZ181/225).

It can not be understood phenomenologically by merely adding, in a mechanical and haphazard way, the various elements encountered in the world. Bringing the various elements together in a structural whole presupposes an "architect's design"—a *Bauplan.* That is, it presupposes the projection of an integrative idea (as Kant would have it) which must be followed. Without such a plan there is no direction to the effort at construction and the result may well be chaos rather than an integrated and meaningful whole.

When we now keep in mind that it is *Dasein* which conceives the ontological structure, and that therefore it is in the Being of *Dasein* that the structural possibilities of the whole are ontologically grounded, then the solution of the problem may well be found through an analysis of what it means for *Dasein* to exist.

Dasein's existence is, of course, a fact. But we must note at once that the question concerning the basic existential structure of *Dasein* is fundamentally different from a question concerning the Being of a mere thing. This is so because the access to *Dasein* is "from itself to itself" and is not in the external mode of science. "In existing, *Dasein* is disclosed to itself in its own Being" (SZ182/226).

We have seen already that State-of-mind and Comprehension constitute the mode of Being of *Dasein*; but *Dasein*'s concern with what is ready-to-hand merely discloses a multiplicity of attitudes and activities, and this multiplicity must be transcended. The question is: Is there within *Dasein* a comprehending state-of-mind in which *Dasein* discloses itself to itself as an integrated unity?

Heidegger maintains that "the phenomenon of *Angst*"—of uneasiness, anxiety, dread—satisfies the methodological requirement. It must be noted specifically, however, that the term *Angst*—as Heidegger uses it—covers all three of the more specific modes just mentioned and that these differ in degree only. The generally accepted translation of Heidegger's term *Angst* is *Anxiety.* I shall follow this tradition but do so only with the understanding that Anxiety—capitalized—is meant to cover all three meanings of *Angst.*

Anxiety must of course be distinguished from *fear* (*Furcht*) which, as we have seen already, is always fear of something specific in the world which is threatening. It is otherwise with *Anxiety*, which provides the phenomenological but subjective basis for *Dasein*'s primordial concern for its own existence (SZ182/227).

It must also be understood at once that, as a basic existential phenomenon, Concern cannot be identified with or derived from will, desire, inclination or a drive of any kind because these are themselves already grounded in Concern.

What is needed, therefore, is "a pre-ontological justification of the existential interpretation of *Dasein* as Concern"; and this interpretation is provided by the fact that when *Dasein* asserts for the first time anything concerning itself it already understands itself pre-ontologically as Concern (SZ183/227). At *Dasein*'s greater maturity, however, the analytic of *Dasein* in terms of Concern is to prepare the basis for the "fundamental-ontological problematic"—that is, for the problem of the meaning of Being in general or of *Being as such*—a meaning which includes everything encountered in "being-in-the-world."

The ontological context of "Concern, Worldness, At-handness and the merely extant (*das Vorhandene*)" leads to a more precise conception of *Reality*—a conception which implies that any *Seiendes* is independent of experience, knowledge, and comprehension. However, "Being 'is' only in the understanding of the *Seienden* to which something like an understanding of Being (*so etwas wie ein Seinsverständnis*) belongs" (SZ183/228). Being can thus be uncomprehended, but it is never completely understood.

There is, however, one of *Dasein*'s possibilities of Being which reveals something to *Dasein* about itself—and that is *Anxiety*. It is the state of mind which can and does reveal "a constant and absolute (*schlechthinnige*) threat to *Dasein* itself—a threat arising from *Dasein*'s ownmost individualized Being" (SZ265/310).

Aristotle rightly regarded anxiety as a kind of depression or confusion. It is a fact which, depending on what is being feared, reveals *Dasein* not only as lost in the They but, beyond this, as facing "the factual self-certain and self-fearing *freedom toward* death" (SZ266/311; SZ255/299). And in this sense *Anxiety* provides the phenomenal basis for an explicit comprehension of *Dasein*'s existence and of the existentially basic phenomenon of *Sorge*—of *Concern* and *Care*. As far as Heidegger is concerned, Anxiety thus entails the question concerning the meaning (*den Sinn*) of Being as such (*Sein überhaupt*) (SZ183/227).

This meaning of "Being" includes not only *Dasein* but also what is "at hand" (*zuhanden*) and what is available or generally extant (*vorhanden*). And this fact requires that we take a new look at the ontological context of Care, of worldliness, at-handness and at what is merely extant or available. When we do so, we obtain a more precise meaning of the concept of *Reality*. We realize that a *Seiendes* is independent of our experience—of knowledge and comprehension—through which it is but discovered and identified. We realize that, as distinguished from any *Seiende*, Being "is" and is the understanding of a *Seiendes* to whose availability "something like an understanding of Being (*ein Seinsverständnis*) belongs" (SZ183/228). This Being of the *Seiende* is never completely understood and may be entirely uncomprehended.

Dasein itself, however, has a mode of Being (*eine Seinsart*) in which it is disclosed to itself as a being which is always its own possibilities and which, in the every-day-ness of its being-in-the-world and being-with-others, is concerned with is ownmost possibilities-for-being (*das eigenste Seinkönnen*). Is it possible to comprehend the whole of this structure of *Dasein*'s every-day-ness?

The wholeness of the structural whole can not be understood phenomenologically by putting the various aspects together because for such a procedure a specific plan—a *Bauplan*—is needed. And we must keep in mind that the question concerning the existentially basic character of *Dasein* is essentially different from that of the Being of what is merely extant. Exhibiting *Dasein*'s Being is a task of finding the most far-reaching and most primordial possibility of disclosure that is entailed in *Dasein* itself. Heidegger identifies it with *Angst*—Anxiety—a basic mood that must not be confused with fear, although it makes fear possible.

That "what for " of Anxiety is not some particular inner-worldly *Seiendes* but *Dasein*'s being-in-the-world as such. That is, Anxiety individualizes *Dasein* in its own-most being-in-the-world. In other words, *Dasein* finds itself *"unheimlich"*—uncomfortable, uneasy, not at home in the world; and this fact is what manifests itself as Anxiety (SZ188/233).

As Heidegger sees it, this feeling of not-being-at-home in the world is "existential-ontologically" "the more basic" (*das ursprünglichere*) phenomenon because it individualizes and, therefore, may well serve as the "phenomenal basis" for an answer to questions concerning the Being of *Dasein*—including *Dasein* as *Care* (SZ191ff/235ff) and *Dasein*'s pre-ontological way of interpreting itself (SZ196ff/241ff).

The hitherto prevailing analysis of *Dasein* does not reveal the originality (*Ursprünglichkeit*), authenticity (*Eigentlichkeit*), and wholeness (*Ganzheit*) of *Dasein*. What is specific here is that, as long as *Dasein* exists, there is still something which it can be but which as yet it is not—which as yet has not been realized (SZ233/276); and Care is *Dasein*'s call to its own-most possibilities to be (SZ317/365). In this anticipatory call is revealed also *Dasein*'s inherent Temporality (*Zeitlichkeit*) (SZ424/477).

Still, the meaning of "the whole of Being" can be understood only when we transcend the innermost sphere of *Dasein* and take into consideration the *Seiende* as an extant context of things (*Seinszusammenhang*). When we do so, Being takes on the meaning of *Reality* (SZ201/245). [See Heidegger's interpretation of Descartes (SZ95-101/128-134).]

We must keep in mind, however, that Reality is not just a mode of Being. As world-at-handness (*Weltzuhandenheit*) it stands ontologically in the relation as foundation to Dasein; and this fact entails the *problem of reality*. The complexity of that problem may be seen in Kant's refutation of idealism. In A375/NKS 349 we read that "outer perception yields immediate proof of something real in space . . . . That is, there corresponds to our outer intuitions something real in space." Heidegger points out, however, that what Kant here actually proves is merely the necessary co-presence of a persistent and changing *Seiendes*, and that the occurring together of the physical and the mental is "ontologically completely different from the phenomenon of Being-in-the-world" (SZ206/249). With *Dasein*'s being-in-the-world, an inner-worldly *Seiendes* is already revealed. And this existential-ontological assertion agrees with the thesis of realism which asserts that the external world *is really there* (*vorhanden*) (SZ207/251).

Compared with this realism, idealism has a superiority (*Vorrang*) in principle —provided it does not misunderstand itself as "psychological" idealism. When idealism asserts that Being and Reality are "only in consciousness," it expresses an understanding of the fact that "Being can not be explained in terms of the *Seiende*." But if this is so, and if reality is possible only within an understanding of Being, then we must ask for the Being of consciousness—that is, of the *res cogitans* itself. Hence, as Heidegger sees it, "only because Being is 'in consciousness' is it understandable within *Dasein*; and *Dasein* can understand such characteristics of Being as independence, Being-in-itself, and reality in general— and can 'conceptualize them'" (SZ207f/251).

It is a fact, however, that reality is an ontological problem only because we encounter it as "resistant to our endeavors." Such encounters are ontologically possible only because of "the disclosedness of the world" to a consciousness which itself is a mode of being-in-the-world (SZ210f/253f).

But consider this: Being in the world, we make judgments about what we encounter; and in making judgments we must distinguish between the psychological event of judging, which is real, and that which is being judged—that is, the ideal content of the judgment. How is this relation of the ideal *Seiende*—that is, of the content of the judgment—to the mental process of judging, which is real, to be understood ontologically? (SZ216/259)

The problem is complicated by the fact that the judgment may be true or not true. And what does this mean?

We must realize that there is truth only insofar as and only so long as there is *Dasein* (SZ226/269). That is, in its mode of Being, truth is always relative to the Being of some *Dasein*. But why do we presuppose that there is truth at all? "Has a *Dasein* ever decided—or will it ever be able to decide—whether or not it itself is to come into *Dasein*? We simply do not know why any *Seienden* ought to be discovered and why truth and *Dasein* must be" (SZ228/271). The limits of our understanding here revealed are encountered again and again (SZ420/472).

All that has been said so far was intended merely to bring *Dasein* as such and as a whole into view. Heidegger now turns to the basic theme of *Dasein*—Time. What he seeks is an answer to the question concerning the meaning of *Being in general*—that is, to the basic problem of all ontology.

This problem, Heidegger believes, can be solved only when *Dasein* is primordially interpreted as to its own Being (SZ231/274); and this can be done only when we have first shown "the Being of *Dasein* existentially in its possibilities of *authenticity* and *totality*" (SZ233/276). We must remember, however, that so long as *Dasein is*, there is also something which it still can be and actually become. There are possibilities of existence yet to be realized. The end of all outstanding possibilities is, of course, death—an event which limits in each case "the possible wholeness of *Dasein* in its development" (SZ234/277).

Even in this perspective it is clear that the primordial ontological ground of *Dasein*'s existence is *Temporality*. And this fact must now be confirmed. It is the central problem of *Sein und Zeit*.

Heidegger starts the discussion with the question "Can *Dasein* as a whole ever become accessible in its being-a-whole?"

Inherent in the basic constitution of *Dasein* is a constant incompleteness (*Unabgeschlossenheit*). So long as *Dasein* is a *Seiendes*, it has not realized all of its possibilities and therefore has not yet attained its wholeness. But when it attains its wholeness in death, it is never again experienceable as existent. And if this is so, is it not a hopeless undertaking to try to find in *Dasein* the *ontological totality of Being*? (SZ236/279f)

Heidegger believes that the situation is not completely hopeless, for we can observe the death of others. "An end of *Dasein* is thus 'objectively' accessible (*zugänglich*) to us" (SZ237/281). But what in that case is actually present is merely a "body-thing" (*ein Körperding*). And thus the *end* of *Dasein* as such is the *beginning* of it as something merely present (*vorhanden*) as a "body-thing." As Heidegger puts it: "The *end* of the *Seiende* as *Dasein* is the *beginning* of the very *Seiende* as something merely present (*vorhanden*)" (SZ238/281). Although being-in-the-world entails that, in many situations, one *Dasein* can take the place of another, this is not possible where death is concerned. "No one can take over the dying of the other" (SZ240/284).

The analysis of the wholeness and the end of *Dasein* leads Heidegger to the consideration of the following three theses:

1. To *Dasein* belongs a "not yet" which includes all possibilities of *Dasein* that have as yet not been realized—*der ständige Ausstand.*

2. Everything which as yet has not come-to-its-end will be coming-to-its-end. [Ed note: Macquarrie and Robinson translate this thesis as "The coming-to-its-end of everything which as yet has not come to its end has the character of no-longer-*Dasein.*"]

3. Coming-to-an-end includes that every particular *Dasein* is in its mode of Being unrepresentable.

Dasein always exists precisely in such a way that its Not-yet (death) belongs to it (SZ243/287). In what sense is death here to be understood as the end of *Dasein*? As Heidegger sees it, in death *Dasein* is neither completed nor has it simply vanished, and certainly it is also already its end. What characterizes *Dasein* as a *Seiendes* is its "*Being-toward-an-end*" (SZ245/289).

To be sure, *Dasein* can be interpreted as "something-living." As a biologico-physiologically integrated whole it belongs to the world of animals and plants. But even then, death remains an ontological problem and "the existential interpretation of death is prior to all biology and ontology of life" (SZ247/291). That is, the existential problematic aims only at the clarification of the ontological structure of *being toward the end* of *Dasein* (SZ249/293). What Heidegger attempts to show is how—in the phenomenon of death—"existence, facticity and decline of *Dasein* reveal themselves." "Death is the possibility of the absolute impossibility of *Dasein*" (SZ250/294). It reveals itself as one's ownmost (*eigenste*), unrelational, unsurpassable possibility. As such it is "a distinctive coming event" (SZ250f/294). As soon as *Dasein* exists it is already thrown into the possibility of death—a fact which reveals itself as anxiety (*Angst*) and which essentially belongs to the having-been-thrownness (*Geworfenheit*) of *Dasein* (SZ251/295). Heidegger can thus accept the thesis that Care (*Sorge*) is the "ontological name for the 'wholeness' of the structural whole of *Dasein*" (SZ252/296); and the analysis of the fact that "one dies" reveals unambiguously "the mode of Being of one's every-day Being-unto-death" (SZ253/297). No one doubts that "one dies"—although not right now (SZ255/299). As the end of *Dasein*, death is intrinsic to the Being of *Dasein* as a *Seiendes*. Or, as Heidegger puts it, "as a Being thrown into the world, *Dasein* is always already delivered onto its death" (SZ259/303). And this ontic reality must be ontologically possible, too (SZ260/304).

With respect to something regarded as possible—such as its death—*Dasein* takes an attitude of *expectation* (*Erwarten*), and every expectation has its "possibility (*sein Mögliches*) as to if, when, and how it will really be present" (SZ262f/306). We must realize, however, that death, as our own-most possibility, is unrelational. It "lays claim to every *Dasein* as individual." As Heidegger puts it: "Death does not indifferently 'belong' to one's own *Dasein* but lays claim to it *as individual*"—a fact which "individualizes *Dasein* as itself" (SZ263/308). This own-most, non-relational possibility can not be overtaken (*es ist unüberholbar*) (SZ265/310). It is certain but, despite its certainty, it is undetermined. We do not know *when* our death will occur.

What Heidegger now seeks is "a proper being-able-to-be" of *Dasein* that is attested to by *Dasein* itself in its existential possibilities—a testimony familiar to us as a voice of conscience (*Stimme des Gewissens*) (SZ268/313)—of a conscience which calls *Dasein* back into its own-most possibilities "out of being lost in the 'They'"—in *das Man* (SZ274/319). That is, in its conscience "*Dasein* calls itself . . . . The call comes *out of me* and yet *from above me*" (SZ275/320).

But what if in the depth of its uncomfortableness (*Unheimlichkeit*) *Dasein* itself were the caller of the "call of conscience"? In that case conscience would reveal itself as "the call of Care" (*als der Ruf der Sorge*). The caller would be the very same *Dasein* that is being called to its own-most ability to be (SZ277/322). This fact clearly indicates that in the very depth of its Being *Dasein is* Care (SZ278/323). But the concept of moral guilt has as yet not been ontologically justified (SZ282/328).

It is Heidegger's thesis that *Dasein*'s "being guilty" (*Schuldigsein*) is not the result of some particular act (SZ284/329). *Dasein* is guilty because, as a *Seiendes*, it is prior to all of what it can project and usually can attain (SZ285/331). But, as Heidegger puts it, *Dasein* can never go back to before its having been thrown into the world (SZ383/434). The crucial fact is that the *Seiende* whose Being is Care *is guilty* in the very ground of its Being. And this *essential* "being guilty" is the existential condition of the possibility for morality (SZ286/332). That is, in its very ground of Being, in "locking itself up" in its own self, *Dasein* is guilty, and its conscience is possible as the call of *being guilty*. And this "being guilty" constitutes the mode of Being which Heidegger calls *Care* (*Sorge*) (SZ286f/332f). Understanding this call, *Dasein* hears "its own-most possibility of existence" (SZ287/333). It can choose itself. This "existential interpretation of conscience" clarifies an actual testimony of the own-most *ability-to-be* within *Dasein* itself (SZ295/341). And the resolve to follow this call is the first "projection and determination of the actual (*jeweilig*) practical possibility"

(SZ298/344f).

The existential specificity of what is possible for *Dasein* is determined in each case by the constitutive moments of the situation in which *Dasein* actually finds itself—a situation essentially closed to the *They*. It is the call of conscience that reveals the situation to *Dasein* (SZ299/346f).

What Heidegger has shown so far is the most elementary structure of *Dasein*'s being-in-the-world. In his analyses of Care, Death, Conscience, and Guilt he has shown how within *Dasein* itself the caring understanding of the ability-to-be and its disclosure have taken over, and that "the entity which in every case we ourselves are, is ontologically what is farthest removed from being clearly understood . . . . *Dasein*'s kind of Being requires an ontological interpretation which exhibits it despite *Dasein*'s tendency to cover it up" (SZ311/359).

Dasein understands itself factually as always already within definite existential possibilities. Expressly or not, adequately or not, existence is in some way also understood. That is, "every ontologically formulated question concerning the Being of *Dasein* is already prepared in advance (*ist vorbereitet*) by the mode of Being of *Dasein*" (SZ312/360). But if this is the case, has *Dasein*'s being-in-the-world a higher proof of its potentiality-for-Being (*seines Seinkönnens*) than its death?

Dasein understands itself as being-in-the-world; and in this situation it encounters a *Seiendes* of the mode of Being of what is merely extant (*vorhanden*) and a *Seiendes* which is also at-hand (*zuhanden*). But even when it understands existence as reality, *Dasein* is not only extant but it has also understood itself in some "mythical" or "magical" explication. This understanding of itself is a basic mode of the Being of *Dasein* and is constitutive of *Care*. This being so, "the most primordial and basic existential truth" aimed at in the fundamental ontological analysis is "the disclosedness (*Erschlossenheit*) of the meaning of the Being of Care" (SZ316/364).

To be sure, in saying "*I*," *Dasein* expresses itself as being-in-the-world. But the reference to the "I" is here ambiguous. It refers at first and most often to the self which, as a *Seiendes* in the world, is like any other object. Basically, however, "I" means the particular *Seiendes* which is concerned about its own Being—a fact which manifests itself as Care (*Sorge*). Care thus provides "the ontological constitution of the independence (*Selbst-ständigkeit*) of *Dasein*" (SZ323/370). [Ed. note: Macquarrie and Robinson translate the passage as ". . . existentiality, as constitutive for care, provides the ontological constitution of *Dasein*'s Self-constancy . . . ."] That is, in existing, *Dasein* understands itself as a *Seiendes* concerned with its own being. To put it existentially: Anticipatory resoluteness with regard to its own Being, formally understood, is *Being toward* our own-most and distinctive potentiality-for-Being.

Dasein's sense of Being is thus grounded in its anticipatory resoluteness which discloses the prevailing (*die jeweilige*) situation of the *Da* in such a way that "its Temporality reveals itself as the meaning of actual Care" (SZ326/374).

We must note, however, that the thematic use of the term "Temporality" excludes as yet any reference to the vulgar conception of time as "future," "past," and "present." To be sure, the "time" of our ordinary understanding is "a genuine phenomenon," but it is one that is derivative and not basic. If resoluteness is the mode of authentic Care but is itself possible only through Temporality, then relatedness as a phenomenon is but a modality of that Temporality which makes Care possible. "The primordial unity of the structure of Care thus lies in emporality" (SZ327/375), and "the primary phenomenon of the original and authentic Temporality is its future" (SZ329/378).

We must note also that reckoning with time is constitutive of being-in-the-world. That is, an inner-worldly *Seiendes* becomes accessible as "being in time" (SZ333/382).

But does not an inner-worldly *Seiendes* become available in space also? Here an essential deficiency of Heidegger's phenomenological position is obvious. Let us note this fact but go on with the Heideggerian thesis.

We then find that "the explication of the Temporality of *Dasein* as 'every-day-ness,' 'historicality,' and 'inner-timeness' gives us for the first time a 'rude' (*rücksichtslos*) insight into the *complications* (*Verwicklungen*) of a basic ontology of *Dasein*" (SZ333/382).

For us to attain this insight Heidegger suggests that we interpret such structural aspects of our Being as understanding, state-of-mind, forfeiture, and speech with reference to time. We then find that the temporal aspects of these phenomena all lead back to one Temporality which entails the structural unity of them all (SZ335/384f).

What is here crucial is that "temporality manifests itself as a whole in every phase of the ecstatic unity" of past, present, and future. This unity implies that "the future is *not later* than the past (*Gewesenheit*)" and the past is not earlier than the present. That is, Temporality reveals itself as "past-actualizing-future" (*gewesende-gegenwärtigende-Zukunft*) (SZ350/401). This "ecstatic temporality" is "what primarily regulates the possible unity of all existential structures of *Dasein*" and of *Dasein*'s being-in-the-world—of what is present in that world and of what is at hand (SZ351/402).

Dasein's circumspective concerns with what is given in the surrounding world includes the understanding of all involvements—the "in-order-to," the "toward-which," and the "for-the-sake-of-which." "That in which the existing *Dasein* understands itself 'is there' (*ist da*) in its factual existence" (SZ364/415f). It is *Dasein*'s world. The existential-temporal condition of the possibility of that world lies in the fact that "temporality has something like a horizon"—a "horizontal schema" involving past, present and future—which is grounded in a prior understanding of the relationships of "in-order-to," "what-for," "toward-this," "for-the-sake-of-which." In these relations *Dasein* understands itself as being-in-the-world. They *are* its world—a world of which *Temporality* is constitutive (SZ365/416f).

Although we are told that "only on the basis of the ecstatico-horizontal Temporality is it possible for *Dasein* to break into space," we are told also that this is so because "the world is not present in space" but "space lets itself be discovered within the world" (SZ369/421).

As will be remembered, the mode of Being in which *Dasein* finds itself at first and most often, Heidegger called *Dasein*'s "every-day-ness"—the kind of existence in which *Dasein* finds itself every day. But this "natural" horizon is "only seemingly self-evident" (SZ371/423). It must be supplemented by an analysis of *Dasein*'s "historicality" (*Geschichtlichkeit*)—which reveals that *Dasein* can exist only historically because "*in the very ground of its Being Dasein is temporal*" (SZ376/428).

But does this mean that *Dasein* is something which merely *has been*—prior; or *that it has been as something which, in the present, relates past and future*—that is, as something which has been in "the temporalizing of its Temporality?" (SZ381/432)

Heidegger, affirming the latter, regards *Dasein* as "primarily historical." He puts it this way: "Only a *Seiendes* which in its Being is essentially *futural* and is equally essentially also something that has been, can transmit to itself an inherited possibility . . . . Only authentic Temporality, which at the same time is finite, makes possible something like fate—that is, authentic historicality" (SZ385/437).

And so it turns out that the finitude of Temporality, as manifest in the authentic Being-toward-death, is the hidden ground of *Dasein*'s historicity (SZ386/438). *Dasein* does not become historical in the repetition of past events; it *is* historical and can repeat itself in its history because it is temporal (SZ388/440). And with *Dasein*'s being-in-the-world what is present and at hand is already included in the history of that world.

Because Temporality is constitutive of the *Da*, it is always known to us and therefore interpretable (SZ408/460). The result is that, as factually thrown into the world, *Dasein* can only "take" or "lose" time, whereas "time" is allotted to *Dasein* as extended Temporality of the *Da* (SZ410/463).

Dasein's having-been-thrown into the world also accounts for the fact that there is "public" time and, with this, something like a "clock" is discovered—that is, "something-at-hand which, in its regular recurrence in the actual present," indicates the passing of time is discovered (SZ413/466). Clocktime, thus, is world-time. It pertains to an inner-worldly *Seiendes* in general and makes it datable. Time, thus, belongs to the world itself (SZ414f/467f).

As the condition of every possible object, "world-time" is essentially *objectified.* But it is also more "subjective" than any possible object because it first makes the Being of all objects possible (SZ419/472).

Of course, the vulgar representation of time has its natural justification. It belongs to the every-day mode of the Being of *Dasein* and to the prevailing understanding of time. Heidegger's point, however, is that Temporality reveals itself as the meaning of the Being of Care (SZ436/486), and that the task now is to clarify the ontologically fundamental questions: "How is a revelatory understanding of Being at all possible? Can this question be answered by going back to the original constitution of Being as Being? . . . Is there a way that leads from original *Time* to the meaning of Being? Does Time reveal itself as the horizon of *Being*?" (SZ438/488)

Heidegger raises these questions but gives us no answer. *Sein und Zeit* can provide an answer.

Four

A FIRST STEP BEYOND *SEIN UND ZEIT*

When I visited Heidegger at his home in Freiburg on 30 May 1937, we discussed at length some of the problems which troubled me in reading *Sein und Zeit*. The problem of time as such, for example, requires further analysis. But then, of course, *Sein und Zeit* is only a fragment. It is clearly marked "Erste Hälfte" (First Half). When I asked Heidegger when we might expect the "Zweite Hälfte," he replied, "It has been written. It is here [pointing to the right-hand top drawer of this desk]. But it will not be published during my lifetime. In complete misunderstanding of my intention I have been decried enough as the philosopher of *Angst* in these 'heroic' times." The sarcasm in his pronunciation of "heroic" was unmistakable. And when I pressed my argument further by asking Heidegger how he would define his basic position, his answer was: "*Das Erwarten des Kommens Gottes*"—"The awaiting of the coming of God." It was clear within the context of our discussion that the coming of Hitler and the Nazis was by no means "the coming of God." (I shall return to this problem later.)

The manuscript found after Heidegger's death has been published as volume twenty-four of the Heidegger *Gesamtausgabe*. It is, of course, his *Grundprobleme der Phänomenologie*—which had served as a basis for his lecture course (*Vorlesung*) of the summer semester of 1927—the year when *Sein und Zeit* was published. As Heidegger himself put it, in the *Grundprobleme* he was giving us "a new version (*eine neue Ausarbeitung*) of the third division of Part I of *Sein und Zeit*" (GP1/1. He now faced the fact that, although "we understand Being, we nevertheless do not comprehend it" (GP389/274).

The understanding of Being is and always has been a problem of ontology. Heidegger, therefore, devotes the first three hundred pages of the *Grundprobleme* to an analysis of three distinct types of traditional ontology. He identifies them as "Scholastic Ontology" (GP108-71/77-121), "Modern Ontology" (GP172-251/122-176), and "The Thesis of Logic" (GP252-320/177-224); but he does not commit himself to any of these. Instead he examines in his own way the basic problems encountered relative to the position he developed in *Sein und Zeit*. The question is: How do we comprehend Being?

1. Time and Temporality

Heidegger asks: "How and where is time?" (GP338/238) How can time be real when its parts—the *no-longer* (the past) and the *not-yet* (the future)—are non-existent, and when only the present—the immediate *Now*—is real? Worse yet: The Now is never the same but is always a new one. There is only a manifoldness of *Nows*; and each new *Now*, we may add, is actual only as a transitory stage in an ongoing process. The temporal aspects of anything which exists imply *sameness* and *unity* of the existing things. When these qualities are absent we can hardly assert that there is something which persists or is in process.

It may be well at this point to ask—as Heidegger does not—just how do we actually experience time? We certainly do not do so in the abstract. Let us, therefore, consider a concrete situation. "Hearing a melody is a hearing, a having heard, and a being about to hear, all at once . . . . Anyone who thinks back to past tones or anticipates coming tones in imagination ceases to hear a melody."[1] Time is evidently characteristic of the actual process, of the uninterrupted sequence of moments, and is not anything like a thing. We do not experience isolated *Nows* but the interwoven sequence of stages in a concrete process; and this is characteristic of all of our experiences.

But let us suppose—and this is Heidegger's example—that we move a pointer from left to right across a screen. In this motion time discloses itself, and we may add, as Heidegger does not, so does space. To be sure, when we stop the motion, time "moves on." But is it actually *time* that moves on? Or are the events around us what move on in time? Moreover, Heidegger himself brings to our attention that the rate of transition from one place to another is velocity—which the physicists define as the distance traversed in a specific time: $V = d/t$ (GP339/239). The formula shows clearly that velocity involves both space and time; and it does so because movement is a process involving both.

Disregarding the involvement of space, Heidegger continues his argument by pointing out that "our clocks tell us 'what time it is'"—as does "the course of the sun"; and that "time is something 'before' and 'after' whenever we encounter motion." And this sequence, Heidegger maintains, "can be understood only as grounded in, and emerging from, *primordial time* (*ursprüngliche Zeit*)—that is, from *Temporality*" (GP342/241). But can we not develop a parallel argument on behalf of space? In the world we live in, there are *Seiende* in front, behind, below, above, to the left or to the right of us; and is not this a display of specific directions emerging from primordial spatiality? The only difference in this respect is that space and spatial relations prevail only as far as a physically real *Seiendes* is concerned, whereas time and temporal relations include the realm of mental and spiritual realities as well. In this respect time is indeed more fundamental than space and requires a special analysis.

Heidegger continues his argument by stating that, *in a purely formal sense*, we can speak of the sequence of *Nows* as a dimension, and that this implies a *continuum* of the *a priori basic context* of any sequence. But must we not ask: What, precisely, is here the "basic context"? Is not that context the reality of the actual process of events in the world we live in? And just as we do not mean an object when we say "here" or "there," but a position in space, so we do not mean an object when we say "Now," but a stage in an ongoing process.

To be sure, Heidegger is right in asserting that time is nothing usable; that it is nothing like a thing (GP370/262); but neither is space. Space and time both transcend *Dasein*, and both involve structural elements. Heidegger admits that when I say "Now," I always mean "now, when this and that occurs"; and when I say "Then," I always mean "then when"—either when something has occurred (past) or when this or that will occur (future). That is to say, every Now and every Before and every Not-yet is always already more or less specifically determined with respect to some occurrence (GP371/263). And this is precisely the point; for it means that all time references pertain only to actual processes in our real world. And what is true with respect to time, is true also with respect to something real: East of the Mississippi, south of Bermuda, to the left of that tree, below the shelf at the right. Although there may be some uncertainty in the actual dating or in the spatial references, every reference reflects the continuity of space as well as of time. And just as the Now of any event is readily understandable for all who live together, and in this sense is public, so also is every Here and every There understandable and public. Both, the Now and the Here, are aspects of real events in a real world. If time has significance as "belonging to the world we live in"—as Heidegger maintains (GP374/264)—then so has space; and must we not conclude that Heidegger's position is here at least one-sided? To be sure, Heidegger is correct in maintaining that "*Dasein* can get as little out of its past as it can escape death" (GP375/265). But this is clearly a reference to the process of living—a process of which time is but an abstract aspect. And is it not equally true that from birth until death *Dasein* can not escape the three-dimensionality of the world in space? Is not the individual's own body proof of this—just as the years of his life are proof of the reality of a process in time?

I am fully aware of the fact that time is much more profoundly involved in *Dasein*'s existence than is space, and shall therefore follow Heidegger's argument more closely—an argument which begins with the question, "Where does that time originate which we first of all (*zunächst*) know and which alone (*einzig*) we know?" (GP374/265) Can the structural aspect of time—and therefore time itself—be understood in terms of what manifests itself in the Now, the Not-yet, and the At-that-time-in-the-past?

It is Heidegger's contention that whenever we are expecting some particular event to happen we have a certain relation to our own *Dasein*. Even when what we are aware of is an event in history, an occurrence in nature, our own *Dasein* is "always conjointly present" and understands itself by way of "its own-most ability to be" (*ibid.*). In thus understanding itself, *Dasein* is "ahead of itself." As Heidegger sees it, "being aware of a possibility I come out of it toward that which I myself am" (*ibid.*). That is, I come toward my own possibility to be. "This coming-toward-oneself out of one's own-most possibility"—which is intrinsic to the existence of *Dasein* and of which all anticipation is a special mode—is "*the Primary concept of the future*" in the ordinary sense of the "not-yet-now" (GP375/265). But let us note more specifically—as Heidegger does not—that *Dasein* is here the *actual reality in process*. As Whitehead put it: The *being* of an *actual entity* is "constituted by its 'becoming.' This is the principle of progress."[2] And *Dasein* is obviously an entity in process. But Heidegger's interest is not—as Whitehead's was—the categorial analysis of process.

The ontological reality of *Dasein* is even more in evidence when Heidegger continues his argument thus: "Retaining what has been forgotten, *Dasein* always relates itself in some way to what it already has been" (*ibid.*). It can get rid of its past as little as it can avoid death. In a very real sense, therefore, "what we have been is an essential determining factor in our existence" (*ibid.*). Or, as Heidegger also puts it, "Having-been-ness (*Gewesenheit*) belongs to the existence of *Dasein*" (GP376/266).

Heidegger continues his argument by asserting that "the original unity characterized by future, past and present is the phenomenon of that primordial time which we call Temporality"; that is, future, past and present "are what they are only because they originate in Temporality"; and "Temporality *temporalizes itself* (*zeitigt sich*) in the prevailing (current) unity of future, past, and present" (*ibid.*). But, surely, there is such a unity only when there exists some ontologically real being—such as *Dasein*—which persists in the process. Take away that reality and what happens to Temporality? Ontologically speaking, where or how *is* time when detached from all processes in the world? Time in itself is quite obviously neither an entity nor a process. It is only a mode of Being of that which is real.

When Heidegger now maintains that "the essence of the future lies in the coming-toward-oneself (*im Auf-sich-zukommen*)," in the "*back to a having-been*," and in "the *being-with* of the present" (GP377/266), this clearly bespeaks an *actual entity in process* and is not simply a manifestation of Temporality as such.

But let us follow Heidegger's argument further.

He calls past, present, and future "the three *ecstases* of Temporality" which "intrinsically (*gleichursprünglich*) belong together" (GP377/267). We must keep in mind, however, that, as Heidegger uses the term, "ecstatic" does not refer to "ecstatic state of mind," but is "related to the term 'existence.'" In fact, it is by way of its "ecstatic character" that Heidegger interprets existence which, "viewed ontologically, is the original unity of *Dasein*'s coming-toward-itself, coming-back-to-itself, and being-present . . . . This ecstatically determined Temporality is the condition of the constitution of *Dasein*'s existence" (GP377f/267).

This Heideggerian statement is in its way quite obviously an acknowledgement that, in its process in time, *Dasein* is the actual reality here and now whose Being is to be clarified. But such clarification requires a meticulous categorial analysis of *Dasein* itself, and such an analysis Heidegger does not give us at any time. He maintains instead that "*Dasein* is intentional only because in its essence it is determined by Temporality" (GP379/268). But would it not be closer to the facts to maintain instead that, in its self-development and in its activities generally, *Dasein* is an actual *reality in process* whose Being requires detailed categorial analysis? But there is not even a hint of such an analysis in any of Heidegger's works.

Heidegger continues by stating that "as ordinarily understood, time in itself is a free-floating (*freischwebende*) sequence of Nows. It is simply there" (*ibid.*). For Heidegger the question, therefore, is "whether we can let the sequence of Nows with respect to its essential structure—that is, with respect to significance, datability, spannedness (*Gespanntheit*) and publicness—arise out of primordial Temporality" (*ibid.*).

In his answer to this question Heidegger points out that "in its very essence every Now is a Now-when"—"a Now-when-this-or-that happens" (GP380/269). Such datability is possible, we are told, because each Now "belongs to a *particular* (*bestimmt*) ecstasis" pertaining to "the making-present (*Gegenwärtigen*) of something . . . of a *Seiendes*" (*ibid.*). That is, "as Now, every Now is a 'Now when this and that'" (GP381/269). And, correspondingly, every reference to the past and every reference to the future implies a "then when this and that." But, we must add, does not Heidegger here admit that the time-reference merely indicates stages in a process of actual events which are ontologically real and are available for categorial analysis—an analysis which Heidegger never attempts?

Every Now, so he tells us, has an "extension" (*Gespanntheit*). Even when the Now is reduced to a millionth of a second it still has extension because "every time determination has intrinsically an extension" (GP381/269f); and this extension is Temporality. As Heidegger puts it: "The character of continuity and extension of time in the ordinary sense has its origin in the primordial extension of Temporality itself as ecstatic" (GP382/270).

Because of the ecstatic character of Temporality "every expressed time-determination is *publicly accessible*," "in the being-together (*Miteinandersein*) of *Daseins* . . . that is, in their sharing being-in-the-world, there is already present the unity of Temporality itself as one that is open in itself" (*ibid.*).

But can not this be said of spatiality also? How would individual human beings share being-in-the-world without there being space and spatiality? And is not their sharing a sharing of events in space-time rather than of time as such or in itself? Heidegger never raises or gives answers to these questions..

But let us continue his argument.

As Heidegger sees it, "the basic constitution of *Dasein* is its being-in-the-world," and being in the world in such a way that, in its very existence, *Dasein* is "concerned with its own ability-to-be-in-the-world (*sein In-der-Welt-seinkönnen*)" (GP383/270). It experiences itself as "being present in the Now, as expecting to be present in the Not-yet, and as having been involved in the At-that-time" (*ibid.*). In these time-dimensions, so Heidegger holds, "Temporality expresses *itself*," and "the time thus expressed is simultaneously that *for* which *Dasein* uses (*verwendet*) itself, and *for the sake of which* it itself is" (*ibid.*).

What concerns Heidegger here—although he does not say so—is obviously *Dasein* as an ontic reality in process—and, as it turns out, in a highly complex process of which Temporality is but one aspect. Moreover, in what sense can it be justified to maintain that "the time thus expressed" is that "*for the sake of which Dasein itself is*"? To this question Heidegger gives us no answer. He does not even raise it.

But let us follow his argument to its conclusion.

Insofar, he writes, as "Temporality makes possible the ontic constitution (*Seinsverfassung*) of *Dasein*" and *Dasein* is a *Seiendes* in time, the existing *Dasein* is appropriately called the "*temporal Seiende in general*" (GP383f/271). And when we accept this stipulation, Heidegger maintains, it is clear why a *Seiendes* such as a stone, which does not move but "is at rest in time, is not called temporal" (GP384/271).

But what do we then say about the whole range of beings between stones and our own *Dasein*? Birds build nests in anticipation of raising their young, and migratory birds—storks, for example—return in the spring to the very nest they had left in the fall. Even bees find their way back to their very own hives. And he who would deny that animals remember the past and anticipate the future has never had a dog for his companion. Are we to classify all of these beings with stones? Or do they represent a class of *Seiende* somewhere between stones and human beings? Are they not also *Seiende* in our actual space-time world? And is not their existence also a *process* in space-time? What is required here is a meticulous categorial analysis which would clarify the complex situation. But for such an analysis we look in vain in Heidegger's publications. We have to look elsewhere. We shall find that being-in-the-world is a highly structured stratification of *Seiende*.[3]

Heidegger continues his argument by asking: How does it happen that in our ordinary understanding of time we know only the irreversible sequence of Nows—"the manifoldness of naked Nows"—which has no further structure? This "covering-up (*Verdeckung*)" of the structural aspects of world-time and of their origin in Temporality Heidegger calls their "deteriorating (*Verfallen*)." Although he gives no further analysis of this problem, he continues his argument by stating that *Dasein* is "at first always oriented relative to *Seiende* in the sense of what exists" (GP384/271), and that *Dasein* thus understands its own Being also as existence. It calls itself "the I, the subject, a *res*, a *substantivum*, a *subjectum*" (GP384/271f). What this means—Heidegger interpolates—is a general indication of *Dasein* understanding itself primarily as if it were a thing, and to "derive the concept of Being from what exists" (GP385/272). The result is the conviction that "*Seiende* are encountered in time"; and that, as Aristotle had it, time is "something connected with motion (*kineseos ti*)" (*ibid.*). But this means, so Heidegger maintains, that "time *is* in the same way" as things are; for when the ordinary understanding of time "knows Being only in the sense of Being-in-extantness (*Vorhandenheit*)," then time, "involved in motion and being publicly accessible," is "necessarily something that is extant" (GP385/272). When *Dasein* encounters time in this ordinary sense, time is interpreted as something which "is somehow *co-extant*, be it in the objects or in the subject or just anywhere" (*ibid.*). The succession of Nows is taken to be an "extant sequence." The Nows come and go like *Seiende*—like what is extant, and then no longer is extant. In our ordinary view we have no understanding of Being except in terms of extantness; and, in this view, time "is simply extant just like space." As Heidegger puts it more explicitly:

It is implicit in the mode of Being of *Dasein* itself that *Dasein* knows the

> sequence of Nows only in the naked form of Nows joined one to another in sequence. Only on this presupposition is the Aristotelian manner of inquiry possible when he asks: Is time a *Seiendes* or is it a *Nichtseiendes*? (GP385f/272)

When we take time to be a *Seiendes*, then that which in relation to the present Now are past and future Nows is not extant, and time is nothing but the present Now. But every Now is in its very essence a transition. To consider it otherwise would be to misunderstand the sequence of Nows and the infinity which it entails. As Heidegger sees it, "time in the ordinary sense is infinite, only because Temporality, properly understood, is finite. The infinity of time . . . characterizes a negative nature of Temporality" (GP386f/273). But, Heidegger insists, "here is not the place to analyze this difficult problem." Why not? To do so, I believe, would give us a better understanding of Heidegger's philosophical position. But he also does not give us the required analysis anywhere else. Instead he now emphasizes that our ordinary understanding "does not expressly (*ausdrücklich*) know the characteristics of the Now—its significance, its datability, its tenseness (*Gespanntheit*), and its publicness" (GP387/273). But we wonder: Is it the Now that has these characteristics or is it the "march of events"—the actual process of real events passing through the Now—that has these characteristics? It would seem that the latter is the case, and that any particular Now is but a transitory phase of actual events in process. Although certain characteristics of a process are thus apparent even when we take "time" to be merely the time with which we ordinarily reckon, this fact can not be the only guide to an interpretation of time as such, for—as Heidegger sees it—"time in the ordinary sense is infinite only because Temporality, properly understood, is finite. The infinity of time . . . characterizes a negative essence of Temporality" (GP386f/273).

This seems to me to be a startling statement; but Heidegger, again, insists that here is not the place "to analyze this difficult problem." He continues his interpretation by asserting:

> To every Now belongs the character of a transition (*Übergangscharakter*) because, as ecstatic unity, Temporality is in itself extended. The ecstatic context of the coming-toward-itself (making itself present) in which *Dasein* simultaneously comes back to itself (retains itself) is what first (*allererst*) provides the condition of the possibility for the fact that the expressed time —the Now—is dimensionally future and past; that every Now as such extends itself as the Not-yet and the No-longer. (GP387/273)

This extension of the Now is what Heidegger calls the tension (*Gespanntheit*) of time. But we wonder: Is it the *Now* that is thus extended or are the things and events extended in time? Would there be an "extended Now" at all if there were not some *Seiende* that could remember and/or anticipate events? It is Heidegger's point that time encompasses *Seiende* in such a way that we know as intratemporal (*innerzeitliches*) what is "possible and necessary because of (*auf grund*) the character of time as world-time" (GP388/274). And, as world-time, time makes it possible for *Dasein* to encounter *Seiende* in the world. But, we may ask, does not space also "encompass" *Seiende* because it is world-space? Although this fact may be irrelevant to Heidegger's intention, it has significance in connection with his crucial argument later.

What is important now is that Heidegger sees time as "approximately a sequence of Nows with respect to its origin in Temporality," and that he thus finds (1) that "the essential structure of Temporality is the self-contained (*in sich geschlossen*) ecstatic-horizontal unity of future, past, and present"; and (2) that "*Temporality is the condition of the possibility of the constitution of the Being of Dasein . . . and also of Dasein's understanding of Being*" (*ibid.*, Heidegger's italics). The question now is: In how far is "time as Temporality the horizon for the explicit understanding of Being itself," if Being is to be the theme of ontology? And let us note that, when time is "to function as condition of the possibility of a pre-ontological as well as of an ontological understanding of Being," Heidegger calls it *Temporality*—capital T.

And this is certainly a step beyond *Sein und Zeit*, where *time* rather than *Temporality* was the ultimate concept.

2. Being-in-the-World

So far it has been Heidegger's thesis that every existing *Dasein* has something like an understanding of Being. We now face the fact that, although we understand Being, we nevertheless do not yet comprehend it. What does "to comprehend" here mean?

As Heidegger sees it, "comprehending is a specific type of cognitive attitude" (GP389/275). But *what* type is it? The question is warranted because in all attitudes toward *Seiende*, be the attitude cognitive-theoretical or practical-technical, we deal with Being, and "only in the light of an understanding of Being can a *Seiendes* be encountered *as something*" (GP390/275). But an *understanding* based upon practical encounters with things is not yet a comprehension of Being. It is therefore necessary to find a "sufficiently original concept of understanding from which (*aus dem heraus*) all modes of cognition can in principle be understood" (*ibid.*).

It is Heidegger's thesis that

> if understanding of Being is constitutive of the ontological constitution of *Dasein*, and if comprehension is included in it, then comprehension is an original characteristic (*Bestimmtheit*) of the existence of *Dasein*. . . . And what is more, in the end comprehension is not primarily a cognition . . . but a basic characteristic of existence itself. (GP390f/275f)

And Heidegger now asks: "In what sense (*inwiefern*) does apprehension belong to the existence of *Dasein* as such, apart from whether *Dasein* is or is not engaged in a comprehending psychology or a comprehending history?" (GP391/276) How is this to be understood? His answer is: "To exist is essentially—even if not entirely—a comprehending."

Heidegger's thesis is that "being-in-the-world belongs to the existence of *Dasein*," and that it does so in the sense that, in *Dasein*'s "being-in-the-world, Being itself is given" (*ibid.*). This means, as Heidegger tells us, that, "in a certain way, *Dasein* has its own Being under control"—in so far, namely, as it can take such or such an attitude towards its own possibility to be "as it has decided for or against it, or this way or that" (*ibid.*). The fact that *Dasein* is concerned with its own Being means that its own *ability-to-be* (*Seinkönnen*) is at issue. That is, "as existent, *Dasein* is free for specific possibilities of itself. It is its own-most ability to be . . . ." (*ibid.*).

Let us pause here for a moment to consider, as Heidegger does not, what "being-in-the-world" means.

The "in" quite obviously means to be spatially as well as temporally within the spatio-temporal world. And "being-in-the-world" also means encountering *Seiende*—stones, water and fish, flowers and bees, trees and birds, cats and dogs, and stars and galaxies of stars—as I have mentioned earlier in a different context. And in this world various forms of determination and dependencies prevail: mechanical, organismic, mental and socio-historical. *Dasein* must adjust to all of these realities, and its adjustments require an understanding of the changing conditions and of the forces which determine those changes. Granted that all encounters in the world occur in time. But they also take place in space, and the interactions are causal as well as holistic and intentional or purposive. If *Dasein* is "free for specific possibilities of itself"—as Heidegger maintains that it is—then it ought to be shown how such freedom is possible despite all the modes of determination which *Dasein* faces. But Heidegger gives us merely the dogmatic assertion that *Dasein* is free for "its own-most possibilities to be"; that "it *is* these possibilities themselves" (*ibid.*).

What Heidegger intends here may in the end be justified; but his statement alone is not sufficient to establish that freedom as a fact. Unless a categorial analysis can reveal *Dasein*'s intrinsic freedom, we can accept Heidegger's thesis only on faith. And this is not changed by his statement that "*the understanding of itself in the Being of its own-most ability to be is the original existential concept of understanding*" (*ibid.*, Heidegger's italics). This understanding of itself he regards as basic to all other modes of *Dasein*'s knowledge, be they exploratory or merely descriptive.

"More precisely speaking," Heidegger states, "'to understand' means '*to project oneself upon a possibility*' and 'to maintain oneself always in a projection'" (GP392/277). But must we not ask here: How do we recognize a possibility upon which we can project ourselves? Does not the projection presuppose a knowledge of the facts and forces which *Dasein* encounters and is yet to encounter in the world? How can I make plans for myself if I cannot first recognize the actualities of given situations and my own bodily and mental abilities in relation to them? In my fantasies I may project myself as a second Einstein or a contemporary of Plato or of Kant; but if I "maintain myself" in such projections would I not be ready for an asylum? Being-in-the-world implies having to face the realities of that world, and of my potentialities or lack of them, before I can make a meaningful projection of myself in that world. And all of this presupposes an analysis of the kind which Heidegger does not even suggest.

He continues his argument thus: "Only in the projection, in projecting oneself upon a can-be (*ein Seinkönnen*), is this can-be—the possibility as possibility—actually there" (*ibid.*). The "can-be" in itself is *actual* only "as possibility," and is so "only in the projection of oneself upon a can-be (*ein Seinkönnen*)" (*ibid.*). But such a projection involves two aspects: (1) "It involves *that toward which* (*woraufhin*) Dasein projects a can-be of itself." (2) "This projection upon something is always a *planning for* (*ein Entwerfen von*)" (*ibid.*).

Insofar as *Dasein* projects itself upon a possibility, it understands and discloses itself in that projection. This disclosure is not a self-contemplation (*eine Selbstbetrachtung*) in the sense that the I becomes an object of just any cognition. The projection is rather a disclosure such that "I *am* the possibility. It is the way in which I exist freely" (GP392f/277). The essential aspect of this projection as an understanding is that, "in it, *Dasein* understands itself existentially"—that it "provides *Dasein*'s insight into itself" (GP393/277). As far as Heidegger is concerned, "this understanding as projection of itself (*als Sichentwerfen*) is the basic mode of *Dasein*'s happening (*Geschehen*)"; it is, as we may also say, the authentic meaning of acting, which characterizes "*Dasein*'s historicity (*Geschichtlichkeit*)" (GP393/277f). That is, the mode of understanding is "not a kind of cognition but is the basic determination of existence." In and through it "*Dasein* becomes what it is, and it is always only what it has chosen for itself—that is, as it understands itself in the projection of its own-most ability to be" (GP393/278).

With this in mind, Heidegger now sees his task to be twofold:

> *To clarify in terms of Temporality this understanding in its possibility* insofar as it constitutes existence; and at the same time so to set it off from the understanding which, in a narrow sense, we describe as understanding-of-Being (*Seinsverständnis*) in general. (*Ibid.*)

Because *Dasein* is essentially a being-in-the-world, the projection of itself reveals in every instance a possibility of being-in-the-world; and with this understanding "*a certain possible Being-toward-intra-worldly Seiende* is projected" (GP393f/278). The existing *Dasein* is thus essentially a "being-with (*ein Mitsein*)." And when Heidegger now says that *Dasein* understands itself, he means that it understands its being-in-the-world, and that it thus has the possibility of being and dealing with intra-worldly *Seiende*.

According to this concept, understanding is "free self-understanding by way of an apprehended possibility of one's own factual being-in-the-world" and, because of this understanding, *Dasein* has the "intrinsic possibility of projecting itself in various directions" (GP394f/279). This means that the factually existing *Dasein* "can understand itself primarily by way of the encountered intra-worldly *Seiende*, and can let its existence be determined primarily not by itself but by the things and circumstances, and by others" (GP395/279).

Heidegger calls this the *inauthentic understanding*. But "inauthentic" does not here mean that it is not a real understanding. It means rather that it is an understanding in which *Dasein* does not understand itself primarily out of "the own-most Being of itself" (*ibid.*).

3. The Problem of Being

Heidegger continues that, "as the projection characterized, understanding is a basic determination of *Dasein*'s existence" (*ibid.*). It pertains to *Dasein* as *Seiendes* and is therefore "an ontic understanding." Heidegger calls it "the existentiel understanding." Insofar as it pertains to *Dasein* as a *Seiendes*, it pertains to "Being in the sense of existence" (*ibid.*). But insofar as *Dasein* is "being-in-the-world" and, as with its existence, "a world and other *Dasein* are disclosed and intra-worldly *Seiende* are encountered," the understanding of *Dasein*'s existence includes "*with equal primordiality an understanding of other Dasein and of the Being of intra-worldly Seiendes*" (*ibid.*, Heidegger's italics).

At first the Being of *Dasein* and of what is extant (*Vorhandenes*) is not differentiated. Being extant, extantness (*Vorhandenheit*), availableness (*Zuhandenheit*), co-existence of other *Dasein*—although not understood in their respective modes of Being—are included in an understanding of Being which "makes possible and guides the experiencing of nature as well as the self-comprehension (*Selbsterfassung*) of the history of being-with-one-another" (GP396/279f). What thus becomes apparent in being-in-the-world is that everything *Seiendes* is disclosed in principle. In it is given an understanding which, as projection, understands not only the *Seiende* but which in some way has also projected Being as such (GP396/280).

In the analysis of the structure of an ontical understanding we thus come upon a stratification of projections which make it possible. But "stratification" is perhaps a misleading image. There is here "no unilinear Interrelation of strata of the projections such that one is the condition of another" (*ibid.*). However, "in this *existentiel understanding*, one's own *Dasein* is experienced as a *Seiendes* and, with this, Being as such (*das Sein*) is also understood" (*ibid.*).

When we now note that, as Heidegger has it, "understanding is a 'projection,'" then the understanding of Being is also a projection: "Being is understood only insofar as it is *projected toward something* (*auf etwas hin*)" (*ibid.*). That toward which it is projected "remains at first obscure (*bleibt vorerst noch dunkel*)." But "[w]e understand a *Seiendes* only insofar as we project it upon Being" (*ibid.*). And if this is so, must not Being itself also be projected upon something? The question of whether or not this recursion (*Rückgang*) from one projection to another involves a *progressus in infinitum*, Heidegger does not discuss. As he puts it: "We seek now only the *relation between* the *experiencing of Seiende*, the *understanding of Being*, and the *projection upon . . .* which is *present in the understanding of Being*" (GP397/280).

Heidegger's thesis is this:

> If *Dasein* harbors within itself the understanding of Being (*Seinsverständnis*) but it is Temporality which makes *Dasein* possible in its ontological constitution, then *Temporality must also be the condition of the possibility*

> *of the understanding of Being* and thus of *the projection of Being upon time*. (*Ibid.*, Heidegger's italics.)

Heidegger insists, however, that this is not to be taken to mean that, in the projection, Being is apprehended as an object. As he sees it, "Being is projected upon something from which it becomes understandable, but in an unobjective way" (GP398/281). Heidegger calls this "the pre-ontological understanding of Being," and insists that, although the experience of a *Seiendes* does not require an explicit ontology, "a general understanding of Being in the preconceptual sense is the condition for a *Seiendes* to be objectified at all" (*ibid.*); and he sees as his task "to inquire even beyond Being as to that upon which Being itself is projected" (GP399/282).

And so, as far as Heidegger is concerned, "the basic condition (*die Grundbedingung*) for a cognition (*Erkenntnis*) of a *Seiendes* as well as an understanding (*Verstehen*) of Being . . . is something upon which in understanding, we have projected what is to be understood" (GP402/284). Or, as Heidegger also puts it:

> In order to be able to experience what is real we must not only understand reality, but the understanding of reality must on its part first of all have its illumination (*Aufklärung*). The understanding of Being moves already within a *light-giving illuminated horizon*. (*Ibid.*)

How is this to be understood?

As Heidegger sees it, "understanding belongs to the basic constitution (*Grundverfassung*) of *Dasein*" and *Dasein* "is grounded in Temporality" (GP405/286). The question is: What precisely does this mean? In what sense is Temporality the condition of the possibility of an understanding of Being? Do we, as Heidegger claims, "understand the being-there of the *Seiende* in terms of time (*aus der Zeit*)?" That is, more specifically, "in what sense (*inwiefern*) is existentiel understanding determined by Temporality?" (GP406/286)

The key to Heidegger's answer to these questions is given in his interpretation of *resoluteness* (*Entschlossenheit*), which "has its own Temporality"—a Temporality that pertains to *Dasein*'s "own distinct (*bestimmte*) present"—a present which Heidegger calls "moment" (*Augenblick*). It is "a modus of the present" but has the "ecstatic-horizontal character of *making . . . present* (*das Gegenwärtigen von . . .*)" (GP406f/287). In any given "moment," "understanding is primarily futural (*zukünftig*)" and is therefore basic to any resoluteness in which

Dasein understands itself as "coming toward itself out of its own-most possibility-to-be." But in this coming-toward itself *Dasein* has also "already accepted (*übernommen*) itself as the *Seiende* which it has been at any time in its past (*je schon gewesen ist*)" (GP406/287).

Does this not imply that the essential mode of *Dasein*'s Being is process? And that *only as process* is *Dasein* "authentically free and open . . . for the factual possibilities of its current (*jeweiligen*) existence" in the world? (GP408/288.) Heidegger does not see it this way. He admits that *Dasein* does not constantly exist "resolute"; that "at first and mostly it is irresolute in the projection of its possibilities" (GP409/288). This means, he assures us, that "Temporality itself is modifiable with respect to its various ecstases, and especially with respect to the future" (GP409/288f).

It seems to me that this statement is simply not defensible; for "Temporality itself" is not modifiable. What is modifiable is the *process of events* as it moves in time through the present into the future. And it is modifiable only with respect to the future. If "dealing with things" is essential to *Dasein*'s projection of its own-most possibility-to-be, and if this projection is to be reasonable and possible of actual achievement, does it not presuppose a careful analysis of the given as well as of the anticipated facts and forces in the real world? Such an analysis can not be provided by Temporality as such but only by a *Dasein* which actually exists as a *Seiendes-in-progress*.

And does not *Dasein*'s anticipation of its own "possibility-to-be" also require analysis and clarification of the values realized or disregarded in the past, and of values to be realized in the future? Is *Dasein* in the projection of its own possibility-to-be to be guided by anticipated pleasures—as the Hedonists have it—or by values that are at one and the same time relative to the individual and also binding to him? Or is there an objectively grounded realm of values confronting *Dasein* in its decisions? Would not a clarification of the value problem be essential to *Dasein*'s decision in resolving the problem of its own-most possibility-to-be? But Heidegger is silent on this crucial point. We look in vain for the least indication of what is to guide *Dasein* in its crucial resolution pertaining to its own ability-to-be.

But let us go on with Heidegger's argument.

We know, he points out, that "in so far as *Dasein* factually exists, it is a *Seiendes* among intra-worldly *Seiende* and a being-with other *Dasein*" (GP409/289). This entails that *Dasein* understands itself usually in its contacts with things. The other human beings are, of course, also there—even when they are not in immediately obvious nearness (GP409f/289). Heidegger's argument is thus concentrated exclusively on *Dasein*'s "understanding attitude (*verstehendes Verhalten*) toward available and extant things" (GP410/289).

He begins his argument by asserting that "we understand ourselves by way of things (*aus den Dingen*) in our everyday being-there" (*ibid.*). This means that we project our own ability-to-be in relation to what is "proper, urgent, unavoidable and advisable in the affairs of our everyday Pursuits" (*ibid.*). That is, "*Dasein* understands itself *via* an ability-to-be which is determined by the success and failure, the appropriateness and inappropriateness of its dealings with things" (*ibid.*). *Dasein* is aware of its own ability-to-be "as the being-able-to-be of a *Seiendes* which relies upon what the things offer or what they refuse" (*ibid.*). It is thus the dealing with things and not *Dasein in itself* that primarily projects *Dasein*'s ability to be. In other words, "simply as being as it is (*wie es ist*)" *Dasein* exists always "as a dealing with things"—which in every case involves the future. But this future may be an "inauthentic future (*uneigentliche Zukunft*)." Heidegger calls it an "awaiting (*ein Gewärtigen*)." It always discloses "a realm (*Umkreis*) from which something can be awaited." *Awaiting* is thus not a degenerate mode of expecting. On the contrary, "expecting is grounded in an awaiting" (GP410f/289)—an awaiting which, on its part, is grounded in our dealings with things.

But in this dealing with things,

> We do not specifically come back to ourselves in an authentic projection of our own-most possibility-to-be . . . . We do not repeat the *Seiende* which we have been, nor do we take possession of ourselves in our facticity. What we are—and this always includes what we have been—lies in some way behind us—is forgotten. (GP411/290)

This forgetting is "an escape"—a running away from our "own-most having-been (*dem eigensten Gewesensein*)." Forgetting has thus "the characteristic of forgetting not only what is forgotten, but of forgetting even the forgetting as such" (*ibid.*). And so "for the ordinary pre-phenomenological understanding it appears as though forgetting is nothing at all (*überhaupt nichts*)" (*ibid.*). But, as Heidegger sees it, "forgottenness (*Vergessenheit*) is an elementary mode of Temporality in which we *are* at first (*zunächst*) and most often (*zumeist*) our own having-been" (*ibid.*). And this implies a distinction between "the by-gone (*das Vergangene*) . . . of which we say that it no longer is," and the "having-beenness (*Gewesenheit*)" as a mode of Being—that is, as "the determination of the way and style (*Art und Weise*) of *Dasein* as existent" (*ibid.*).

Having made this distinction, Heidegger now asserts that "a thing which is not temporal, whose Being is not determined by Temporality but which is merely extant (*vorkommt*) in time, can never have been because it does not exist" (*ibid.*).

This, surely, is a very puzzling statement unless we regard it as essentially a definition of what Heidegger means by "not existing." In fact, he himself admits as much when he states that "only that which intrinsically has a future (*was in sich selbst zukünftig ist*) can have been; things have at best (*allenfalls*) simply disappeared" (GP412/290).

A close scrutiny of this statement reveals that it entails a firm commitment to an ontology which sees *process* as the ultimate character of reality. Although Heidegger does not say so, this interpretation is confirmed by his statement that "only on the basis of this primordial oblivion (*Vergessenheit*) which belongs to an actual *Dasein* is it possible for *Dasein* to remember something of which it has just been aware" (*ibid.*). Understanding oneself is thus a "making-present (*ein Gegenwärtigen*) that is equally original with future and past" (*ibid.*), and thus reveals the *fundamental process of Dasein's existence.*

4. Temporality and Being: I

Heidegger asserts that the temporal characterization of an inauthentic understanding just given "has clarified only one possibility of the existentiel (ontic) understanding of *Dasein* as an extant *Seiendes*" (GP412/291). What he is now seeking is "*the condition of the possibility of that understanding-of-Being* (*Seinsverständnis*) *which understands Seiendes in the sense of what is available* (*zuhanden*) *and is extant* (*vorhanden*)" (GP413/291, Heidegger's italics). A *Seiendes* of this type is "encountered in our every-day dealings with it"—that is, in encounters which are "grounded in the basic constitution of existence, in our being-in-the-world" (*ibid.*).

The *Seiende* with which *Dasein* is concerned are thus intra-worldly (*innerweltlich*). But "being-in-the-world, although unitary, is stratified (*gegliedert*)," and the task is "to understand the stratified whole of the structure in terms of Temporality (*aus der Zeitlichkeit*)"—which means "to interpret, along with it, the phenomenon 'world' in its temporal constitution" (*ibid.*).

There can, of course, be no objection to such an attempt. But, surely, the structure of the world in its totality is not merely temporal. The spatial aspect of its structure is equally obvious, if not more so. And more important than both the temporal and the spatial aspects is the dynamic stratification[4] within the spatio-temporal framework as manifested in the interrelations and interactions of forms and forces of determination ranging from the purely mechanical to the organismic, the mental, and the socio-historical. But this aspect of the world we live in Heidegger neglects completely. What alone interests him is "the connection between Temporality and transcendence insofar as being-in-the-world is the phenomenon in which is revealed how far, by its very nature, *Dasein* is 'beyond itself'"—both in remembering and in anticipation (*ibid.*). And this leads Heidegger to the problem of "the interrelation of an understanding of Being, of transcendence, and of Temporality" (GP413f/292); and on this basis he attempts to characterize "Temporality as horizon of the understanding of Being" an attempt by which he hopes to come to "the definition of the concept of Temporality" (GP414/292).

What *Dasein* "first encounters" in being-in-the-world, we are told, are things in the form of what is *usable*. We may well question this assertion. We encounter many things that are not usable. But let us follow Heidegger's argument according to which "the *Seiende* is not merely extant but, in conformity with its character as usable, belongs to a *context* of the usable—a context within which each *Seiendes* has its specific function as something usable—a function which primarily constitutes its Being" (*ibid.*).

Taken in this ontological sense, the usable is "everything of which we make use domestically or publicly . . . bridges, streets, light-generating establishments, and so forth" (*ibid.*). All these *Seiende* Heidegger calls "the available (*das Zuhandene*)." What is essential here is not that the usable is directly available but that it is extant somewhere; and that, in making use of what is available, *Dasein* is always already also with other human beings—"whether [they are] actually present or not" (*ibid.*). We may interpolate: because they are in part responsible for the actual presence of something which is available.

And now Heidegger maintains that the "individuation" of something useful is "not primarily determined by space and time" but by "the character of the context of the usable" (GP414f/292). And this character is "constituted" by what Heidegger calls "functionality" (*Bewandtnis*). What we "use as hammer or as door" has a specific function. It is "in order to (*um zu*)." But this statement has "an ontological and a merely ontic significance," which means that

> a *Seiendes* is not what and how it is (a hammer, for example) and is in addition also something "with which to hammer," but what and how it is as *Seiendes*, its being-what and being-how, are constituted by the in-order-to (*um-zu*)—that is, by functionality. (GP415/292f)

We may readily grant the distinction which Heidegger here makes between the "ontic" and the "ontological." Quite obviously, however, the ontological aspect presupposes the ontic. For example, we can not use a rubberband as a hammer, or a brick wall as a door. To understand what a *Seiendes* can be "used for" presupposes an understanding of its ontic character; and such an understanding assumes a categorial analysis of its Being—be that analysis ever so sketchy. Heidegger's statement that "we can use what is usable only when we have already *projected it upon a functionality relation*" (GP415/293) is, of course, true enough. But it is precisely this projection which presupposes an ontic understanding based on a categorial analysis of a *Seiendes* that makes the projection meaningful. Heidegger never even mentions this fact. He states instead that "the being-what and the being-how" of what is usable is constituted by the "in-order-to"—that is, "by its functionality" (*ibid.*). But is just *any Seiendes* usable for just *any* purpose? Or is its usability, and therefore its relation to functionality, in any given situation conditioned by the ontic reality of the involved *Seiende*? You surely would not use a hammer as a suitable key to a lock—at least not in an ordinary situation; and even Heidegger could not possibly ride on a broomstick.

We can make use of the usable only when we already have projected the relevant *Seiende* with respect to its *usableness*. This anticipatory projection Heidegger calls *letting-function* (*Bewendenlassen*)—a term that has "ontological meaning" only. In using a thing, we are aware of its "what-for." Only in keeping this in mind do "we first understand the usable as usable in its specific functionality-relation (*Bewandtnisbezug*)" (GP415f/293).

But this "awareness of the what-for is not a contemplation of purpose; and even less is it the expectation of success" (GP416/293). It does not have "the character of an ontical apprehension," nor is it a "contemplative dwelling (*betrachtendes Sichaufhalten*) with something." Thus,

> [w]hen I am completely engrossed in dealing with something and, in doing so, make use of some particular usable thing, I am not directed toward the usable thing as such—say toward a tool. And neither am I directed toward the work to be done. Instead, I am *in* the functionality relation as such . . . . in the in-order-to. (*Ibid.*)

As Heidegger sees it, this understanding of functionality and of the letting-function has a temporal constitution "which *points back* to a more primordial Temporality" (GP416/294), and it is his contention that "only when we have grasped this more primordial Temporality are we able to survey in what way the *understanding of the Being of a Seiendes*—of the 'thingness' of available things and of their availableness [Ed. note: Hofstadter translates this passage as "here either of the equipmental character and *handiness* of handy equipment or of the thinghood of extant things and the *at-handness* of the at-hand"]—is made *possible* and transparent *through time*" (GP416/294).

Leading up to the main argument, Heidegger now reminds us of his earlier statement that "*as usable*, everything usable is within the context of the usable" (GP417/294). This context is not a supplementary (*nachträgliches*) product of what is available as usable, "but every usable thing as such is available or extant only within the context of the usable" (*ibid.*). An understanding of this context "is antecedent to every specific use of the usable." An analysis of the understanding of the context "in the wholeness of its functionality (*Bewandtnisganzheit*)" thus leads to an analysis of "the phenomenon of the world." And, so Heidegger continues, "in so far as the world is a structural element of *Dasein*'s being-in-the-world, and being-in-the-world is constitutive of the ontological constitution of *Dasein*, we come with the analysis of the world also to an understanding of our being-in-the-world as such and of its possibility, and we do so by way of time (*aus der Zeit*)" (*ibid.*). And with this interpretation of the possibility of being-in-the-world on the basis of Temporality, "the Being of *Dasein*, the Being of *fellow-Dasein*, and the Being of all *Seiende* ever encountered as extant and available for use is also understood" (*ibid.*).

But this understanding, Heidegger points out, is most of the time oriented with respect to that *Seiende* in which *Dasein* "at first and for the most part has lost itself" (*ibid.*). This orientation was the basis for the ontological interpretation of Being at the beginning of philosophy in Antiquity and in the Orient. But it becomes "philosophically insufficient," Heidegger insists, "when it attempts to broaden itself universally and, using this concept of Being as guide, attempts to understand *existence*" (GP417f/294).

5. The Horizontal Schemata of Ecstatic Temporality

Heidegger now finds it necessary to clarify "in principle" the concept of *Dasein's transcendence*; for it is only after we have done so that we can inquire back to the Temporality of the understanding of Being.

As Heidegger sees it, "in dealing with the *Seiende* in nearest proximity—that is, in dealing with what is actually available," *Dasein* understands functionality as an "in-order-to" (*ein Um-zu*). "The relations of the 'in-order-to'—but also the purpose-free and the purpose-less relations—are either initially or ultimately rooted in the *for-the-sake-of-which* (*im Worumwillen*)" (GP418/295). This means, so Heidegger explains, that they are understood only when *Dasein* understands something like "for-the-sake-of-itself"; and *Dasein* understands this because "its own being is thus determined." That is, "only insofar as the for-the-sake-of an ability-to-be is understood can something like an in-order-to (*ein Bewandtnisbezug*) be unveiled . . . as created or extant for the purpose of *Dasein*" (*ibid.*).

Heidegger continues:

> Insofar as *Dasein* exists as a *Seiendes* which, in its being-there, is concerned with its own can-be, it has already understood something like "for-the-sake-of-itself." Only on the basis of this understanding is existence possible. *Dasein* must give itself the understanding of its own ability-to-be. (GP419/295)

Dasein's ability to do so Heidegger calls *significance* (*Bedeutsamkeit*). He sees it as the structure of what he regards as "*world in the strictly ontological sense*" (GP419/296, Heidegger's italics).

Heidegger has argued earlier that *Dasein* understands itself "first and for the most part" by way of dealings with things and of encountering other *Dasein*. These relationships entail *Dasein*'s understanding of its ability-to-be as a "being-with-others." That is, "*Dasein* is essentially open to being-with-others"; and this means that, "explicitly or not, the factual *Dasein* is for-the-sake-of-being-able-to-be-with-one-another (*um-willen des Miteinanderseinkönnens*)" (GP419f/296). But this is possible only, Heidegger insists, because *Dasein* itself is "inherently (*von Hause aus*) determined by being-with-others" (GP420/296). To say that *Dasein* exists for the sake of itself is thus "an ontological determination of existence"—as distinguished from mere ontic extantness. It does not mean that, in the ontic sense, "the factual purpose of the real *Dasein* is primarily and exclusively to be concerned about itself and to use things as tools" (*ibid.*). Such "factual-ontical (*faktisch-ontische*) interpretation" is possible only "on the basis of the ontological constitution of *Dasein*"—a constitution which includes "essential existential relations to others" (*ibid.*).

We already know that in its very existence *Dasein* is concerned about its being-able-to-be in the world and has already projected itself upon this. The existence of *Dasein* thus includes "something like an antecedent understanding of world, of significance"; and in this sense "world is a determination of the Being of *Dasein*." That is, "only so long as *Dasein* is—that is, so long as it exists—is a world given" (*ibid.*). And insofar as an understanding of the world includes "the relation of in-order-to, [that is,] of functionality, and for-the-sake-of-which," it is essentially a *self-understanding*; and self-understanding is an understanding of *Dasein* (GP420f/296). And this, in turn, includes "an understanding of being-with-others, of what will be usable, and of a dwelling with what is available" (GP421/296).

The world in which all of this is encountered is extant. It is already "a world which one shares with others." But only because *Dasein* is in itself constituted as being-in-the-world can it existentially communicate something factually (*faktisch*) to others. But this factual existential communication is not what "first constitutes the possibility of one *Dasein* sharing a world with another *Dasein*" (GP421/297). There are various ways of actually being with others. They constitute

> the factual possibilities of the extent and the genuineness of the disclosure of the world, the different factual possibilities of inter-subjective confirmation of what has been discovered, the inter-subjective founding (*Begründung*) of the unanimity of the understanding of the world (*des Weltverständnis*), and the factual (*faktischen*) possibilities of the pre-givenness (*Vorgabe*) and guidance of existentiel possibilities of the individual. (*Ibid.*)

But, Heidegger points out, it is also no accident that what is meant by "world in the ontological sense" first becomes clear to us primarily through our contact with intra-worldly *Seiende*—involving not only things that are available or are at least extant, but also other *Dasein*. "Fellow human beings (*Mitmenschen*) are simply also present and, together with us, constitute the world" (GP422/297). This ordinary comprehension sees the world as a *cosmos* which includes not only all plants and animals, but "primarily the existence of human beings in the sense of God-forsaken (*gottverlassenen*) man in his association with earth, stars, animals and plants"; and "only when there is a world and *Dasein* exists in the world is an understanding of Being possible" (*ibid.*).

I am sure that no one will disagree with this assertion. But Heidegger gives it a special twist:

> Self and World belong together in the one *Seiende* which is *Dasein*. Self and world are not two *Seiende*, like subject and object, also not like you and I. In the unity of the structure of being-in-the-world self and world are the basic determination (*Grundbestimmung*) of *Dasein* itself. That is, only insofar as the "subject" is determined by being-in-the-world can it as this

> self become a thou for another *Dasein*. Only because I am an existing self am I a possible thou for another self. The basic condition for the possibility of the self to be a possible thou in co-existence (*Mitsein*) with others is grounded in the fact that, as the self which it is, *Dasein* is such that it exists as being-in-the-world. (GP422/297f)

In brief, *Dasein*'s existence includes being-in-the-world. "Self and world belong together in the unity of the basic constitution of *Dasein*, which is being-in-the-world" (GP423/298).

Heidegger's question now is: "How is *the whole of the structure*, the being-in-the-world, grounded in *Temporality*?" (*ibid.*).

We have just seen that, as far as Heidegger is concerned, the unity of self and world belongs to the constitution of *Dasein*. Together they determine the "subject." And this implies that "the *Seiendes* which we ourselves are is 'the *transcendent*'" (*ibid.*). But what does "transcendent" here mean?

To the "popular philosophical sense," so Heidegger points out, it means a *Seiendes* which "lies beyond" . . . that is, the "things in themselves," as Kant had it[5] (GP424/298) But let it be noted that things never transcend. They never "go beyond" themselves, in a strict sense, therefore, they are not what "transcends." What does transcend is *Dasein*—which in dealing with what is available for use, always already understands the context of usableness, significance, and world. The usable is "always encountered as intra-worldly *Seiende*," and "world is already understood when objects confront us" (GP424/299). In a certain sense, therefore, "world is 'further out' than the objects." (*ibid.*) It is more "objective" than all objects, but it does not have the mode of Being of objects, that is, of available things. Still, "the world exists." In the ordinary conception of transcendence it is even more transcendent than are objects. "It is the genuine transcendent (*das eigentlich Transcendente*)." At the same time, however, "as existing, this 'beyond' is the basic determination of the being-in-the-world, of *Dasein*" (GP424f/299).

But if the world is transcendent in this sense, then that which truly transcends is *Dasein*; and it does so "*in the genuine ontological sense of transcendence*" (GP425/299). That is, being in the world, *Dasein* goes beyond itself in its Being. It is "a *Seiendes* which in its very Being is beyond itself (*über sich selbst hinaus*)." And this implies that "one *understands one-self* in terms of one's relation to a world (*aus einer Welt*)" (GP425/300). "The selfhood of *Dasein* is thus grounded in its transcendence" (*ibid.*). And this means more specifically that *Dasein* is not first an "I-myself (*ein Ich-Selbst*)" which then transcends something, but that it "can exist as a self" only as transcendent (GP425f/300). As basis of *Dasein*'s selfhood this transcendence is the presupposition of the fact that *Dasein* has "various possibilities of being itself and of losing itself (*sich zu eigen zu sein und sich zu verlieren*)" (GP426/300). Or, as Heidegger puts it more specifically,

> *Dasein* does not exist, to begin with (*zunächst*), in some mysterious (*rätselhaften*) way in order to take the step beyond itself to others or to extant things (*Vorhandenem*), but its existing (*Existieren*) always already means: to step beyond (*Überschreiten*) or, better, to have stepped beyond (*Überschrittenhaben*). (*Ibid.*)

This transcendence makes it possible for *Dasein* to take an attitude toward things, toward other human beings, and toward itself. It is the "*being-there*," the "openness," in which *Dasein* exists for itself and "encounters what is available and extant." Or, as Heidegger puts it more specifically, "in the structural aspects (*Strukturmoment*) of toward-itself, of with-others, and of among-the-available is implicit the character of stepping-beyond (*des Überschritts*), of transcendence" (GP428/301).

The "unity of these relations" Heidegger calls the "Being-in (*das In-sein*) of *Dasein*"—meaning more specifically that *Dasein* has an "original familiarity with itself, with others, and with what is available and is extant." In brief, it is a "familiarity within a world" (*ibid.*).

But let us pause for a moment to consider more closely what is involved in this "familiarity."

Granted that in its encounter with other *Seiende*—with things and with other human beings—*Dasein* transcends itself. But such encounters are possible only within a framework of space and spatial relations. An encounter is not just a matter of *Now*, but is one of *Here-Now* or *Now-Here*. When we do not take the spatial aspects of an encounter into consideration we can at best attain only a distorted conception of transcendence. And we must also keep in mind that a simple encounter with things and other human beings does not constitute being-in-the-world, for the conception of "world" includes dynamic as well as spatio-temporal relationships—that is, relationships which in themselves are categorially and dynamically interrelated in complex ways. Only a detailed analysis of these relationships can give us a truly meaningful conception of the world in which we find ourselves. That *Dasein* transcends itself in developing such a conception is, of course, quite obvious. And that we face here a highly complex problem concerning the ultimate meaning of Being is equally obvious. But Heidegger disregards all of this completely.

To be sure, there is also another mode of transcendence. *Dasein* is capable of transcending any actual moment—any given *Now*; and it is capable of doing so in two opposite directions—that of the *past* and that of the *future*. We can agree with Heidegger that "the ecstatic character of time makes possible *Dasein*'s specific character of going-beyond (*Übergangscharakter*), its transcendence" (GP428/302). But does this really justify his conclusion that "in its specific wholeness (*Ganzheit*) the transcendence of being-in-the-world is grounded (*gründet*) in the original ecstatic-horizontal unity of Temporality" (*ibid.*)? Is not this transcendence grounded in the nature of the ontically real *Dasein*? And *Dasein*'s nature is quite obviously determined also by factors other than mere Temporality. Stones, for example—although "there" in time—have to our knowledge no relation of transcendence (in the strict sense) to anything. Their "being there" differs in crucial respects from *Dasein*'s "being there." These respects pertain not to the Now in which both, stones and *Dasein*, "are there," but to the difference in categorial structure of stones and of *Dasein*. In the case of stones, the categories of the physical and chemical, and the modes of determination which these entail, are sufficient to determine the "being there." But in the case of *Dasein* these categories, although valid within a limited range, are insufficient to account for its existence and its actions. Here the categorial structure is vastly more complex. It includes not only the physico-chemical categories, but the organismic, the mental, and the intellectual or spiritual as well. Only because of this stratified structure does *Dasein* rise above the inertness of stones. And only because of this structure is *Dasein* capable of making decisions and of determining its own actions. *Dasein*'s existence in the flux of time—its Temporality—is only a minor aspect of its existential structure.

6. Temporality and Being: II

Heidegger completely disregards the problem of constitutive categories and now attempts to show how, on the basis of Temporality—which he regards as the basis of *Dasein*'s transcendence—*Dasein*'s Temporality "makes possible *Dasein*'s understanding of Being (*Dasein's Seinsverständnis*)" (GP429/302). What must be shown explicitly, he states, is "how the understanding of availability of the available usable (*die Zuhandenheit des zuhandenen Zeugs*) as such is an understanding of 'world' (*ein Weltverstehen*), and how, as transcendence of *Dasein*, this understanding of 'world' is rooted in the ecstatic-horizontal constitution of *Dasein*'s Temporality" (GP429f/302).

The presupposition of Heidegger's argument seems to be that "understanding of the availability of what is available *has already projected its Being upon time*" (GP430/302f). He continues:

> This interconnection (*Zusammenhang*) of Being and time is not totally hidden from *Dasein* but is known in a very much misunderstood and mistaken interpretation. In some way (*in gewisser Weise*) *Dasein* understands that the interpretation of Being is in one form or another (*in irgendeiner Form*) connected with time. Pre-philosophical as well as philosophical knowledge customarily differentiates a *Seiendes* as to its mode of Being (*Seinsart*) with regard to time. Ancient philosophy already defined the *Seiende* which in the primary sense (*in erster Linie*) and truly *is*—the *aei on*—as the *ever*-Being (*das Immerseiende*), and distinguishes it from the changeable which only occasionally *is*, and occasionally *is not*. In ordinary discourse one calls this *Seiende* a temporal being. "Temporal" here means "running its course in time" (*in der Zeit verlaufend*). From this delineation of the Everlasting-Being (*dem Immerseiendem*) and the temporal *Seiende* the characterization then goes on to a determination of the timeless *Seiende* and of the supra-temporal Being. We call the mode of Being of numbers, of pure space-determinations timeless. The eternal in the sense of *aeternitas* as distinguished from *sempiternitas* [we call] supra-temporal (*überzeitlich*). In these distinctions of the various modes of Being with respect to time, time is taken in the common (*vulgär*) sense of intra-Temporality. (GP430/303)

With this as background Heidegger now attempts to show how "*a Temporal interpretation of the Being of the nearest extants, availability*," is possible (GP431/303, Heidegger's italics).

He begins by reminding us of what he has said previously about the "characteristic Temporality of dealing with the usable" and he invites us to the "workshop of a shoemaker" as "a trivial example" of how we get acquainted with *Seiende* (GP431-304). In the shop we find "all kinds of extant things"; but all have at first "the character of unfamiliarity (*Unvertraulichkeit*)" (GP432/304). What there is and how it is *as usable* unveils itself to us only in dealing appropriately with the tools and with what is usable as leather and shoes. To be sure, we can be told about the use of various items and, on the basis of such information, we can in imagination carry out the actual use of the things. But only within the narrowest regions of the *Seiende* known to us are we so familiar with what is available that we can make *appropriate* use of it. "Much of what exists, even that which has already been discovered, has the character of unfamiliarity" (*ibid.*). In fact, unfamiliarity is characteristic of a *Seiende* in general as we first encounter it. We must, therefore, "in principle (*grundsätzlich*)" keep in mind that "the usual approach of epistemology, according to which a manifoldness of arbitrarily occurring things or objects is supposed to be homogeneously given, does not do justice to the primary facts" (*ibid.*). The result is that the epistemological problem is from the very first an artificial one. "The *original* familiarity with *Seiendes* is grounded in an appropriate dealing with them" (*ibid.*).

We can readily agree with Heidegger that the original *familiarity* with *Seiende* "lies in the appropriate dealing with," but familiarity is obviously *not the first encounter with Seiende.* As we enter the shoemaker's shop we encounter a variety of things with which we are not familiar; but *there they are.* And before we can even think of using some of them we must know something about them—such as their size, shape and texture; and these are characteristics of the *Seiende* themselves, and so do not depend on our familiarity with them. On the contrary, the things which we encounter as we enter the shoemaker's shop—or which we encounter anywhere else—are first of all *mere things.* And, as mere things, they are already proper objects for epistemological consideration. It is simply not true, as Heidegger asserts, that "the *whatness* of the *Seiende* which confronts us every day is delimited (*umgrenzt*) by the character of being usable" (*ibid.*) —by "*usableness.*" Do we not daily encounter some *Seiendes* which is not usable at the time of the encounter or, for that matter, at any time, but which is nevertheless a legitimate object of epistemological consideration?

To be sure, Heidegger specifically states that "we are now interested solely in the mode of Being of the usable in its *availability with regard to its Temporal possibility*—that is, with respect as to how we understand availability as such in terms of time (*zeitlich*)" (GP433/305).

Because of a possible change from what is available to what is not available we already know that "availability and unavailability are specific variations of a basic phenomenon"—a phenomenon generally known as *being present* or *being absent.* Heidegger calls this phenomenon *praesens.* He uses the Latin expression to characterize the interpretation which terminologically follows from the time-determination of Temporality thus far characterized (*ibid.*).

Heidegger said earlier that the mode of Being in the temporal sense is a characteristic "*ecstatic-horizontal* unity." The question is: What connection does *praesens* have with the mode of Being? It would contribute little to Heidegger's argument. As he uses the term *praesens*, it is the condition of the possibility of an understanding of availableness as such. He explains:

> Everything available is, to be sure, "in time," . . . "is now," "was then," or "will then be" disposable (*verfügbar*). When we describe the available as intra-temporal, we already presuppose that we understand the usable *as usable*—that is, that we understand this *Seiende* in the mode of Being of availableness. This antecedent understanding of the availableness of what is available is to become possible directly through *praesens*. As a determination of time as intra-Temporality, the Now can not take over the temporal interpretation of the Being of *Seiende*, here of availableness. In every Now-determination (*Jetzt-Bestimmung*), in all ordinary (*vulgär*) determinations of the time of what is available—when the available is already understood otherwise—time is used in a more basic (*ursprunglicher*) sense. This means that the ordinary characteristic of the Being of *Seiende (die vulgäre Charakteristik des Seins des Seinden)* guided by time (*am Leitfaden der Zeit*)—that is, temporal, timeless, supra-temporal—is for us untenable. This is not an ontological but an ontic interpretation in which time itself is taken as a *Seiendes*. *Praesens* is a more basic phenomenon than the Now. (GP434/305f)

But more basic than the Now is also the Moment; for it is "a mode of the being-present of something (*des Gegenwärtigens von etwas*) which can express itself in saying Now (*dem Jetztsagen*)" (GP434/306). This means that we "come back to the present"; and the question is: is *praesens* identical with present? Heidegger states emphatically that it is not; for the present, along with past and future, is "one of the ecstases of Temporality," whereas *praesens* is not an "ecstatic phenomenon." And yet, "there exists a *connection between present and praesens* which is not accidental" (GP435/306). As Heidegger sees it, "the temporal ecstasis of the present as such is the condition of the possibility of a specific 'beyond itself (*über sich hinaus*)' of transcendence, of the 'projection upon *praesens*,' and as this condition of the possibility of this projection, the ecstasis of the present has in itself a schematic pre-design (*schematische Vorzeichnung*) of the *where-to* of this 'beyond-itself'" (*ibid.*). What determines the *where-to* of the beyond itself is "the *praesens* as horizon." As basic determination of the horizontal schema of an ecstatic *praesens* is part of the total temporal structure of the present, and of the other two ecstases—past and future—as well.

In order not to confuse our understanding "too much" as to what is involved here, Heidegger limits the analysis to an explication of the present and its ecstatic horizon, the *praesens*. Let us follow his argument in some detail:

> As removal to . . . (*Als Entrückung zu . . .*), the present is a being-open for what is *encountered* and is thus *understood antecedently with respect to praesens*. Everything encountered in what is present (*im Gegenwartigen*) is understood as to its being present (*auf Anwesenheit hin*) on basis of the horizon already removed in the ecstasis, the *praesens*. Insofar as availableness and non-availableness signify something like presence and absence—that is, *praesens* as so and so modified and modifiable—the Being of the *Seiende* encountered in the world is *praesential*—which means that, in principle, it is projected as Temporal. Accordingly, *we understand* Being from the primary (*ursprünglich*) *horizontal schema of the ecstases of Temporality*. The schemata of the ecstases can not be detached structurally from them, but the understanding orientation (*verstehende Orientierung*) can be turned primarily toward the schema as such. The Temporality thus accepted primarily with respect to the horizontal schemata of Temporality as condition of the possibility of an understanding of Being, constitutes the intent of the universal concept of Temporality. *Temporalität* is Temporality with respect to the unity of the horizontal schemata belonging to it—in our case, it is the present with regard to *praesens*. Depending on the mode of temporalizing Temporality, which always manifests itself in the unity of its ecstases in such a way that the pre-eminence (*der Vorrang*) of one ecstasis always modifies the others also, so that the inner temporal context of the horizontal schemata of time also vary. (GP436/306f)

Just what is Heidegger telling us here? As I read him, he is saying: The present moment is "open to" what is actually encountered. That is, *Dasein* encounters *Seiende* only in the *Now*. This Now is antecedent to *praesens* as the *horizon* of whatsoever is actually present in the encounter. To put it differently: Every *Now* is in itself but an unextended and empty point in time. What we actually experience is a moment in time when past, present, and future fuse in the passing storm of events. The unity of this process in a given moment is what is meant by "the horizon of the *praesens*"—a *praesens* whose temporal content varies with the flux of events and constitutes the content of *Temporalität*.

In the ecstatic-horizontal unity of *praesens* thus described *Zeitlicheit* is the basic condition of that transcendence which is "constitutive of *Dasein* itself." Or, as Heidegger puts it, "*Zeitlicheit* in itself is the original (*die ursprüngliche*) self-projection" which "makes the *Da—(the being-there of Dasein)*—at all possible in its unveiledness" (GP436f/307). This implies, of course, that time is in some sense disclosed in every projection; that somewhere and somehow time is revealed—even in our ordinary understanding and misunderstanding. "Wherever a *Da* is intrinsically (*in sich selbst*) unveiled, time manifests itself" (GP437/307).

We may, of course, grant all of this; but what bearing does it have upon the ontological problem of Being simply *as* Being? Since *Dasein* is an actual human being—that is, a bodily existent being—does not this mean that in its existence *spaciality* also "manifests itself"? I at least know of no *Dasein*—of no human being—that exists in time only; and I am sure that neither do you nor does anyone else. It does not seem likely, therefore, that Being, as manifest in *Dasein*'s existence, can be interpreted in terms of time only. In fact, to understand what it means to exist as a human being, a categorial analysis of our complex physico-organismic-mental-intellectual-and-morally responsive mode of existence is required, and this Heidegger does not give us.

But let us continue with his argument.

Heidegger specifically points out that when he takes time to be "the primordial (*ursprüngliche*) constitution of *Dasein*," and therefore to be also "the origin (*Ursprung*) of the possibility of an understanding of Being," Temporality is "necessarily richer and more pregnant (*trächtiger*) than anything that may arise from it"; and this fact, Heidegger adds, is "relevant to all dimensions of philosophy." It implies that "in the realm of the ontological (*innerhalb des Ontologischen*) the possible is higher than anything real (*höher als alles Wirkliche*)" (GP438/308).

This is, of course, a bold assertion. Its justification would require a detailed categorial analysis of the relationships of possibility and reality—an analysis which Heidegger does not give us, and for which we must look elsewhere. But such an analysis is especially needed in the face of Heidegger's further contention that "all origination (*alles Entspringen*) and all genesis in this realm of the ontological (*im Felde des Ontologischen*) . . . arises *out* of (ent*springt*)—that is, in a sense *escapes*, removes itself from, the superior power of the source" (*ibid.*). But may we not ask, what is the *Seiende* which thus escapes? Is it *Dasein*? Is it simply a *Seiendes*? And what is the source from which it "escapes"? It may not be Being, for a *Seiendes is something extant. It has* Being and has not "escaped" from it. To be sure, a *Seiendes* can be encountered as what it is and how it is only when this encounter is "illuminated by a *praesens* which somehow is understood"—a *praesens* which is "the horizontal schema of the ecstasis which primarily determines the temporalizing of Temporality (*die Zeitigung der*

Zeitlichkeit) dealing with what is available (*mit dem Zuhandenen*)" (*ibid.*). And since the ecstasis of the *praesens* is thus leading in our dealings with what is available,

> *the availableness of the available, the Being of this* Seiende, *is understood as* praesens—*a* praesens *which, non-conceptually understandable, is already disclosed in the self-projection of Temporality through the temporalization of which something like the actual dealing with the available and the extant becomes possible.* (GP438f/309, Heidegger's italics)

What a sentence! When we analyze it, it merely means that, in dealing with what is available, that which is extant and is available must already be present non-conceptually. The truism of such a statement is obvious. It is merely obscured by Heidegger's style and terminology.

But let us continue with his argument.

"'Availability" formally means *praesens*, being-present (*Anwesenheit*), but a *praesens* of its own kind" (GP439/309). What, then, is so special about it? As Heidegger sees it, "implicit in the *praesens* which belongs to availability is a wealth of complicated (*verwickelt*) structures" (*ibid.*). What is positive in these structures becomes "particularly clear" when it is seen from the "private point of view (*vom Privativen*)." But why this is so Heidegger does not tell us. He avoids the issue by stating that—"incidentally (*beiläufig gesagt*)"—the reason for these structures lies "in the essence of Temporality and in the negation rooted (*verwurzelt*) in it" (*ibid.*).

He concludes his argument by emphasizing that the *Seiende* which we encounter in our everyday dealings with it, has "in a pre-eminent sense the character of unobtrusiveness (*Unauffälligkeit*)." We do not perceive it always, not continually. It is simply part of a familiar environment. And it is precisely because of this fact that "we have things around us just as they are in themselves (*wie sie an sich sind*)" (*ibid.*). The presupposition for this is, among other matters, our *undisturbed* dealing with them.

Basic to this "undisturbed imperturbability (*ungestörten Gleichmütigkeit*)" in our dealing with things is a "unique Temporality (*eigentümliche Zeitlichkeit*)" which makes it possible for us "to take the usability-context (*Zeugzusammenhang*) of what is available in such a way that we lose ourselves in it" (GP440/309). The Temporality of this dealing with the usable is "primarily a making-present (*ein Gegenwärtigen*)"; and this "making-present" is possible on the basis of a "special *praesential* constitution of the horizon of the present, on the basis of which the specific presence of the available—perhaps in distinction from the extant—is antecedently (*im vorhinein*) *understandable*" (*ibid.*). The undisturbedness in dealing with the usable becomes evident when we contrast it to a disturbance which proceeds from the *Seiende* with which we are just then dealing.

It is characteristic of the context of the usable that "the individual usable things are among themselves adjusted with respect to one another (*unter sich auf sich eingespielt*) not only in general with regard to their own specific factual character, but also so that each usable thing (*jedes Zeug*) has its own specific place (*seinen ihm zugehörigen Platz*)" (GP440/310). As Heidegger puts it: The characteristic aspect of the context of availableness within which the individual usable thing has its place is that "the *place of the usable thing* within [the context] is always determined with regard to the handiness (*Handlichkeit*) prescribed and required by the total usableness (*Bewandtnisganzheit*) of what is at hand" (*ibid.*).

We may readily grant that ideally and in an organized workshop this is so. But we must note even then that such placement of what is usable for specific purposes is essentially a *spatial* placement of the extant things to be used for specific purposes—and the more so since these things co-exist in time. The fact is so obvious that we wonder why Heidegger does not even mention it. Could it be because it is not resolvable into an aspect of Temporality?

7. Phenomenological Clarification

Before proceeding further in his argument Heidegger summarizes the exposition thus far given in a retrospective sense. The "availability of what is available," he points out, is determined by a *praesens* which, as horizontal schema, "belongs to a present moment and reveals itself as am ecstasis in the unity of Temporality" which makes possible a dealing with what is available (GP443/312). In this fact is grounded our understanding of Being (*unser Seinsverständnis*).

Heidegger has stated earlier that *Dasein* is that *Seiende* whose existence includes an understanding of Being; and we may grant that this is so. But should not a sufficiently penetrating analysis of *Dasein*'s basic constitution provide further clarification and proof of this understanding in terms of "the horizontal schema of Temporality"—that is, in terms of "*Temporalität*" (GP444/312)? Instead of giving us such an analysis, Heidegger now asks: Why does it lead us back to a "bringing forth," to a creating? But this is only part of the problem—a problem which also includes a question concerning "the origin of the ontological structure of reality."

When Kant stated that existence is not a real predicate, he assumed that it is generally understood what reality is. But Heidegger suggests that we first inquire into the ontological basis of the concepts *essentia* and *existentia*, and their possible connection.

In order to clarify the problem at issue, I now turn to the hitherto neglected Part One of the *Grundprobleme*, beginning with GP175/124 and Heidegger's reference to Husserl, who in the *Ideen zur einerreinen Phänomenologie und phänomenologischen Philosophie* maintained that "the theory of categories must begin absolutely (*durchaus*) with this most radical of all distinctions of Being—Being *as consciousness* (that is, as *res cogitans*) and Being as it 'manifests' itself in consciousness, as 'transcendent' Being (that is, as *res extensa*)" (GP175/124). And, following Descartes, Husserl maintained throughout that "there exists a veritable abyss of meaning between consciousness (*res cogitans*) and reality (*res extensa*)" (GP175f/124f). However, in itself the distinction between *res cogitans* and *res extensa* leads into a blind alley; and the problem of the unity of the concept "Being"—of the *Seinsbegriff*—is all the more urgent.

Kant, following Descartes, regarded the *I* as a *res cogitans* which knows itself as a subject that perceives, judges, and acts. In brief, he regarded the *I* "as a thinking being," and as a "substance" (A348/NKS333)—"as something which does not belong to thought as a mere predicate" but is not itself "a *self-subsistent* being or substance" (B407/NKS369). And "the proposition that in all the manifold of which I am conscious, I am identical with myself is . . . an analytical proposition" (B408/NKS369). In its empirical character, this subject must "conform to all the laws of causal determination" (A540/B568/NKS468). But in its intelligible character "this same subject must be considered free from all influence of sensibility and from all determination through appearances" (A541/B569/NKS469).

As Heidegger sees it, "*primordial synthetic unity of apperception* [and of action] is the *ontological* characteristic of the distinctive subject" (GP180/127). And this subject is not a *Seiendes* in the sense in which *objects* are *Seiende*, but is the ground of the possibility of all perceptions and all representations and, "as the original synthetic unity of apperception, [it] is the ontologically basic condition of Being" (GP181/128). To put it differently: "The I is not one of the categories of *Seiende*, but is the condition of the possibility of categories in general" (GP181/129). And in this sense "the I is the ontologically basic condition (*Grundbedingung*)—that is, it is the transcendental which is basic to every particular *a priori*" (GP182/129). As such it must not be confused with the empirical subject, which is the object of psychological investigations.

The statement "I am conscious of myself" contains a twofold reference to the I: (1) to the I as object; and (2) to the I as subject. And yet, there is the *basic unity* of the I. As Heidegger sees it—and Kant did not—"the true and central characteristic of the I . . . lies in the concept of *personalitas moralis*" (GP185/131), for it is here that man is most distinctly separated from animals. It means that the true concept of personality "includes not only rationality but responsibility [and accountability] as well" (GP186/132). This moral self-consciousness is not only a matter of empirical cognition or factual experience, and it certainly is not sensory perception. Kant spoke here of a "moral feeling"—a feeling which, as he saw it, is a feeling of respect—of respect for the moral law.[6]

This respect for the law is one which reason imposes upon itself. As a motive for action, respect for the law first constitutes the possibility of that action. Having this respect, the I "becomes in a specific way revealed to itself" as "the one who acts;" and "this respect for the law is respect of the acting subject for itself as a self" (GP191/135). Kant put it this way: "The moral law . . . is even subjectively a cause of respect,"[7] for ". . . respect for the law is not the incentive to morality; it is morality itself, regarded subjectively as an incentive, inasmuch as pure practical reason, by rejecting all the rival claims of self-love, gives authority and absolute sovereignty to the law."[8] And, "the consciousness of a free submission of the will to the law, combined with an inevitable constraint imposed only by our own reason on all inclinations, is respect for the law."[9] Heidegger states it this way: "the specific feeling for the law which manifests itself in respect is a submitting of oneself. In this submitting of myself I am manifest to myself, that is, I am as myself" (GP192/135). Or, as Heidegger also states, "the respect reveals dignity before which and for which the self knows itself as responsible" (GP194/137).

The morally responsible being, this *Dasein*, is in itself a purpose and "belongs to the realm of ends as a member."[10] As Heidegger puts it, this realm of ends is "the *being-with-one-another* . . . the realm of existing persons among themselves" (GP197/ 139). But we must keep in mind the ontological distinction which Kant made between persons and things as two basic kinds of *Seiende* which led him to the assertion that "a completely isolated metaphysics of morals, mixed with no anthropology, no theology, no physics or hyperphysics, and even less with occult qualities . . . is not only an indispensable substrate of all theoretically sound and definite knowledge of duties; it is also a *desideratum* of the highest importance to the actual fulfillment of its precepts."[11]

But Heidegger regards Kant's interpretation of personality as problematic.

The problem he sees here is this: According to Kant the moral person is "a thing, *res*, something which exists as its own purpose (*was als Zweck seiner selbst existiert*)"; but does this really "clarify the mode of Being of *Dasein*?" (GP199/140f). Kant uses the term "existence" indiscriminately when speaking of things and persons as existing. "Never does he say that the concept of existence has a different meaning than has *Dasein*. Kant shows only that the *essentia* of the human being as purpose is determined otherwise than the *essentia* of things and of the things of nature" (GP200/141). The interpretation of the self as moral person gives us "no really informative disclosure" of the mode of being of the I (GP201/142). And why are the categories of nature not applicable to *Dasein* itself? In his "third paralogism" Kant gives us at least a partial answer to this question. There he says: "The identity of the consciousness of myself at different times is only a formal condition of my thoughts and their coherence, and in no way proves the numerical identity of my subject" (A363/ NKS342). In fact, "so long as we do not go beyond mere thinking, we are without the necessary condition for applying the concept of substance, that is, of a self-subsistent subject, to the self as a thinking being" (B413/NKS372).

As such, the "I" is the ontological ground and condition of the possibility of the categories, and is not subject to them. What alone can be said of this "I" is "I think," "I act." Or as Kant himself put it: "All that I can do is to represent to myself the spontaneity of my thought . . . ; and my existence is still only determinable sensibly, that is, as the existence of an appearance. But it is owing to this spontaneity that I entitle myself an intelligence" (B158n/NKS169n). This means, of course, that we have no perception (*Anschauung*) of ourselves; for all perception is of something given in space and time, and the categories pertain only to what is experienced in that way. But if the categories are not applicable to the subject, to the "I," is it not a necessity to inquire how the "I" is to be understood? (B155ff/NKS167ff.)

8. Temporality and Being: III

In *Sein und Zeit* as well as in his *Grundprobleme* Heidegger's question was: What does existence mean? What are the essential aspects of existence? I shall now try to clarify his answer.

Let us note, to begin with, that even a *Worterklärung*—that is, a purely linguistic explanation—of *actuality* leads back to an *act* of some unspecified subject (GP143/101). In Heidegger's terminology this implies that what is available for use is, in its very existing, related to something for which it is usable. That is, even the seemingly objective interpretation of Being as *actuality* refers to a subject and does so, not to a merely comprehending subject, but to an active and creative (*herstellendes*) one. The question is: Is this interpretation of existence as actuality obtained simply by way of an analysis of words, or can it be shown to be rooted in the "constructive attitude (*das herstellende Verhalten*)" of *Dasein* (GP143/102)? If the latter is the case, then it must be possible to render the concepts "reality" and "essence"—and all concepts related to them—intelligible through a reference to that attitude.

By way of an introduction to this problem let us ask first: How do the traditional interpretations of existence and reality—the Kantian (grounded in perception and comprehension) and the Medieval (based on a constitutive attitude) —fit together? Are both actually necessary? And if so, why? How did it come about that, despite their respective one-sidedness, both could come to dominate the ontological problem of Being in general?

Heidegger deals with this problem by asking first: What is the origin of the concept "existence"? In an attempt to find an answer to this question he turns to the phenomena involved in the problem.

He notes first that, roughly speaking, *existentia* is understood as *Wirklichkeit* or *actuality*, and is thus related to *wirken* or *acting*, "actus, agere." (GP144/102).

In this sense, reality is understandable to everyone as related to a creator—human or divine—and is so without an adequate conception of it. It also leads into a blind alley, not to a solution of the problem. Although Kant had maintained that "the concept of action (leads) to the concept of force, and thereby to the concept of substance," and that "wherever there is action . . . there is also substance," (A204/B249f/NKS228f) he had added that *a priori* we have not "the least conception" of "how anything can be altered." "For that we require knowledge of actual forces, which can only be given empirically" (A206f/B252/NKS230). And Kant stated specifically: "'Being' is obviously not a real predicate . . . . It is merely the positing of a thing, or of certain determinations, as existing in themselves. Logically, it is merely the copula of a judgment" (A598/B626/NKS504).

Still, effective interactions of things are possible only when what interacts really exists. And the problem is: How is the reality of these interacting things to be understood?

Since the days of Thales the traditional view has in effect been to interpret Being in terms of *Seiende*. The question has been: "What are *Seiende* as *Seiende?* (*Was das Seiende als Seiendes ist?*)" (GP454/319) Precisely what does this mean?

Heidegger explains: "The difference between Being and *Seiende* is there *pre-ontologically*—that is, without a specific concept of Being—*latent in the existence of Dasein,*" and therefore can become an "*explicitly understood difference*" (*ibid.*). To put it differently: "On the basis of Temporality and an understanding of the immediate unity of Being and attitudes toward *Seiende* as belonging to the existence of *Dasein*'s existence can it be explicated in different ways" (GP454/319). When the distinction is actually made, we recognize it as an "ontological difference."

As a matter of fact, so Heidegger asserts, "the *concept of philosophy*, as well as that of the *non-philosophical sciences*, can be expounded (*exponiert*) only by way of the (*aus dem*) properly understood concept of *Dasein*" (GP455/320). Science, Heidegger continues, is "a kind of cognition," and cognition has "the basic character of an unveiling" of something which we call "truth." This truth is "a determination-of-Being (*eine Be-stimmung*)—a warranty (*Gewähr*)—of *Dasein*, that is, a free and freely apprehensible (*eine freie und frei ergreifbar*) possibility of its existence" (*ibid.*). What is thus "unveiled" is simply (*lediglich*) *manifest* in its "pure factuality (*purn Sachheit*) and in its specific mode of Being (*Seinsart*)" (*ibid.*). "A *scientific investigation* [thus] *constitutes itself* in the *objectification of what previously* (*zuvor*) *had somehow already been unveiled*" (GP456/320, Heidegger's italics). This means that "a *Seiendes* and its Being, although still undifferentiated, are unveiled in an equally primary way (*gleichursprünglich*)" (*ibid.*). And because

> the distinction of Being and a *Seiendes* always takes place within the Temporality of *Dasein, Temporality* is at the same time *(zugleich) the root and the ground for the possibility* and, understood rightly, *for the actual (faktische) necessity of the objectification of the pre-given* (*vorgegebenen*) *Seiende* and the pre-given Being. (GP456/321, Heidegger's italics)

Heidegger's problem now is "the objectification of Being as such" (GP458/322). A *Seiendes* is not only known but is actually present. *Dasein* can and does take attitudes directly towards it. But it is otherwise as far as Being is concerned. "The direction of the possible projection of Being as such is doubtful, indefinite and insecure" (*ibid.*). "Misinterpretations of transcendence, of *Dasein*'s basic relationship to the *Seiende* and to itself, are not merely failures in thinking and sagacity. They have their basis and their necessity in the historical existence of *Dasein* itself" (GP458f/322). And "we can be sure (*ruhig überzeugt sein*) that even in the temporal interpretation of Being as such there is hidden a mistaken interpretation (*eine Fehlinterpretation*), and again not an arbitrary one" (GP459/322).

The history of philosophy is evidence of the fact that all ontological interpretations are more like "a groping about (*ein Herumtappen*)" than "a univocal methodological questioning" (*ibid.*). Even the basic act of the constitution of ontology—that is, "*the projection of Being upon the horizon of its understandability* (*Verstehbarkeit*)"—is "delivered up (*überantwortet*) to uncertainty and is always in danger of a reversal because this objectification of Being must necessarily move in a projective direction which is contrary to the daily attitude toward any *Seiende*" (GP459/322f). Because of this fact, the projection of Being itself becomes either "an ontic one, or it takes the direction toward thinking, comprehending, mind, soul, spirit, or subject without the necessity of a primary preparatory (*ursprünglich vorbereitenden*) ontological adjustment (*Zurüstung*) of understanding precisely these areas—that is, to take the work seriously" (GP459/323).

It is Heidegger's conviction that the "objectification of Being can be accomplished first of all (*zunächst*) with respect to *transcendence*." But "transcendence on its part is rooted in *Temporalität*." And this implies that "*time is the primary horizon of ontology*" (GP460/323). It is for this reason, Heidegger tells us, that "the First Part of *Sein und Zeit* was entitled 'The Interpretation of *Dasein* in Terms of Temporality, and the Explication of Time as the Transcendental Horizon for the Question of Being.'"[12] (GP460f/323f.) The implication is, of course, that "all ontological propositions are temporal propositions." And since "*a priori*" means "from the earlier," the ontological propositions "are and must be *a priori* propositions" (GP461/324).

But the time-determination "earlier" can not here mean an order in time in the ordinary sense of time. As Kant put it: "To cognize something *a priori* means to cognize it from its mere possibility."[13] Heidegger takes this to mean that "only by way of (*aus*) the *Temporality of the understanding of Being can it be explained why the ontological determinations of Being have the character of apriority*" (GP462/325, Heidegger's italics).

In his justification of this position Heidegger points out that in all our attitudes toward *Seiende* we already understand Being—not just incidentally but "necessarily precursorily (*vorgängig*)," for "the possibility of attitudes toward any *Seiendes* demands a precursory understanding of Being. And this possibility of the understanding of Being demands in turn (*hinwiederum*) a precursory projection upon time" (GP462f/325). But "earlier than every possible earlier of whatever kind (*irgendwelcher art*) is time, because it is the basic condition for any earlier as such" (GP463/325). But this does not mean that "time is ontically the first *Seiende*." In fact, "it can not at all (*überhaupt nicht*) be allowed to call time a *Seiendes*" (*ibid.*).

"*Dasein* dwells daily (*alltäglich*) and first and most of the time (*zumeist*) solely with *Seiende*," although in doing so "it must already have understood Being." But because *Dasein* "loses itself in the *Seiende*—in itself as well as in the *Seiende* which itself is not"—*Dasein* does not know "that it already has understood Being" (GP463/325f). Therefore, if Being is to become an *object* its discernment must have "the objectification of that *prius* (*dieses Früheren*)—of that which was forgotten—that is, it must have the character of a coming-back (*eines Zurückkommens*) to what was earlier and was already understood in advance" (GP463/326). Plato, "the discoverer of the *a priori*," so Heidegger points out, "also has seen this character of the objectification of Being when he characterized it as *anamnesis*, as recollection" (GP463f/326).

This reference to Plato, Heidegger maintains, is meant "to make known the *connection of apriority with Temporalität*." "All *a priori* temporal—that is all philosophical —concept formation . . . requires further penetration into the riddles of apriority and the method of *a priori* cognition" (GP465/327). But this penetrative inquiry Heidegger does not give us. He merely asserts that, "as method, the *method of ontology* is nothing other than the step by step approach to Being as such, and the working-out (*Ausarbeitung*) of its structures" (GP466/328).

Such an *Ausarbeitung* we find in Nicolai Hartmann's detailed categorial analysis which is representative of a "new ontology."[14]

Five

THE EMERGENCE OF HEIDEGGER II

In §44 of *Sein und Zeit* (SZ212/256), entitled "*Dasein*'s Disclosedness and Truth," Heidegger maintains (1) that "to say that an assertion is *true* signifies that it uncovers an entity as it is in itself" (SZ218/261); (2) that "all truth is relative to *Dasein*'s Being" (SZ226/269); and (3) that "because *Dasein*, on its own part, cannot first be subjected to proof, the necessity of truth cannot be proven either" (SZ229/271).

Actually, as Heidegger asserts, "there 'is' truth" only in so far and so long as there is *Dasein*:

> Newton's law, the principle of contradiction, any truth whatever—these are true only as long as *Dasein* is. Before there was any *Dasein* there was no truth; nor will there be any after *Dasein* is no more. For in such a case truth as *disclosedness and discovery cannot be* (SZ226/269).

This statement clearly implies a distinction between *truth* and *validity*. The Newtonian laws, for example, were certainly valid before Newton found a formula to express them. It is thus obvious that the conception of truth requires clarification. Heidegger himself realized this and dealt with the problem in a lecture delivered in 1930 at Bremen and Freiburg, entitled "Vom Wesen der Wahrheit"—"On the Essence of Truth."[1] Prior to its publication in 1943 the lecture was, as Heidegger states in a closing Note, "repeatedly revised, though the arrangement, structure and general trend of it was preserved" (E350).

The revisions were made in connection with Heidegger's lecture course of the winter semester 1937-38 entitled "Aus einer Erörterung der Wahrheitsfrage"—a discussion of the question of truth—and with his lecture course of 1940 entitled "Die europäische Nihilismus," a section of which was devoted to "Die Wesens-bestimmung des Menschen und das Wesen der Wahrheit" (EN193-99).

Here Heidegger points out that modern metaphysics, as "metaphysics of subjectivity," takes as self-evident the opinion that the essence of truth and the explication of Being through man are the proper subject-matter of analysis. But the question is: Is not in that case the momentarily prevailing explication of man and of being human the consequence of the prevailing conception of the "essence" of truth and of Being as such? If this is so, then the essence of man can never *adequately* and *fundamentally* be determined by a metaphysical interpretation of man as "rational animal" (EN193). Insight into this fact, Heidegger tells us, initiated his writing of *Sein und Zeit*—the thesis of which is: "The essence of man determines itself out of the essence (taken verbally) of the truth of Being through Being as such" (EN194). That is, in *Sein und Zeit* the attempt was made to determine the essence of man "by way of his relation (*aus seinem Bezug*) to Being, and only in terms of this." But, Heidegger confesses,

> in the past (*den abgelaufenen*) 13 years it has not been possible to awaken even an initial (*ein erstes*) understanding for posing this questioning (*Fragestellung*) . . . . But more important than anything else is the fact that this way is disrupted (*abgebrochen*) at a decisive point. This disruption is grounded in the fact that the intended way and attempt (*der eingeschlagene Weg und Versuch*) against its intention comes into danger to become merely a solidification (*Verfestigung*) of subjectivity (EN194).

It is readily seen that, in principle, "*Vom Wesen der Wahrheit*" is a pivotal work. The basic theme now is not the Being of *Dasein* but *Being as such*. This change of focus is a genuine transformation of thought and marks the beginning of Heidegger II.

Ordinarily we understand by truth *what makes something true*. "True joy," for example, is actually and only joy; and "true gold" is genuine gold as distinguished from false gold. In other words, we say of something that it is true when it is "as it should be" (*die Sache stimmt*). "A statement is true when what it means and says is in agreement with that about which the statement is made" (B119/E321f). Or as Heidegger, referring to the traditional definition of truth, put it: "Truth is the approximation (*Angleichung*) of the subject-matter (the object) to knowledge." But it can also be taken to mean the approximation of "knowledge to its subject-matter" (B120/E322). In either case a proposition and what it refers to are "fitted to each other."

So understood, truth has its opposite: *untruth*—which is "the non-accordance" of a statement with the matter "about which it presumably is a statement" (B121/E325).

Suppose we say of a coin, "This is round." Heidegger points out the obvious facts that (1) "the coin is of metal" and the statement about it is not; that (2) "the coin is round" and the statement is not spatial at all; and that (3) "the coin is a means of payment for something bought," and the statement is not. The question is: "How can what is completely dissimilar, the statement, correspond to the coin?" (B122/E326)

The "essence of this correspondence" depends on the kind of relation between statement and thing. The thing is presumably what the statement about it presumes; and this is possible only when the "thing" presents itself as an "object" in our experience. And this is a relation in which the "thing" stands opposed to the subject and, as object, is a *Seiendes*—that is, it is the "whatever-is" toward which any subject can take a stand and toward which it can adjust itself. The question is: How can such an adjustment be brought about?

Making the adjustment obviously requires freedom on the part of the subject which is making the adjustment. Heidegger can therefore affirm that "*the essence of truth* is freedom" (B125/E330). And this means that the truth is "submitted to human caprice" (B126/E331).

But truth holds sway "beyond" man. The question, therefore, is: How is this "beyond" possible? Heidegger's answer is: It depends on the essence of freedom—a freedom which "reveals itself as letting a *Seiendes* be what it is as a *Seiendes*" (B127/E333). This "letting be" is no mere absence of restraint, but is a "positive freedom" in the sense of being an engagement in the disclosure of what-ever-is-as-such (*das Seiende als ein solches*) (B128/E334). In this sense, truth "is in its very essence freedom" (B128/E325)—a freedom which lets a *Seiendes* be, and which discloses it as a whole. As Heidegger puts it: "In the ek-sistent freedom of *Dasein* thus comes to pass (*ereignet sich*) a concealedness of *whatever is in its totality*" (B129f/E337).

This concealedness of the *Seiende* as a whole is "the one mystery" which "holds sway throughout *Dasein*'s experience." It is "unexperienced domain of the truth of Being" (B133/E342).

But man is always related to the *Seiende*—that is, to what is readily available and controllable. These *Seiende* include what is "puzzling, unexplained, undecided, questionable" (B134/E343). However, the questions concerning the *Seiende* are merely transitional points on the way from what is familiar to what is essential. In this transition the mystery of *Dasein*'s own existence may be forgotten but is not eliminated. It persists as "unessential."

By turning to what is readily available man turns away from the mystery of Being; and this, according to Heidegger, is a basic error. As he puts it: "Man is always in errancy"—in an errancy which "belongs to the inner structure of *Dasein*" (B135f/E344f). But errancy is also "the essential counter-essence (*das wesentliche Gegenwesen*) of the primordial essence of truth" (B136/E345). Mistakes in judgment and false "knowledge" are but superficial modes of errancy.

But, "by leading him astray, errancy dominates man through and through" (B136/E346).

When Heidegger wrote *Sein und Zeit* he was sure that the distinction between "truth" and "untruth" lies in the constitution (*Seinsverfassung*) of *Dasein* as a "*thrown projection.*" But he now maintains that "the thinking of Being" is "the liberation which provides the basis for history" (B137/E347). In other words, the essence of truth is not the empty "generality" of an "abstract" universal, but is the unremitting history of the disclosure of the "meaning" of what we call Being—that is, of that which "for a long time we have been accustomed to consider only as *a Seiendes in its totality* (*ein Seiendes im Ganzen*)" (B139/E350).

Here, then, in 1930, in the lecture "Vom Wesen der Wahrheit," we have Heidegger's initial step beyond *Sein und Zeit.* But the real transition from Heidegger I to Heidegger II occurs in the lecture course (*Vorlesung*) entitled "Einführung in die Metaphysik" given at the University of Freiburg in the summer semester of 1935.[2] Here Heidegger raises the question "Why is there *Seiendes* at all rather than nothing?" and takes it to be the basic question of metaphysics (EM1).

The totality of what exists is encountered by us "in moments of great despair" as well as in "moments of rejoicing" and of "boredom." It is the most far-reaching problem because

> it confines itself to no particular *Seiendes.* Everything, even *nothing*, is covered by it. And the question about Being is thus "the most profound" question, for it is not concerned with mere particulars but pertains to the primordial ground (*Urgrund*) of all *Seiende* (EM2).

And it is also "the most fundamental question"; for it is the question concerned with man himself—that is, it is the question concerning the *Seiende* which asks the question (EM3).

If we take the question "Why is there *Seiendes* rather than nothing?" in the fullest sense, we must avoid all particular *Seiende.* And when we take the whole of *Seiende* into consideration, "What indeed is man? . . . And what is *the* extension of human life amid all the millions of years?" (EM4) Only when we ask questions concerning the *Seiende* as a whole can we have a perspective on Being.

Of course, the "things in the world" as such are not affected by our asking the question "Why is there *Seiendes* rather than nothing?" and the question concerning the *Seiende* in its totality is not a mere playing with words. "It opens up its own ground" and is therefore "the most fundamental of questions" (EM6).

For anyone to accept the Bible as divine revelation the question "Why is there *Seiendes* rather than nothing?" has a simple answer: "God has created it" (EM7). But, as Heidegger points out, quite aside from whether or not the Biblical statement that "in the beginning God created heaven and earth" is true "for faith," it can supply no answer to his question—which would pertain to the Being of God himself.

The question which Heidegger has given first rank is simply this: Why is there *Seiendes* rather than nothing? (EM20) From the point of view expressed in *Sein und Zeit* this simply means an inquiry into Being as such (SZ20f/42), aiming at "a *disclosure* of Being as such."

But when Heidegger now asks "Why are there things rather than nothing?" he expresses a resolve to let *Dasein* come "to stand in truth"—to endure it. To be sure, he who has information about things may have "learned a few practical tricks but will still be perplexed in the presence of real reality" (EM21). But he may be able to learn; and this presupposes the ability to inquire. Such an inquiry includes two aspects: (i) "what is put into question"—that is, what is being questioned; and (ii) "what is asked for"—that is, what is it being asked about (EM22).

The basic question is simply: Why is there *Seiendes*? The addition "rather than nothing" is essentially meaningless; for as Heidegger himself puts it, "he who speaks of nothing does not know what he is doing" (EM23), and "speaking of nothing is in general repellent to thought" (EM24). For "we cannot talk about nothing as if it were something like rain or a mountain or any other object whatsoever" (EM25).

But when we ask about a thing, that thing is "held out into the possibility of non-being (*Nichtsein*) . . . . It is torn away from the possibility of non-being." And why does it "not simply fall back into non-being?" (EM28). There is one *Seiendes* which for me—and for you, if you do the analyzing—provides the ground for what is present in my experience—or yours: our own *Dasein* which is "extant by virtue of its essential relation to Being in general" (EM29). That is, *Dasein* cannot meaningfully question its own being-there. Hegel, it will be recalled, had called it "the immediacy of being there." In our being-there we encounter *Seiendes* everywhere. "It sustains and drives us, enchants and fills us, elevates and disappoints us" (EM31). The question is: Wherein consists its Being? And how shall we inquire into, let alone find, the ground for the Being of *Seien-des*? (EM32) What is the Being of *Seiendes*? What is the Being which we are striving to understand?

Heidegger is right, of course, when he answers that, "if anything belongs to *Seiendes*, it has Being; yet we do not find this Being inside the *Seiende*" (EM33). Neither can we see or touch it as we can see and touch *Seiendes*. Yet, a mountain range *is*; and so is a cloud in the sky. "The door of an early Romanesque church is a *Seiendes*." And even "a state—*is*," as is Van Gogh's painting of a pair of peasant shoes (EM35).

What in all these things is the Being of the *Seiende*? It remains unfindable —"almost like nothing, or ultimately *quite* so" (*ibid.*). For Nietzsche, Being is thus "a delusion that should never have come about" (EM39). Why, then, and how did it come about?

The old and familiar view is that "Being" is the most universal concept. Anything that is being thought or spoken of *is* in this sense "something." This implies that the concept "Being" is the most indeterminate and empty concept. But Heidegger insists that he is asking "What is Being?" "not in order to set up an ontology in the traditional style" but "to restore man's historical *Dasein*" (EM39)—to open up the process of human *Dasein* in its essential relations (EM44).

To inquire into these "essential relations" is especially necessary in our "darkening Times"—a Time of "the flight of the gods, the destruction of the earth, the standardization of man and the preeminence of the mediocre" (EM45). An Age in which spirit is identified with intelligence and thus falls "to the level of a tool . . . the manipulation of which can be taught and learned" (EM47). "Poetry and art, statesmanship and religion become subject to deliberate cultivation and planning . . . . The spiritual world becomes culture" (EM47f).

But, as Heidegger pointed out in his Rektoratsrede of 1933: "spirit is neither empty cleverness nor irresponsible play of wit . . . . (It) is a fundamental, a knowing resolve toward the essence of Being."[3] And the task thus indicated is a fact inherent in our *Dasein*.

The pursuit of this task requires first of all that we clarify the basic meaning of the term "Being" ("*Sein*"). "And here the first step must be a real revolution in the prevailing relation to language" (EM53)—a revolution which Heidegger himself starts, but which leads him only to the twofold conclusion that (1) the word "Being" ("*Sein*") "becomes a name for something indeterminate"; and (2) the meaning of "*das Sein*" is "a compromise and mixture of three different root-meanings." Statements (1) and (2) together give us (3) "an adequate explanation" of the fact that "the word 'Being' ('*Sein*') is empty and that its meaning is a vapor" (EM74).

To be sure, we use the word "Being" ("*Sein*") like any other word; but such use is deceptive. Still, our own *Dasein is there*—and in this sense it has Being. Heidegger faced the problem here involved in *Sein und Zeit* (SZ39/63). But let us ask again: Is "Being" an empty word? If it is not, then what is its meaning?

In his attempt to find an answer to this question Heidegger suggests that we consider the word "watch" ("*Uhr*"). We may take it (1) in its audible and visible aspects; (2) in respect to the meaning it has for us; and (3) as referring to a thing—to this particular watch. Aspect (1) is a sign for (2) which, on its part, indicates (3). And presumably we can do the same with the word "Being" (EM87). But is "a Being" a thing like a watch or like any other "thing"? Evidently it is not. As Heidegger puts it: "*In each of its inflections the word 'Being' bears a relation to Being itself that essentially differs from the relation of all other nouns and verbs to any Seiendes that is expressed in them*" (EM88, Heidegger's italics).

And Heidegger now bids us to consider the following statements:

> "God is." "The earth is." "The lecture is in the auditorium." . . . "The cup is of silver." "The book is mine." . . . "The dog is in the garden." "*Über allen Gipfeln ist Ruh'.*" (EM89)

In each case the "is" is meant differently, and the question is: Does the "is" become manifold in meaning because of the context in which it is used? Heidegger points out quite rightly that "the diversity of meaning is not an arbitrary one" (EM91). The term "Being" has a similar variety of meanings. Our discourse shows this clearly, for we "differentiate between being and becoming, between being and appearance, between being and thinking, between being and the ought" (EM93).

Having indicated these distinctions, Heidegger discusses now in detail "being and becoming," "being," and the "ought" (EM95-203). He concludes that "*the sense of Being which has been accepted until now does not suffice to name everything which 'is'*" (EM204, Heidegger's italics). And this includes his own discussion of it in *Sein und Zeit*. The problem of Being must be considered anew.

But is this the right time to do so? As Hölderlin put it: "The mindful God abhors untimely growth" (EM206).

The basic change in Heidegger's way of thinking is evident in *Vom Wesen der Wahrheit* and his *Introduction to Metaphysics*. It is evident also in his lecture entitled "Der Ursprung des Kunstwerkes" ("The Origin of a Work of Art"), delivered in 1935 but not published until 1950. We understand the argument of this lecture best when we read it after we have examined what Nietzsche had to say about the origin of a work of art, for Heidegger obviously responded to Nietzsche's thesis.

In the winter semester 1936-37 Heidegger gave a lecture course at the university entitled "Der Wille zur Macht als Kunst." The section of this *Vorlesung* entitled "The Five Propositions About Art" (WMK82-91) is especially relevant here.

Proposition 1: "The phenomenon 'artist' is the most easily understood (*durchsichtig*)." "To be an artist is to be able to create something (*ein Hervorbringenkönnen*)" (WMK82).

Proposition 2: Being an artist is "the most transparent (*die durchsichtigste*) and best known form of the Will to Power" (WMK83).

Proposition 3: It is decisive for Nietzsche's point of view that he sees "art and its very essence from the perspective of the artist." That is, the question concerning art is the question concerning the artist as creator (WMK84).

Proposition 4: The *Seiende* which has not been produced by artists has the mode of Being of that which the artist has created—that is, it has the mode of Being of a work of art. And so the world is seen as "a work of art which gives birth to itself (*als ein sich selbst gebärendes Kunstwerk*)" (WMK85). That is, "art in the broadest sense as creative is the basic character of the *Seienden*" (WMK86). And in this sense "art is the distinguished (*ausgezeichnete*) counter-movement of Nihilism. The artist is what is creating and form-giving" (WMK87).

Proposition 5: Art is "the greatest stimulus to life." It is "a form of the Will to Power" (WMK90).

Although Heidegger does not accept all of Nietzsche's "propositions," he in effect regards Proposition 3 as the prevailing view about art; that is: "The work of art arises out of, and by means of, the activity of the artist." Heidegger insists, however, that "in reality there is something prior to the artist's activity which gives the artist and his work their names—namely art" (UK7/149).

But when we maintain that what art is should be inferable from a work of art, and what a work of art is from the activity of the artist, we obviously are moving in a circle (UK8/149).

To be sure, works of art are things. But what "in truth" is a thing? In what consists the "thingness" of a thing?

As Heidegger sees it, "the word 'thing' designates whatever is not simply nothing" (UK11/152). What we mean by the "thingness of a thing" may be reduced to its characteristics:

A block of granite, for example, is a mere thing. It is hard, heavy, extended, bulky, shapeless, rough, colored . . . . These traits signify something proper to the stone itself. They are properties of the stone. (UK12/153)

This is the way we ordinarily look upon things and is what we commonly mean when we speak of a thing: a certain "something" which has discernible "properties." But, Heidegger asks, what comes first—"the proposition-structure or the thing-structure?" (UK13/154) His reply is that "both, sentence-structure and thing-structure, derive from a common and more basic source" (UK14/154f).

Although the concept "thing as bearer of specific qualities" is generally accepted, it cannot be used to distinguish "singly-things" from "non-singly-beings"— such as animals and plants and human beings. Moreover, although the prevailing thing-concept fits every thing, it does not account for the thing "in its own being" (UK14/155); for we encounter a thing only within a "situation"—that is, in "what the sense of sight, hearing, and touch convey." In other words, the thing is "that which is perceptible by sensations in the various senses pertaining to sensibility" (UK15/156).

But this is not the whole story; for sensations change but the thing "must be accepted in its own constancy" (UK16/157). Moreover, "the thing is formed of matter," and has its specific "form." And so, Heidegger concludes, "in this synthesis of matter and form a thing-concept has finally been found which applies equally to things of nature and to utensils" (*ibid.*).

In this perspective we can and do understand the "thingly" (*dinghaft*) aspect of a work of art. That is, "the distinction of matter and form is *the conceptual schema which is quite generally used in the greatest variety of ways for all art theories and aesthetics*" (*ibid.*, Heidegger's italics). But the question is: "Where does the matter-form structure have its origin—in the 'thingly' character of the thing or in the 'workly' character of the art-work?" (UK17/158)

Consider a jug, an ax, a shoe—they are all matter in some form; and the interfusion (*Vermischung*) of form and matter prevailing in these things is determined in advance by the purposes which they are to serve—that is, by their anticipated usefulness. Matter and form are thus "in no case original determinations of the thingness of mere things" (UK18/159). But in occupying an intermediate position between a mere thing and a work of art, what is usable, makes it possible to comprehend any *Seiendes* in terms of its matter-form structure (UK18/159). [The word "Zeug" has generally been translated as "equipment." But this translation is far-fetched. It is simpler, clearer, and more suggestive to translate it as "the usable."]

We thus can recognize three modes of defining "thingness": the thing (1) as a bearer of traits, (2) as the unity of a manifold of sensations, and (3) as formed matter (UK20/160).

But now the question is: How do we discover what the usable really is?

In his answer to this question Heidegger suggests that we consider "a pair of peasant shoes"—more specifically Van Gogh's painting of such a pair.

The quality "usableness" of a pair of shoes exists, of course, in its usefulness. But what about this usefulness as such? In the case of shoes it is determined by walking in them. Although Van Gogh's painting merely represents a pair of shoes, it at least implies the usefulness of such shoes (UK23/163). And in this sense "the work of art reveals in its own way the truth of these *Seiende*" (UK25/164).

A Greek temple reveals perhaps better the point which Heidegger intends to make.

The temple portrays nothing. It just stands there, enclosing the figure of a god. In a sense the god is present in the temple, and the whole represents the world of a historical people. That is, the temple, simply by standing there, "opens up a world" (UK32/169), giving to *Seiendes* its appearance as the view of a world, and to man a view of himself in historical perspective. "To be a work of art" thus means "to set up a world" (UK33/171); and it "lets the earth be an earth" (UK35/171). This implies that what conforms to our cognition—in this case, the awareness of Greek culture—occurs within a "clearing" in which its *Seiendes* is "unconcealed in varying degrees" (UK41f/175). [The German term "*Lichtung*" means a region in the woods that has been cleared of its trees and bushes. It is a *clearing*.]

This "clearing" is never a rigid stage with a permanently raised curtain on which the play of *Seiendes* runs its course. It is, rather, "a denial of a double concealment that belongs to the essence of truth as unconcealedness" (UK43/176).

As we have seen in the first part of the present chapter, the essence of truth subsists between clearing and concealing. It is an "open region in the midst of *Seiende* in which 'world' and 'earth' are in conflict . . . . Earth juts through the midst of the *Seiende* in which 'world' and 'earth' are in conflict . . . . Earth juts through the world and world grounds (*gründet*) itself on the earth" in several ways. In one of them "work is fighting the battle in which the unconcealedness of the *Seiende* as a whole—that is, truth—is won" (UK44/177). This happens, for example, in Van Gogh's painting of the shoes. It reveals the shoes as something usable. That is, in the counter play of world as idea and earth as reality we experience an unconcealedness which is beautiful. "*Beauty is thus one way in which truth occurs essentially as unconcealedness* (*Schönheit ist eine Weise, wie*

Wahrheit west)" (UK44/178, Heidegger's italics).

The createdness of the work of art can obviously be understood only in terms of "the process of creation"—that is, in terms of the activity of the artist (UK46/179). But to create is to bring forth or to let emerge something as a thing in which truth is grounded. That is, truth establishes itself in the world as the strife (conflict) of the idea (world) and the reality (earth). And, as we contemplate a work of art, we realize that "art is the becoming and happening of truth" (UK59/183). And since this is the case, Heidegger now maintains that "*in essence, all art is poetry*." It "lets truth originate" (UK59/184).

The interpretations of the essence of truth and of a work of art quite obviously reveal a transformation of the position and role of man in the world. Heidegger himself concedes as much.

In the otherwise unchanged 1957 edition of *Sein und Zeit* Heidegger states (xxi) that "the problematic of *Sein und Zeit* is supplemented in a decisive way . . . . The supplementation for the first time yields the adequate determination of *Dasein*, that is, of the essence of man as seen in the truth of Being as such." [Ed. note: No confirmation of this citation could be found.]

The clearest evidence of the change to which Heidegger here refers is found in his "Brief über den Humanismus" ("Letter on Humanism") of 1947. There he points out that ordinarily "we view action only as causing an effect"; but the essence of action is accomplishment—to bring something "into the fullness of its essence" (BH193). And this presupposes an adequate understanding of what man is.

After a critical survey of various historical conceptions of man, Heidegger comes to the conclusion that "just as little as the essence of man consists in being an animal organism can the insufficient definition of man's essence be overcome or offset by outfitting him with an immortal soul, the power of reason, or the character of a person" (BH205). In *Sein und Zeit* Heidegger had stated emphatically (that is, in italics) that "the essence of *Dasein* lies in its existence." (SZ42/67) That is, "man occurs essentially in such a way that he is 'the there' (*das Da*) which is the clearing (*Lichtung*) of Being" (BH205). But *Dasein* itself occurs essentially as "thrown into the world" (BH207). *Vom Wesen der Wahrheit* and "Der Ursprung des Kunstwerkes" have shown that man is thrown into the world by *Being as such* and that, as existing, he manifests the truth of Being. But what is the Being which is so manifested? It is "not God and not a cosmic ground" (BH210). How is it related to the existence of man?

In *Sein und Zeit* (SZ212/255) Heidegger had asserted that "only so long as *Dasein is* . . . 'is there' Being." And he had elaborated: "Entities with *Dasein*'s kind of Being cannot be conceived in terms of Reality and substantiality; we have expressed this by the thesis that *the substantiality of man is existence*" (*ibid.*). The *Da* in *Dasein* expresses the nearness of Being—*Dasein* = *being-there*. It means existence. And this existence "consists in man's dwelling in the nearness of Being" (BH222)—a situation which clarifies the relation between subject and object in actual experience. That is, man's existence in the "openness of Being" clarifies "the 'between' within which a 'relation' of subject to object can 'be'" (BH229). It is a relation of transcendence. With this understanding of transcendence we first achieve an adequate conception of *Dasein*. With respect to this conception "it can now be asked how is the relationship of *Dasein* to God ontologically possible?" We must keep in mind, however, that "the thinking which ponders the truth of Being" is "neither theoretical nor practical" but is antecedent to such distinctions, for "it is a *recollection* of Being and nothing else" (BH236).

In this situation language plays a special role; for, as Heidegger sees it, "language is at once the house of Being and the home of human beings" (BH239)—quoting Aristotle's *Poetics*: "poetic composition is truer than any exploration of Reality" (BH240).

This is a position which differs in fundamental respects from that developed in *Sein und Zeit*. It introduces us to problems discussed in the next chapter.

Six

ON THE WAY

In the *Vorwort* to his *Nietzsche*, volume one, Heidegger wrote: "This publication, viewed as a whole, would like to give at the same time a view of the way of thinking (*den Denkweg*) I have gone from 1930 until the "Letter on Humanism" (1947)."[1] Let us note also his confession that *Vom Wesen der Wahrheit* (published in 1943) was "actually worked out in 1930/31."[2]

In 1936 Heidegger gave a single lecture entitled "Nietzsche's Word 'God is Dead.'" At the same time he was preparing a lecture course (*Vorlesung*) to be given during the first semester of 1940, entitled "The European Nihilism." Of the lecture Heidegger himself says that "this elucidation remains in its intension and scope within the range of the experience within which *Sein und Zeit* has been thought" (NW195). But we must in this chapter consider Nietzsche's discussion of "The European Nihilism"—the very meaning of which is characterized by the assertion that "God is dead."

In the lecture of 1936 Heidegger quoted at length Nietzsche's characterization in *The Gay Science* (1882) of "the mad man" (*der tolle Mensch*) who, on a bright morning, lantern in hand, ran to the market place crying, "I seek God. I seek God: where has he gone? I will tell you. *We have killed him*—you and I." (NW198)

> The holiest and the weightiest which the world has possessed up to now has bled to death under our knives . . . . With what water can we cleanse ourselves? . . . Is not the greatness of this deed too great for us? Must we ourselves not become gods in order to appear worthy of it? And now, since God is dead, what are the churches if they are not the graves and monuments of God? (NW198f)

In 1886, in the added fifth book of *The Gay Science*, Nietzsche added to this view of the present condition in the world an aphorism (No. 343) in which he states: "The greatest of the newer events—that 'God is dead,' that faith in the Christian God has become unbelievable—this fact begins already to cast its first shadow over Europe" (NW199). The cultivation of religion is being replaced by "an enthusiasm for the creation of a culture or the expansion of civilization"

(NW203). The highest values are devalued. "The goal is lacking: there is no answer to the question 'Why?'" (NW205). Nihilism is "the fundamental process of Occidental history and, at the same time, the lawfulness of history" (NW206).

Nietzsche concludes his *Thus Spoke Zarathustra* with the statement "Dead are the *Gods*; now we will that the *Above-man* (*der Übermensch*) live" (NW235). And this entails the positing of new values the principle of which is the conception of the Will to Power.

As Heidegger puts it in the lecture course of 1940 ("The European Nihilism"): "Since God is dead, that which for man is to be the measure and center can be only man himself." That is, "the only 'goal' is to create the hitherto existing man 'beyond himself.' The goal consists in the vision of 'Superman'" (EN39). "Not 'humanity' but 'Superman' is the goal" (EN40).

The moving force in the argument is the Heidegger/Nietzsche challenge to contemporary Nihilism. Let us view it in its proper perspective.

According to Nietzsche, Nihilism is that historical process in which even the *Seiende* itself loses its meaning and value (EN33). "All hitherto prevailing goals of *Seiende* have become frail (*hinfällig*)" (EN34). There is no longer a lasting goal (EN45). The human will, however, "needs a goal—and wills *the Nothing* (*das Nichts*) rather than *not* to will" (EN65).

As to the hitherto prevailing values—well, we realize that it was *we* who in the past placed them into the world (EN80). Nihilism is but the reversal of these values.

In the past "we have measured the value of the world in terms of categories *which pertain to a purely fictitious* (*fingierte*) *world*" (EN85)—that is, to an imagined "everlasting beyond (*ewiges Jenseits*)" (EN87). Once we realize this fact, the values associated with it have lost their compelling power and "*a new principle of positing values becomes necessary*" (*ibid.*). For Nietzsche this new principle is the Will to Power (EN90). As basic character of the *Seiende as a whole*, this Will to Power is also the determining factor in the very essence of man (EN91). And the aspect of value is "necessarily a constitutive aspect of the metaphysics of the Will to Power" (EN97).

A value has value only because it is posited as valid; and values are so posited because they are seen as conditions for the preservation and enhancement of life (EN102). That is, science, art, the state, religion, culture in general—all of these are valid as values in so far as they are "conditions by virtue of which (*kraft dessen*) alone what takes place in the world is reality" (EN107). Without these value-orientated aspects the *Seiende* as a whole is without values.

However, as conditions of preservation and enhancement, values pertain essentially to man (EN108).

The so-called "good man" of conventional morality, seen metaphysically, is one "who has no notion of the origin of the values to which he submits as to unconditional ideals" (EN120). He remains imprisoned in this naive point of view so long as he does not take seriously the knowledge that "it is *he alone* that posits values" (EN122).

With this challenge to prevailing metaphysics Nietzsche challenged Occidental metaphysics as a whole and, understood properly, marked the end of metaphysics itself (EN192).

In his own way Heidegger did the same. He stressed, for example, that "the essence of man can never be determined *with sufficient originality* by the hitherto prevailing—that is, the metaphysical—explication of man as rational animal" (EN193); and, Heidegger added, "the insight into these connections (*Zusammenhänge*) is the impulsion for the treaty *Sein und Zeit.* The essence of man determines itself out of the essence (essence taken *verbally*) of the truth of Being itself" (EN194). In other words, in *Sein und Zeit* the attempt was made to determine the essence of man *in terms of his relation to Being and only in terms of this.* But, Heidegger admits, "this way breaks off at a decisive point." This "break-off" is grounded in the fact that "the way decided upon . . . comes against all intention in danger of becoming again but a solidification of subjectivity" (*ibid.*). And Heidegger himself now refers to his book *Vom Wesen der Wahrheit* as "a new approach."

The question is: What does the new approach ultimately come to?

When I visited Heidegger in May of 1937, I had no knowledge of his lecture of 1936 ("Nietzsche's Word 'God is dead'"), and certainly not of his work on the projected lecture course on European Nihilism. But I had ample time to discuss with him some of the problems which had troubled me while reading *Sein und Zeit.* When I left, Heidegger gave me a copy of his recently published *Hölderlin und das Wesen der Dichtung.* This slender publication (sixteen pages) and the text of his lecture of 1936 give us proof of Heidegger's changed position.

Why discuss Hölderlin and the essence of poetry? The answer to this question is stated quite clearly on page fifteen of the essay: "it is the time of the escaped gods (*der entflohenen Götter*). It is the needy time (*die dürftige Zeit*) because it stands in a double Want and Need: in the *No-longer* of the Gods that have escaped, and the *Not-yet* of the coming God" (HWD44/313).

In "The European Nihilism" Heidegger stressed that ours is the time of a prevailing Nihilism; and it is in this perspective that his essay on Hölderlin's poetry must be read. But why select Hölderlin? Why not Goethe or Shakespeare or Dante? In Heidegger's view "Hölderlin is in a distinguished sense the *poet of poets*" (HWD32/295). But why deal with poets at all?

Heidegger answered this question in 1950, in an essay entitled "Wozu Dichter?"—"What are Poets for?" Here he states that, for Hölderlin,

> the appearance and the sacrificial death of Christ mark the beginning of the end of the day of the gods . . . . Not only have the gods fled, but the divine radiance has become extinguished in the world's history. (WD91)

Ours is the "destitute time" when Nihilism "stands at the door," and Nazism is obviously no shield against it.

But let us first take a look at "Hölderlin und das Wesen der Dichtung." In this essay we are told that "poetry is completely harmless," for "it remains a mere saying and speaking" (HWD33/295. But it is also "the most dangerous of goods" (HWD33/297). How can that be?

Hölderlin sees man—as distinguished from "the rose, the swan, and the red deer in the woods"—as the one who "dwells in cottages." He is "the one he is in the attestation (*Bezeugung*) of his own *Dasein* . . . as belonging to the earth" (HWD34/297). Man's belonging to the *Seiende* entails his history; and in order for this history to be possible "man has been given language"; and "language is the danger of all dangers" for it is "what first of all (*allererst*) creates the possibility of danger." In language "the purest and the most hidden as also the most confused and ordinary find expression" (HWD34/298). That is, the pure and the ordinary are in the same sense "something said (*ein Gesagtes*)." But as *mere* word, a word never guarantees that it is essential or that it is a mere delusion (HWD35/299).

To be sure, language serves mutual understanding and is, therefore, a value. But the fact that language is a means of communication does not fully express its essence; for in its very essence language is "what first vouchsafes the possibility to stand in the midst of the openness of the *Offenheit von Seiendem*" (*ibid.*) That is, "only where there is language is there world . . . . And only where there is a world (as distinguished from mere 'earth') is there history" (HWD35/300). Language is what makes it possible for man to exist historically; and this is crucial. Hölderlin could therefore say

> Much has man experienced.
> Of the Heavenly he has named many.

> Because we are a conversation (*ein Gespräch*)
> *And can* hear from each other. (HWD36/300)

This statement clearly transcends the fundamental thesis of *Sein und Zeit* according to which *Dasein*'s existence is rooted in time. Heidegger now recognizes that "the Being of man is grounded in language" which itself is actual "only in conversation (*im Gespräch*)" (HWD36/301). And this means that conversation and its unity support our *Dasein* as human beings.

Where there is to be a conversation, the essential words and phrases must for all participants refer to the same subject matter. Without such shared reference a meaningful conversation is not possible. But a reference to one and the same subject matter is possible only where there is something which endures and is in itself constant. This aspect of a conversation can be realized only where "flowing time" bridges past, present, and future at least for a moment. Only under this condition is it possible to agree on some thing which persists. And this entails that "being a conversation"—that is, using language—and being historical belong together and are in a profound sense one and the same (HWD37/302).

Hölderlin now argues that man, having experienced much, "has named many of the Heavenly" and has himself posited the values he lives by. In this fact and in the world's becoming embodied in language consists "the conversation which we ourselves are" (HWD36/302).

But who, specifically, is naming the gods? Who extracts from the flux of time what is permanent? Who posits the highest values? In the simplicity of his poetry Hölderlin tells us that "the poets originate what is permanent (*das Bleib-ende*) in the stream of time"; that "poetry is the origination of Being through the word ([*die*] *worthafte Stiftung des Seins*)" (HWD38/3094f. Poetry is not merely an accompanying ornament but is "the supporting basis (*der tragende Grund*) of history" (HWD39/306).

This is so because "poetry is the original speech (*die Ursprache*) of the people" (HWD40/307) which, in its primitive way, names the essence of all things and of Being. But the poetic word has the power to do this only "when the gods themselves bring us to language" (HWD42/311); and this occurs only in a "conversation" in which the poet plays a special role. He interprets the "hints of the gods" and makes them effective for his people. He does so by putting into words "what he has seen," and thus says in advance what has not yet been realized. "Like eagles in thunderstorms the daring spirit (of the poet) flies, prophetically, ahead of the coming gods" (HWD43/311).

Hölderlin found his own age to be a "time of need"—"the time of the gods that have fled *and* of the God that is coming." It is the time of a double *Not* (*Nicht*); of the no-more of the gods—the ideals—that have fled, and the Not-yet of the God—the ideal—that is coming" (HWD44/313).

When Heidegger told me in May of 1937 that he was "awaiting the coming of God" he obviously thought of the present age also as a "destitute time"—a time awaiting the positing of new ideals. This inference finds confirmation in his essay "Wozu Dichter?"—"What are Poets for?"

In that essay Heidegger argues that although the Christian relationship with God is living on in individuals and in churches, "the divine radiance has become extinguished in the world's history." "The world's night is approaching midnight" (WD91).

Our times are destitute "not only because God is dead, but because mortals are hardly aware . . . of their own mortality" (WD96). "Even the trace of the holy has become unrecognizable" (WD97). The question is: Is there a poet who speaks for our destitute time?

Heidegger regards Rainer Maria Rilke as such a poet, and quotes Rilke's *Sonnets to Orpheus* as evidence. But even more to the point than these sonnets are the "improvised verses" of Rilke's *Briefe aus Muzot*. There we are told that "*Nature* ventures us," and we "go *with* this venture—we will it" (WD99). The very essence of man is identified with everything natural. As the Being of beings *Nature* manifests itself as "the *vis primitiva activa*"—that is, as Will. Every positing of Being "is as something willed" (WD100f).

What Rilke calls Nature is quite obviously not the subject matter of our natural sciences but the very ground for history and art and our natural sciences. That is, Nature is "the *Urgrund*"—the "pristine ground" of everything that exists, including ourselves. And this Nature, this Being of beings, is a venture which "resides in the will"—which "exists as the Will to will" (WD102). Although the venture sets free what is ventured, it holds at the same time in balance that which is ventured (WD105). Everything ventured thus "reposes in the ground of the whole" (WD106).

But there are differences which "lie in the different degrees of consciousness" (WD107). Plants and animals are thus "in this world," whereas man "stands over against the world" (WD108). As Rilke put it:

> Nature gives the other creatures over to the venture of their own delights . . . . (But) we, more eager than both plant and beast, go *with* this venture . . . . (WD109)

Actually, of course, man "sets up the world toward himself"; where Nature is not satisfactory to him he "redisposes" it—transposing things and producing new ones (WD110). The earth and all it contains and provides thus "becomes mere raw material for modern technical production" (WD112).

But Heidegger points out quite rightly that, "generally, the utilization of machinery and the manufacture of machines is not yet technology as such" (*ibid.*). A further step toward the end is taken when

> the humanness of man and the thingness of things dissolve into the calculated market-value of a market which not only opens the whole earth as a world-market but, as the Will to will, trades in the nature of Being and subjects all things to the trade of a calculation that dominates most tenaciously in the areas where there is no need for numbers. (WD114f)

We thus face the danger that man will lose his selfhood to unconditional production (WD115). And this means that self-asserting man is in danger of becoming the mere functionary of technology.

Hölderlin had written: "Where there is danger, there grows also what saves" (WD118). But as far as Rilke is concerned, man is "ventured into unshieldedness." He

> moves within the medium of "business" and "exchange." . . . He lives essentially by risking his nature in the vibration of money and the currency of values . . . . Man is the merchant. (WD135)

But the poets in these destitute times "bring to mortals the trace of the fugitive gods, the track into the dark of the world's night" (WD141).

Hölderlin was such a poet in destitute times; and if Rilke is also one, then destiny decides what remains fateful within his poetry (WD142).

Hölderlin had written: "Poetically man dwells." Heidegger, in his essay titled after this statement of Hölderlin, now asks "how is man—and this means every man and at all times—supposed to dwell poetically?" (PMD213) As Hölderlin saw it, man has always "measured himself against something heavenly" (PMD221). That is, man has always pursued values. He measures himself in terms of values; and it is the poet who reveals what these values are. But the measure of the values is neither a quantum nor a number. It is instead "the godhead"; and the question is: "What is God?" (PMD225)

To this question Hölderlin's answer was

> . . . As long as Kindness,
> The Pure, still stays with his heart, man
> Not unhappily measures himself
> Against the Godhead. (PMD228)

This is a theme which, in effect, goes back to Sophocles's statement: "For kindness it is, that ever calls forth kindness." And Heidegger concludes that only the spirit of Hölderlin and only so long as kindness endures "does man succeed in measuring himself not unhappily against the godhead" (PMD229).

By contrast we have Rilke's thesis that "man moves within the medium of 'business' and 'exchange'"; that "he lives essentially by risking his nature in the vibration of money and the values of currency," and that "man is the 'merchant'" (WD235).

This is a radical interpretation of our own times, indeed. It neglects completely that ours is also the Age of Technology and of technological exchanges. Even business and commercial transactions depend largely on the production of goods—a production which is largely technological. It is small wonder, therefore, that Heidegger found it necessary to augment Rilke's conception of our "destitute time," and to deal with man's existence in the Age of Technology in his essay "Die Frage nach der Technik"—"The Question Concerning Technology."

Heidegger begins his interpretation by asserting that there are two definitions of technology which belong together. One implies that technology is simply "a means to an end," while the other points out that technology is "a human activity" (FT4). Although interrelated, the two definitions actually stress quite different aspects of our prevailing technology. According to one definition technology is simply an instrumentality (FT5). We must realize, however, that "wherever ends are being pursued and means are employed . . . there reigns causality" (FT6). But suppose now, Heidegger states, that "on its part, Causality is veiled in darkness with respect to what it is" (*ibid.*). Philosophical tradition distinguishes between material and formal causes, and also between formal and efficient causes. And it is the efficient cause that "sets the standard for all causality" (FT7).

Together, the four causes bring something specific about. Or, as Heidegger puts it, they reveal something by bringing it "out of concealment" (FT11). But what has the essence of technology to do with revealing? Heidegger's answer is: "everything." That is, "technology is a way of revealing" (FT12). It makes something available for use. And in this respect man is challenged to exploit the energies of nature. But does not this imply that he himself "belongs even more originally than does nature within the standing-reserve?" (FT18). That is

> when man—investigating, observing—ensnares nature as arena of his own conceiving, he has already been claimed by a way of revealing which challenges him to approach nature as an object of research until even the object disappears into the objectlessness of a standing-reserve—of that which is not yet revealed. (FT19)

As a revealing of what is concealed in nature as "standing-reserve" modern technology is thus "no merely human doing" (*ibid.*). Its essence is itself nothing technical but is a challenge to man to reveal the real by arranging familiar things which are "standard parts of an assembly—such as rods, pistons, and chassis"—into functional wholes" (FT20). Heidegger's argument here parallels what he had said in *The Origin of a Work of Art*—that it is Art which is constitutive of both, the artist and the work of art.

In the connection Heidegger uses the term "*Gestell*"—which means *something made by man*, "some kind of apparatus"—and he maintains that in its ancient meaning the term can be taken in vague parallel to Plato's *Idea* as "that which constitutes what in some way is accessible" (*ibid.*). In this sense Heidegger uses the term "*Gestell*" as "the name for the *essence* of modern technology" which, as such, is nothing technical (FT22). [The word "*Gestell*" requires a brief explanation. Basic to its meaning is the verb "*herstellen*," which means "to make" or "to construct" something; and "*Gestell*" thus means "that which has been constructed." As projection it means what is to be constructed. Hence the "vague parallel" to Plato's *Idea*. When Heidegger spells it "*Ge-stell*," he obviously means to preserve the implied verb-form of "*herstellen*" in reference to what *has been "hergestellt"*—what has been made or constructed.]

What then, precisely, is the essence of modern technology? It reveals itself in the *Herstellen* or making of a multitude of technical objects or things, but in itself it is "nothing technological, nothing of the order of a machine" (FT23). On the contrary, the essence of modern technology reveals to man that "the real becomes everywhere more or less distinctly a standing-reserve" (FT24). Although this revealing holds sway over man, it is never a fate that compels. Man "becomes one-who-hears (*ein Hörender*) but not one-who-is-forced-to-obey (*ein Höriger*)" (FT25).

Still, the very essence of technology places man in a precarious position. He now faces two possibilities: (1) the possibility of deriving all his standards on the basis of "pursuing and pushing forward" in technical construction; and (2) that "man might be admitted more and sooner and ever more primarily to the essence of that which is unconcealed." Placed between these two possibilities, Heidegger points out, man is "necessarily in danger" (FT26); and because he is thus threatened, he "exalts himself to the posture of lord of the earth." In truth, however, "*man today no longer encounters himself*" (FT27), for he is threatened in his very essence. This threat does not come from "the potentially lethal machines." It is inherent in the very essence of technology, which threatens to prevent man from experiencing "the call of a more primal truth" (FT28). In other words, technology demands of man that he think in a specific way of what is meant by *essence*—that is, by what is permanent. While particular things are but transitory manifestations of *Ideas*, technology is ambiguous "in a lofty sense" (FT33). It pertains to things—yes; but it also "points to the mystery of all revealing—that is, to the mystery of truth" (*ibid.*). Technology in its very essence is like a realm of art. And the more questioningly we ponder the essence of technology, the more mysterious becomes the essence of art and of truth. And "questioning is the piety of thought" (FT35).

Seven

A STOP ON THE WAY

I have discussed already Heidegger's essay "Nietzsche's Word 'God is Dead.'" But we now know that at that time he was also preparing a lecture course to be given at the university during the first trimester of 1940, entitled "The European Nihilism." In this lecture course Heidegger devoted a large section to the problem of determining the essence of man and of truth. His point is that modern metaphysics, which dominates our thinking, entails as "self-evident" the opinion that the essence of truth and the explication of Being are the proper subject matter of philosophy. But is not the prevailing interpretation of man himself always a consequence of the prevailing conception of the "essence of truth and of Being"? (EN193).

Heidegger now tells us that the insight into these interrelations is what led him to the writing of *Sein und Zeit* and the thesis that "the essence of man determines itself out of the essence (taken verbally) of the truth of Being through Being itself" (EN194). That is, in *Sein und Zeit* the attempt was made to determine the essence of man in terms of his relation to Being—and in terms of this relation only. The relation was expressed in a firm and circumscribed meaning of "*Dasein*" (*ibid.*).

> But despite the simultaneous (because necessary) development of the conception of truth, it has not been possible (in the past 13 years) to awaken even a first understanding for the *asking of this* question. (*Ibid.*)

The reason for this lack of understanding is the unextirpatable and solidifying custom of the modern way of thinking of man as subject, and of all of his contemplations as anthropology (*ibid.*).

A second reason for not understanding what was intended may be seen "in the attempt itself"—an attempt which, although rooted in history, intended to say something new. But even more important is the fact that "this way breaks off at a decisive point" (*ibid*). This "breaking-off" (*Abbruch*) is the result of the fact that the way entered upon comes against its will in danger of becoming again a mere fortification of subjectivity. All turning to "objectivism" and "realism" remains "subjectivism." And the question about Being as such remains outside the subject-object relation (EN194f).

However, we cannot escape the distinction between *Sein* and *das Seiende*—between *Being* and *what is extant* (EN240).

> Being is at the same time the emptiest and the richest, also the most universal and the unique, the most understandable and the most undefinable concept . . . the most dependable and the most precipitous . . . the most spoken of and the most discrete (EN253).

But are these aspects really antithetical within the very essence of Being itself?

In our actions and attitudes we stand only on one side of these antitheses. "Ever since Plato interpreted the *Seiende* as *ἰδέα* until the Age when Nietzsche interpreted Being as value," Being has occupied the metaphysicians as "the *Apriori* toward which man as a rational being takes an attitude" (EN254). And now "the century of the completion of metaphysics" forces us anew to consider the problem of Being (EN256). In this new orientation Nietzsche is the pioneer.

In his essay "Der Spruch des Anaximander" of 1946 Heidegger had claimed that *Dasein* is "the shepherd of Being (*der Hirt des Seins*)."[1] And in his "Letter on Humanism" of 1947 he asserted that "the world's destiny is heralded in poetry." He had added:

> Homelessness is coming to be the destiny of the world . . . . The estrangement of man has its roots in the homelessness of modern man. (BH219)

Rainer Maria Rilke had said as much in his poetry. But Heidegger encountered the most forceful description of this situation when, in the *Vorlesung* of 1940—"The European Nihilism"—he dealt with Nietzsche's characterization of the European Nihilism.

Nietzsche's premise is that "God is dead"; or, as Heidegger puts it: "The Christian God has lost his power over the *Seiende* and over the destiny of man" (EN33). And Nihilism is but the historical process in the course of which the dominance of the "supersensible" ceases and even the *Seiende* loses its meaning and value. All hitherto accepted goals have become perishable. At the same time, however, this Nihilism also sets for man the task of positing new values. That is, as Heidegger puts it, "classically conceived, Nihilism means the liberation from hitherto prevailing values as liberty for a transvaluation of all values" (EN35).

Such "transvaluation" requires, of course, a *new principle*; and such a principle Nietzsche found in the Will to Power as "the basic character of all *Seiende* (considered as taken) *as a whole*" (EN36).

So understood, the Will to Power is a constant *enhancement* of Power (*ibid.*). That is, the whole of whatever exists, in so far as it *is* and is *as* it is, is Will to Power; and as this Will it posits values. But since Power is Power only as enhancement of Power (*als Machtsteigerung*), the Will to Power as "principle of a new positing of values" tolerates no goal outside the *Seiende* as a whole and, in effect, is "a constant (*ständiges*) becoming which never can turn toward a goal outside itself" (EN37).

But the term "Will to Power" tells us only what the *Seiende* in its very essence *is*. The idea of "a transvaluation of all hitherto prevailing values" challenges man to "set the field-markers" for a new order of the *Seiende* as a whole. Since "God is dead," what for man is to be the "measure and center" of everything can only be man himself. And so the only goal of positing new values must be "to create man beyond himself." That is, to create the *Übermensch*—the man above present-day man. As Nietzsche had Zarathustra put it: "God died; now *we* will that the Superman live"—the man above present-day man "is the goal" (EN39f).

And what does Nihilism have to do with all of this? Quite simply: Nihilism is the occurrence of the devaluation of the highest values. "The goal is lacking; there is no answer to the question Why?" (EN45). But the human will *needs* a goal. "It wills Nothingness (*das Nichts*) rather than not to will" (EN65).

And what is the cause of Nihilism? "We have hitherto measured the values of the world in terms of categories which pertain to a *purely fictitious* world" (EN85); and by discarding that fictitious world we have transformed our actual world here and now into "the only whole of all *Seiende*" (EN87). But since the Will to Power is the basic character of the *Seiende* as a whole, it is also the determining factor in the very essence of man (EN91).

Within this context a value *is* a value because it has been posited as value—that is, as a condition of the preservation and enhancement of life (EN102). This means that all science, art, religion, and culture in general are values in so far, and only in so far, as they are conditions that are determinative of human existence. The *Seiende* as such and as a whole "stands outside all valuation" (EN107).

Seen metaphysically, the "good man" of traditional morality is he who has no understanding of the origin of the values to which he submits himself. He remains in this unique state of mind so long as he does not realize that it is he alone who posits values (EN122).

Of course, in modern history man has attempted everywhere and always to bring himself as center and measure of all things into "the position as master" (EN146). And so, as Heidegger sees it, "what began metaphysically with Descartes has found in Nietzsche's metaphysics its historical completion"—placing man at the center (EN149). This is, as Heidegger sees it, the inner connection of the basic positions of Descartes and Nietzsche which characterizes modern (*neuzeitliche*) metaphysics (EN193).

> Insight into these connections [we are told] has been the impulsion (*der Anstoss*) for the treaty *Sein und Zeit.* That is, the essence of man determines itself out of the essence (understood verbally) of the truth of Being through Being itself. (EN194)

It is of special significance that Heidegger now admits that "this way breaks off at a decisive point"; and that "this disruption" occurs because "the adopted (*eingeschlagene*) way and attempt comes, against its will (*wider seines Willens*), in the danger of becoming itself but a mere solidification of subjectivity" (EN194). Nietzsche, of course, who quite early regarded his own philosophy as "the reversal of Platonism," developed in his conception of the Will to Power a "metaphysic of unconditional subjectivity" (EN200).

But so far we have considered only part of Nietzsche's thesis. The conception of the Will to Power is not the only characteristic of his doctrine. Actually, there are five basic conceptions which, together, constitute his metaphysics: the Will to Power, Nihilism, the Eternal Recurrence of the same, the *Übermensch*, and righteousness. All of these are closely interrelated as basic conceptions, and only when, in thinking any of them, we think also of the others do we get the full meaning of Nietzsche's intent.

To be sure, Nietzsche sees the Will to Power as the basic character of all *Seiende* as such. Everything alive is Will to Power. "To have and to want to have more—in a word: growth—that is Life itself" (EN267). And in every will there is "estimation"; for "it is the Will that wills *Values*" (EN271).

And what is Nihilism? It is the fact that "the highest values *devalue* themselves." "The goal is lacking; there is no answer to the 'Why?'" (EN275). This devaluation of the hitherto prevailing values entails that "the world seems worthless." And so the necessity for a new valuation arises (EN277).

The "essence proper of Nihilism" is thus the "affirmative liberation" from the values of the past which have revealed themselves as unattainable (EN279).

Nihilism affirms that "there are no 'eternal' values" (EN280). Its fundamental principle of faith is "the absolute valuelessness—that is, the senselessness and the lack of any goal in itself" (EN283). And this entails that "the *Seiende*, taken as a whole (*im Ganzen genommen*), can only be the recurrence of the same." And, contrariwise, "the *Seiende* which, *as a whole*, is eternal recurrence of the same must have the basic character of the Will to Power" (EN284). In fact, the idea that "*everything returns* is the most extreme approximation of a world of Becoming to a world of Being" (EN288).

Within this perspective Nietzsche now admonishes us: "The *Übermensch* —the new and higher man—*must be* the meaning of the earth" (EN293). And we must remember that "reason is living only as embodied (*leibend*) . . . . The body is a great Reason"; and "what you call spirit—your reason—is but a tool (*ein Werkzeug*) of your body" (EN294). Nihilism thus recognizes the unqualified affirmation of the body as "the command-position (*Befehlsstelle*) of all interpretations of the world" (EN300).

This "collapse of the priority of reason" entails, as Nietzsche himself points out, "the death of the Christian moral God" (EN302). The question is: What is taking its place? Nietzsche's reply to this question is: Man himself—because man "alone is capable of projecting and pursuing the highest completion (*Vollendung*) of his own essence." He alone is the "value-positing Will in the midst of all *Seiende*" (EN303); and having this Will, man is capable of going beyond present-day man to what is above that man—Superman.

Superman not only transcends present-day man by devaluing the traditional values and setting new ones, but he is the very meaning of the whole of the *Seiende*. And it is in this sense that "not 'mankind' but Superman is the goal" (EN303f).

However, this interpretation must not be taken to be an expression of "overbearing." Superman lives only in so far as a new humanity takes "the Being of any *Seiendes* as the Will to Power," and "wills this Being because humanity itself is willed by that *Seiendes*" (EN304). And it is in this sense that Zarathustra exclaims: "Dead are all gods; now we will that the Superman live—let this be some time on the great mid-day our last Will" (*ibid.*). Let Superman be "the meaning and goal of all *Seiende*" (EN304).

It is in this sense that Zarathustra-Nietzsche exclaims:

> All the beauty and sublimity which we have loaned to actual and imagined things I want to demand as property and creation of man; as his most beautiful apology. Man as poet, as thinker, as God, as Love, as Power—:

> oh about his kingly largess with which he has richly endowed all things but to empower himself, to feel miserable! It has so far been his greatest selflessness that he admired and worshipped and knew how to hide that it was *he* who has created what he admired. (EN305)

What Nietzsche aims at is to "humanize" the world—that is, to let us feel ever more as its master. And Superman must *not* be taken "to be a coarse enlargement of the arbitrariness of the customary deeds of violence (*Gewalttäten*) of the hitherto existing man" (EN307). Superman means rather man's concentration upon the goal: "*The master of the earth*" (EN308). "The greatness of Superman consists in this: that he places the essence of the Will to Power in the will of humanity" (EN312).

As part of the enhancement of power, "truth is essentially related to art as enhancement of Power." Indeed, "truth and art are *essentially the same* (*wesensgleich*) because of the unity of the Will to Power" (EN319) which supports both. And the turning away from Christianity means nothing if not prior to it, and in place of it, a new essence of truth has been found—a truth which encompasses all *Seiende* "unconditionally and completely as subjectivity" (EN321). And when this happens, a new freedom begins to develop its very essence into the law of a new order in which the Will to Power is elevated to a new lawfulness (*Gesetzlichkeit*).

This new "constructive thinking holds on to what is supportive of the world but rejects what endangers it. Construction of the future requires this" (EN323). And in this sense we must understand what Nietzsche wrote in 1881-82:

> The time comes when the fight about the mastery of the world must be fought.—It will be fought in the name of philosophically basic doctrines. (EN333)

And in these doctrines there is nothing brutal and inhuman.

Eight

THE END OF THE TRAIL

When I visited Heidegger in May 1937, he made two statements which impressed me in particular. Although I have quoted them already, they deserve repetition because, as far as I am concerned, they have a distinct bearing on the Heidegger-Nazi issue which has become a much discussed problem. The two statements are: (1) "In a complete misunderstanding of my intention I have been decried enough as the philosopher of *Angst* in these 'heroic' times." When I asked him what his basic position was, he replied (2) "The awaiting of the coming of God." Both statements obviously entail that at that time Heidegger was not committed to Hitlerism.

Recently, however, I have come across Victor Farias's book *Heidegger and Nazism*[1] with its thesis that throughout his life Heidegger was deeply involved in the Nazi Party; that he was not only in sympathy with Nazi ideology but was predisposed toward it by his cultural background, and that he remained in sympathy with it even after 1945. This is a challenging thesis. But, as Fred Dallmayr and others have pointed out, Farias's book is "an intensely polemical work, exuding a prosecutor's zeal." It is "a jumble of truths, half-truths, insinuations, and innuendoes—all presented . . . with the same unquestioned authority."[2]

The literature on Heidegger's relation to Nazism is, of course, immense and represents a variety of points of view; and, to be sure, it is not easy to obtain a clear view of the facts. But an attempt must be made to see all of it in proper perspective.

That during the time of the Weimar Republic of Germany many observers shared the sense of crisis—of the approaching Nihilism in Europe, as Nietzsche called it—is understandable; and it would be strange if Heidegger would not have shared it. But it was also the time of the rise of National Socialism as a political factor. And many prominent persons—scientists, writers, artists, and university professors—saw Hitler's takeover of the government as the salvation for Germany.

Heidegger joined the Nazi Party on 1 May 1933, and kept up the payments of Party dues until 1945. The question is: How "good" a Nazi was he?

There is evidence to show that he distinguished between National Socialism as an ideal and the Nazi movement as a political reality. In his *Einführung in die Metaphysik*, for example, he wrote:

> The works that are being peddled about nowadays as philosophy of National Socialism . . . have nothing whatever to do with the inner truth and greatness of this movement (namely the encounter between global technology and modern man) . . . . (EM152/199)

That Heidegger believed that the ideal of National Socialism might be the salvation of a disintegrating Germany can not be denied. In his *Rektoratsrede* of 1933[3] he admonished his audience:

> We want our people to fulfill its genuinely historical mission. We do will ourselves.[4]

But he added:

> Let not the "dogma" and "idea" be the rules of your Being. The *Führer* himself, and only he, *is* the present and future German reality and the law. . . . [F]rom now on, everything demands decision, and all action demands responsibility. Heil Hitler![5] [Ed. note: Werkmeister accepts uncritically Ott's quotation of this passage as from the *Rektoratsrede* of 1933. Ott gives no citation, and Heidegger's son, Hermann Heidegger, disputes this passage's attribution to his father's address: "The words 'National Socialism' and 'National Socialist' do not occure in this address; the 'Führer,' the 'Chancellor of the *Reich*,' or 'Hitler' are not mentioned."[6] Ott's reply: "This is specious nonsense, of course, since Heidegger uses these words often enough in his other speeches, proclamations and writings . . . ."[7]]

This statement seems to imply a firm commitment to National Socialism; and it is a legitimate question to ask: To what extent was Heidegger a convinced Nazi? What was his reaction to the consequences of Hitler's seizing power—to the Nürnberg Laws and the horrors of the extermination camps? All of this was obviously not the realization of the dream of a renewal of the spiritual and moral strength that Heidegger had hoped for. It was rather a complete distortion of that dream.

It is Farias's thesis that Heidegger was predisposed toward National Socialism by his background; and that he was completely and unqualifiedly involved in it and remained so to the end of his life.[8] But is this really the truth?

In his *Einführung in die Metaphysik* Heidegger had stated:

> This Europe in its ruinous blindness always on the point to plunge a dagger into itself (*sich selbst zu erdolchen*) lies today in the great pincers between Russia on one side and America on the other. Seen from the point of view of metaphysics, Russia and America are one and the same; the same disconsolate (*trostlose*) frenzy of the unchained (*entfesselt*) technology and the bottomless organization of the common man (*des Normalmenschen*). When the farthermost corner of the earth has been technologically conquered and economically exploited; when every happening whatsoever at any place whatsoever can be communicated to the rest of the world at any desired time . . . then, yes then, above all this spectre there arises like a ghost the question: What for?—Whither?—and What then? (EM28f/37f)

> We are caught in a pincer. Our people, standing in the center, experience the sharpest pressure of the pincers. We have the most neighbors and are the most endangered. And in all of this we are the most metaphysical people. Only when we comprehend our tradition creatively can we bring about the unfolding (*Entfaltung*) of the new historico-*spiritual* forces from the center . . . and can put an end to the dreary technological frenzy that has affected Russia and America. (EM29ff/38ff)

But we have already seen earlier that, as far as Heidegger is concerned, our Age of Technology leaves man in a precarious position. His very existence *as human* is at stake. And it seems clear that, at the beginning, Heidegger regarded the Nazi Movement as a spiritual renewal of the German people in the face of the tragic conflict of technology and the essence of man. So understood, the Movement did have intrinsic greatness and dignity. Unfortunately, the Hitler version of Nazism did not in the least resemble such an ideal; and Heidegger must have realized this fact. Did his rejection of the radicalism of Nazism ultimately stem from his own idealistic radicalism, as Hugo Ott maintains?[9] But be that as it may, there is evidence to show that even as early as 1934 Alfred Rosenberg, the Nazis' chief ideologist, started a file on the increasingly suspect Heidegger.

To be sure, Heidegger had written that in these times "a man without a uniform gives the impression of being something unreal which no longer belongs."[10] But in a letter to Karl Jaspers, dated 1 July 1935, he wrote:

> What is being passed around today expressly as a philosophy of National Socialism has absolutely nothing at all to do with the inner truths and greatness of National Socialism; that is fishing in the muddy waters of "values" and "integrities."[11]

As far as racism—an essential part of the Nazi doctrine—is concerned, Heidegger seems to have shared Nietzsche's view that "the conception of race (*der Rassengedanke*) has not a biological but a metaphysical meaning."[12] But we may well ask: Is one view worse than the other? Still, in 1933-34 Heidegger defended Jewish colleagues as "noble Jews" of "exemplary character,"[13] although he did not visit Husserl who still lived in Freiburg.

In his book *Heidegger on Being and Action from Principle to Anarchy*, Reiner Schürmann informs us that "in 1935 Heidegger still trusts that if modern man can come to grips with technology it will be through National Socialism."[14] And the question is: "How far did his disillusionment really go when he resigned from the university rectorate a year later?"[15] As Schürmann sees it, Heidegger "can and should be criticized for having treated the problem of so-called practical philosophy all too allusively"; and that as a result he "became an unwitting apologist for that peculiar reference to a first—the call for a leader."[16] Still, as Michael E. Zimmerman sees it, Heidegger's early—that is, 1933-36—confidence in National Socialism "gradually waned. Like other intellectuals, he began distinguishing between the historical reality of National Socialism and its 'inner truth.'"[17]

However, Karl Löwith, who had been one of Heidegger's students in 1928 but was now in exile, reports that when he met his former teacher in 1936 Heidegger "left no doubt about his belief in Hitler . . . . He was still convinced that National Socialism was the path that was mapped out for Germany."[18]

National Socialism, yes—but "Hitlerism"? As Heidegger told me in 1936, he was still "awaiting the coming of God." And Otto Pöggeler, who is well known for his comprehensive and detailed study of the development of Heidegger's thinking,[19] points out that in the years 1936-38, "in total isolation," Heidegger wrote his *Contributions to Philosophy* in which he "offers a sharp criticism of National Socialism, and of 'Liberalism' and Bolshevism as well."[20]

As Pöggeler sees it, "around 1938, Heidegger had no political alternative to National Socialism; nevertheless, he condemned this totalitarianism in formulations that might well have cost him his life, had they come to light in the darkness of those days."[21] Hitler was obviously not the "God" Heidegger was waiting for in 1937.

Hugo Ott has suggested that Heidegger rejected the radicalism of the Nazis because "he was radical in his own independent way, a way that soon became a nuisance to the National Socialists."[22] But, as Max Müller points out, although Heidegger recognized already in 1934 that he had chosen the wrong party, "he kept the belief that something could still be done with the so-called Führer." That is, Heidegger "did not back the Party but one person and the direction, the 'movement.'"[23]

What this comes to is that Heidegger's attitude toward existing political conditions, as generally understood, was by no means completely clear. In 1945 the university "*Säuberungsausschuss*"—an investigative body—in its routine procedure asked Heidegger to answer twenty-three questions of a general *Fragebogen* concerning his relation to the Nazis. He broke down completely and was taken by Dean Beringer to Badenweiler, where Heidegger stayed from 10 February until the end of May 1946, when he returned "a healthy man." But the "psychotherapeutic treatment continued,"[24] and Heidegger's relation to Hitler and the Nazis was still muddled.

In the interview with the editors of *Der Spiegel,* Heidegger attempted to clarify his position; but the interview, given in 1966, was at his request not published until after his death in 1976.

As I read the interview, it pertains to two issues: (1) Heidegger's assertion that he "was in no way politically active before (he) became rector" (DS41); and (2) his thesis that as yet we have no way of dealing effectively with "the essence of technology" (DS55).

With regard to the first issue Heidegger admits that in 1933, "in the general confusion of opinions and political tendencies," he believed it to be "necessary to find a national, and especially a social, point of view" (DS44); and he believed "that in the questioning confrontation with National Socialism a new path . . . to a renewal might possibly open up" (DS46). But, Heidegger insisted, "the university was to have renewed itself through its own reflection, not with National Socialists," to avoid "the danger of the politization of science" (DS45); and he claimed that his lectures on Nietzsche, given in 1936, were for "all who could hear a confrontation with National Socialism" (DS51). As a consequence, he was "constantly under surveillance" (*ibid.*).

For Heidegger the "decisive question" was "how any political system—and which one—can be adapted to an epoch of technology?" (DS54) He was not convinced that it was democracy. But was it Nazism?

As Heidegger saw it, the paramount problem of the future of Western civilization was the problem of technology: "Human beings are caught, claimed, and challenged by a power that is revealed in the essence of technology" (DS57). In this situation the individual can do little more than "keep[ing] himself open to the arrival or absence of God" (DS58). And in this respect "traditional metaphysics . . . no longer offers us any possibility to experience the fundamental characteristics of the technological Age—an Age that is only beginning through thinking" (DS59).

Only a new way of thinking could "awaken, clarify, and fortify" our readiness for the New Age (DS60). Although National Socialism *pointed in the right direction* of "an adequate relationship to the essence of technology," its adherents

> were much too limited in their thinking to give a really explicit relationship to what is happening today and what has been under way for three centuries . . . . They are still entangled in a thinking—pragmatism—that fosters technological operations and manipulating, but simultaneously blocks the path toward a contemplation of what is characteristic of modern technology. (DS61)

In fact, Heidegger concludes,

> as far as I can see, no thinker yet speaks who is great enough to place thinking directly and formatively, before its subject matter and therefore on the path. The greatness of what is to be thought is too great for us today. (DS66)

As Heinrich W. Petzet has pointed out:

> A swelling hate arose against Heidegger's inconvenient call for a change in thinking and for a new beginning, a hate that was evident in numerous attacks, misinterpretations, even personal slights that were directed against the thinker in the fifties and on into the sixties.[25]

When the *Spiegel* interview was finally published it had a "clarifying effect" but "could not completely silence the accusations" brought against Heidegger.[26]

However, on 30 October 1955, Heidegger gave the "Memorial Address" at Messkirch honoring the 175th birthday of the composer Konradin Kreutzer. It was published in 1959 as Chapter One of *Gelassenheit*—that is, of serenity, a calmness in resignation to a prevailing situation. And what is the situation to which Heidegger here responds?

It is, of course, the time after World War II—a war which decided nothing as far as human destiny on this planet is concerned. Crowded in "the turmoil of large cities" countless numbers of people still live in "the wastelands" of industrial regions. Hourly and daily "chained to radio and television," transposed by movies into a world of imagination which is not a real world, they are essentially victims of modern technology. In other words, as Heidegger saw it, "man is today threatened at his very core" (G48f). There has been a radical revolution in outlook, in philosophy—a revolution which entails "a completely new relation of man to the world and to his place in it" (G50). The world is taken as merely an object for calculating thinking, and nature is but an energy source for modern technology and industry which, in turn, determine the relation of man to whatever exists. This basic technological interest is not only ruling the whole earth, but already leads man to begin to advance beyond the earth into outer space (*ibid.*). This technological advance "will move faster and faster and can never be stopped" (G51). All we can do is accept it in calm resignation—in *Gelassenheit*—and return to *meditative thinking* (G53).

We can use technical devices as they ought to be used and deny them the right to dominate us (G54); but for the time being "man finds himself in a perilous situation" (G55).

> The approaching tide of technological revolution in the Atomic Age could so dazzle and beguile man that merely calculative thinking may someday be accepted and practiced as *the only* way of thinking. (G56)

But if this happens, man will have denied and discarded his own essential nature—his nature as "*a meditative thinker*." And so "the issue is to keep meditative thinking alive" (*ibid.*).

This theme of *Gelassenheit* reflects in at least one respect what Heidegger had said in his lecture course of 1944, entitled "Die seinsgeschichtliche Bestimmung des Nihilismus":

> The half admitted, half denied *Heimatlosigkeit* (homelessness) of man with respect to his *essence* is replaced by his *Einrichtung* (establishment) of the conquest of the earth as a planet and the *Ausgriff* (the reaching out) into cosmic space. Through the success of this achievement arranging the *homeless*, man lets himself be driven into flight from his own essence in

order to imagine this flight to be his coming-home (*Heimkehr*) to the true humanity of *humano humanus*.[27]

As we know from the *Spiegel* interview, Heidegger doubted that it would be democracy that would be appropriate to this technological age. Was this doubt the inspiration for his belief in an *ideal* of National Socialism? And when this ideal was shattered by the realities of the Nazi regime, there was nothing left for Heidegger but the “awaiting of the coming of God”—as he expressed it to me in 1937.

NOTES

Notes to Guest Preface

1. E. F. Kaelin, *Heidegger's Being and Time—A Reading for Readers* (Tallahassee: Florida State University Press, 1988), p. 1.

2. Karen Horney, *Neurosis and Human Growth* (New York: W. W. Norton, 1950).

3. Thomas Langan, *The Meaning of Heidegger* (New York: Columbia University Press, 1959), p. 215.

4. E. F. Kaelin, *Heidegger's Being and Time: A Reading for Readers*, p. 293.

5. W. H. Werkmeister, *Nicolai Hartmann's New Ontology* (Tallahassee: Florida State University Press, 1990).

6. Nicolai Hartmann, *Ethics*, trans. Stanton Coit, three volumes (London: George Allen & Unwin, 1932), vol. 2, p. 431.

7. Immanuel Kant, *Critique of Pure Reason*, A529-532/B557-560.

8. Below, p. 125, n. 2.

9. Kaelin, "Guest Foreword," below, p. xxx.

10. *Ibid*, p. xxxiii.

11. See below, p. 101.

12. See Martin Heidegger, *Sein und Zeit*, in Edmund Husserl's *Jarhbuch für Philosophie und phänomenologische Forschung*, Band 8, 1927, pp. 10-11.

13. See Martin Heidegger, *Being and Time*, trans. John Macquarrie and Edward Robinson (New York: Harper & Brothers, 1962), pp. 307-309.

14. Thomas Langan, *The Meaning of Heidegger*, p. 7.

15. W. H. Werkmeister, *An Introduction to Critical Thinking* (Lincoln, Nebraska: Johnson Publishing Company, 1948).

16. Below, p. 59.

17. In *Nicolai Hartmann's New Ontology*, p. 192, Werkie writes:

Hartmann's *Ethik* has been much neglected. The only significant discussion in English that I know of is Eva H. Cadwallader's *Searchlight on Values: Nicolai Hartmann's Twentieth Century Value Platonism.* But even German-language discussions of Hartmann's *Ethik* are scarce.

18. W. H. Werkmeister, *Nicolai Hartmann's New Ontology*, p. xiv.

19. *Ibid.*

20. *Ibid.*, p. xiii. The "30" is a reference to Martin Heidegger, *Die Grundprobleme der Phänomenologie*, in *Gesamtausgabe*, vol. 24, ed. Friedrich Wilhelm von Hermann (Frankfurt am Main: Vittorio Klostermann, 1975).

21. W. H. Werkmeister, *Nicolai Hartmann's New Ontology*, p. xvi.

22. *Ibid.*, p. xvii.

Notes to Guest Foreword

1. See Ralph Manheim, trans., in Martin Heidegger, *An Introduction to Metaphysics* (New Haven, Conn.: Yale University Press, 1959), p. ix, *passim.*

2. See Martin Heidegger, "Vom Wesen und Begriff der Physis: Aristoteles Physik, Book 1," in *Wegmarken* (Frankfurt am Main: Vittorio Klostermann, 1967), pp. 309-371.

3. See A.-T. Tymieniecka, *Why Is There Something Rather Than Nothing?* (Assen: Van Gorcum, 1966).

4. Martin Heidegger, *Der Satz vom Grund* (Pfullingen: Günther Neske, 1957).

5. Martin Heidegger, *Unterwegs zur Sprache* (Pfullingen: Günther Neske, 1959).

6. Hans-Georg Gadamer, *Heidegger's Ways* (Albany: SUNY Press, 1994).

7. See William J. Richardson, S.J., *Heidegger from Phenomenology to Thought* (The Hague: Nijhoff, 1963).

8. Victor Farias, *Heidegger and Nazism* (Philadelphia: Temple University Press, 1989).

9. Guido Schneeberger, *Nachlese zu Heidegger* (Bern: Schneeberger, 1962).

Notes to Chapter One: *INTRODUCTION*

1. Martin Heidegger, *Unterwegs zur Sprache* (Pfullingen: Günther Neske, 1959), p. 98.

2. Robert Mugerauer wrote: "It seems a reasonable question: 'Does Heidegger make sense?' His etymologies disturb the scholars; his method of 'argument' wrests a moan from the logicians; his talk of will, releasement, region, and horizon offends the clear-headed; words often appear to be shuffled together in combinations so various that they strike even the sympathetic reader as attempted chance poetry or word magic." See Mugerauer, *Heidegger's Language and Thinking* (Atlantic Highlands, N. J.: Humanities Press International, 1988).

Rudolf Carnap regarded Heidegger's work as "a paradigm case of metaphysical nonsense." See Carnap, *Scheinprobleme in der Philosophie* (Berlin: Weltkreis, 1928); *Logical Structure of the World [and] Pseudoproblems in Philosophy*, 2nd ed., trans. Rolf A. George (London: Routledge and Kegan Paul, 1967); "Überwindung der Metaphysik durch logische Analyse der Sprache," *Erkenntnis*, 2 (1931): 219-241.

Werner Marx found that "the consequences of Heidegger's conception that scandalize us lie precisely in the fact that poet and thinker can fall into evil, error and sham 'with impunity.'" See Marx, *Heidegger und die Tradition* (Stuttgart: Kohlhammer Verlag, 1961); *Heidegger and the Tradition* (Evanston: Northwestern University Press, 1971).

And Julius Kraft added: "It is a crushing testimony to the freedom from want at the present time that it elevates this kind of triviality to its religious symbols." See Kraft, *Von Husserl zu Heidegger* (Frankfurt am Main: Offentliches Leben, 1957).

3. Nicolai Hartmann, *Grundzüge einer Metaphysik der Erkenntnis*, 2nd ed. (Berlin and Leipzig: Walter de Gruyter, 1925).

4. See W. H. Werkmeister, "The Structure of the Real World," chap. 2 in *Nicolai Hartmann's New Ontology* (Tallahassee, Fla.: Florida State University Press, 1990).

5. René Descartes, *Meditations on First Philosophy,* Meditation 1, in *The Philosophy of the 16th and 17th Centuries,* ed. Richard H. Popkin (New York: The Free Press, 1966), pp. 130f.

Notes to Chapter Two: *HEIDEGGER AND KANT*

1. See W. H. Werkmeister, *Nicolai Hartmann's New Ontology* (Tallahassee, Fla.: Florida State University Press, 1990), p. xi.

2. Immanuel Kant, *Kants Opus postumum*, presented and critiqued by Erich

Adickes (Berlin: Verlag von Reuther & Reichard, 1920), p. 653. See also KPM29/37. Also see W. H. Werkmeister, *Kant: The Architectonic and Development of His Philosophy* (La Salle, Ill.: Open Court, 1980), pp. 176f.

3. Immanuel Kant, *Logik*, vol. 8 of Kant's *Werke*, ed. Ernst Cassirer (Berlin: Bruno Cassirer, 1922), p. 344.

Notes to Chapter Three: *THE PROBLEMATIC OF* SEIN UND ZEIT

1. *Being and Time, Macquarrie and Robinson, p. 17.*

2. E. F. Kaelin, *Heidegger's Being and Time—A Reading for Readers* (Tallahassee, Fla.: Florida State University Press, 1988). But let the reader of Kaelin's book keep in mind from the beginning that he states on page 304 his basic thesis: "What, in the end, was the achievement of Heidegger's *Being and Time?* It invented a hermeneutical phenomenology and so broadened the scope of phenomenological inquiry. It gave renewed impetus to the existential movement begun by Kierkegaard . . . and as the Hegelian unhappy consciousness, he brought to life once more Kierkegaard's depiction of the ultimate paradox—that the Eternal should become historical . . . ." See in this connection Thomas Langan, *The Meaning of Heidegger: A Critical Study of Existentialist Phenomenology* (New York: Columbia University Press, 1959). When I visited Heidegger in 1937, knowing that Jean-Paul Sartre had been his student, I asked Heidegger about his relation to existentialism. His reply was an emphatic "My God, that I have never intended."

3. G. E. Moore already claimed that our knowledge of the external world is presupposed by the simplest of our actions. See Moore, "Refutation of Idealism," in *Philosophical Studies* (Paterson, N.J.: Littlefield, Adams & Co., 1959), pp. 1-20.

4. For an overview of Heidegger's change in philosophical style see William J. Richardson, S.J., *Heidegger Through Phenomenology to Thought*, in *Phaenomenologica*, vol. 13 (The Hague: Nijhoff, 1963). The argument is that Heidegger's "reversal" is a change from phenomenologist to "thinker."

Notes to Chapter Four: *A FIRST STEP BEYOND* SEIN UND ZEIT

1. Victor Zuckerkandl, *Sound and Symbol: Music and the External World*, trans. Willard R. Trask (New York: Pantheon Books, 1956), pp. 234f.

2. Alfred North Whitehead, *Process and Reality* (New York: The Macmillan Company, 1929), pp. 34f. I am here reminded also of Hegel's statement that "as the unity

of being outside itself, time is also . . . the Being which in so far as it is *is not*, and in so far as it is not *is*—the intuited Becoming." G. F. W. Hegel, *Enzyklopädie der philosophischen Wissenschaften im Grundriss*, ed. V. G. Boland (Leiden, 1906), secs. 254 ff.

3. Nicolai Hartmann, *Der Aufbau der realen Welt*, 2nd ed. (Meisenheim am Glan: Westkulturverlag Anton Hain, 1949).

4. For a detailed analysis of this stratification see *ibid.*

5. Immanuel Kant, *Critique of Pure Reason*, trans. Norman Kemp-Smith (New York: St. Martins Press, 1961), chs. 1 and 2.

6. Immanuel Kant, *Critique of Practical Reason*, trans. Lewis White Beck (Chicago: University of Chicago Press, 1978), pp. 181 ff.

7. *Ibid.*, p. 182.

8. *Ibid.*, p. 183f.

9. *Ibid.*, p. 187.

10. Immanuel Kant, *Foundations of the Metaphysics of Morals*, trans. Lewis White Beck (Indianapolis, Ind.: Bobbs-Merrill, 1959), p. 91.

11. *Ibid., p. 70.*

12. This is the exact title of the First Part, as it appears on p. 7, "Table of Contents" of the English translation of *Being and Time,* trans. Macquarrie and Robinson (New York: Harper, 1962).

13. Immanuel Kant, *Metaphysische Anganfsgründe der Naturwissenschaft*, in Kant's *Werke*, vol. 4, ed. Ernst Cassirer (Berlin: Bruno Cassirer, 1913), p. 372.

14. See Werkmeister, *Nicolai Hartmann's New Ontology.*

Notes to Chapter Five: *THE EMERGENCE OF HEIDEGGER II*

1. Heidegger himself tells us in the closing Note to "Vom Wesen der Wahrheit" that the crucial question in *Sein und Zeit* (SZ151\192) has been "intentionally left undeveloped." See "Vom Wesen der Wahrheit" (B140/E351).

2. A completely reworked text of these lectures was published under the title *Einführung in die Metaphysik* (Tübingen: Niemeyer, 1953). A translation by Ralph Manheim was published as *An Introduction to Metaphysics* (New Haven, Conn.: Yale University Press, 1959). See list of Abbreviations at the front of this book.

3. Martin Heidegger, "Die Selbstbehauptung der deutschen Universität," trans. by Karsten Harries as "The Self Assertion of the German University," *Review of Metaphysics* 38 (1985), p. 474. [Ed. note: Translations are Werkmeister's own.]

Notes to Chapter Six: *ON THE WAY*

1. Martin Heidegger, *Nietzsche*, 1 (Pfullingen: Günther Neske, 1961), p. 10.

2. *Ibid.*

Note to Chapter Seven: *A STOP ON THE WAY*

1. Martin Heidegger, "Der Spruch des Anaximander," in *Holzwege* (Frankfurt am Main: Vittorio Klostermann, 1950), p. 321.

Notes to Chapter Eight: *THE END OF THE TRAIL*

1. Victor Farias, *Heidegger und der Nationalsozialismus* (Frankfurt am Main: Mischer, 1989); trans. as *Heidegger and Nazism*, Joseph Margolis and Tom Rockmore, eds. (Philadelphia: Temple University Press, 1989).

2. Fred Dallmayr, "Heidegger and Politics: Some Lessons," in *The Heidegger Case*, Tom Rockmore and Joseph Margolis, eds. (Philadelphia: Temple University Press, 1992), p. 283.

3. Martin Heidegger, *Die Selbstbehauptung der deutschen Universität* (Breslau: Verlag Wilhelm Gottleib Korn, 1933), pp. 1-22; trans. Karsten Harries as "The Self-Assertion of the German University," *Review of Metaphysics* 38 (1985), pp. 470-80.

4. *Ibid.*, p. 480.

5. Hugo Ott, *Martin Heidegger, Unterwegs zu seiner Biographie* (Frankfurt/New York: Campus Verlag, 1988); trans. Allan Blunden, *Martin Heidegger: A Political Life* (New York: Basic Books, 1993), p. 164.

6. Hermann Heidegger, "Preface," in Heidegger, "The Self-Assertion of the German University," p. 468.

7. Ott, *Martin Heidegger: a Political Life*, p. 242.

8. Farias, *Heidegger and Nazism*, pp. 4-8.

9. Hugo Ott, "Biographical Bases for Heidegger's 'Mentality of Disunity,'" in *The Heidegger Case*, Rockmore and Margolis, eds., p. 108

10. Martin Heidegger, "Überwindung der Metaphysik," in *Vorträge und Aufsätze* (Pfullingen: Günther Neske, 1954), p. 89; trans. Joan Stambaugh, "Overcoming Metaphysics," in *The End of Philosophy* (New York: Harper & Row, 1973), p. 108.

11. Ott, "Biographical Bases for Heidegger's 'Mentality of Disunity,'" p. 108.

12. Martin Heidegger, "Nietzsches Metaphysik," *Nietzsche*, 2 (Pfullingen: Günther Neske, 1961), p. 309.

13. Otto Pöggeler, "Heidegger, Nietzsche, and Politics," in *The Heidegger Case,* Rockmore and Margolis, eds., p. 138.

14. Reiner Schürmann, *Heidegger on Being and Action from Principle to Anarchy* (Bloomington, Ind.: Indiana University Press, 1990), p. 14.

15. *Ibid.*, p. 15.

16. *Ibid.*, p. 291.

17. Michael E. Zimmerman, "Ontological Aestheticism: Heidegger, Jünger, and National Socialism," in *The Heidegger Case*, Rockmore and Margolis, eds., p. 53.

18. Karl Löwith, "Last Meeting with Heidegger," in *Martin Heidegger and National Socialism*, Günther Neske and Emil Kettering, eds. (New York: Paragon House, 1990), p. 158.

19. See Otto Pöggeler, *Der Denkweg Martin Heideggers*, 2nd ed. (Pfullingen: Günther Neske, 1983); trans. Daniel Magurshak and Sigmund Barber, *Martin Heidegger's Path of Thinking* (Atlantic Highlands, N.J.: Humanities Press, 1987).

20. Pöggeler, "Heidegger, Nietzsche, and Politics," in *The Heidegger Case*, Rockmore and Margolis, eds., p. 134.

21. *Ibid.*, p. 138.

22. Hugo Ott, *Martin Heidegger, Unterwegs zu seiner Biographie* (Frankfurt/New York: Campus Verlag, 1988); trans. Allan Blunden, *Martin Heidegger: A Political Life* (New York: Basic Books, 1993).

23. Max Müller, "Martin Heidegger: A Philosopher and Politics: A Conversation," in *Martin Heidegger and National Socialism*, Neske and Kettering, eds., p. 182.

24. Hugo Ott, "Biographical Bases of Heidegger's 'Mentality of Disunity,'" in *The Heidegger Case,* Rockmore and Margolis, eds., pp. 93f.

25. Heinrich W. Petzet, "Afterthoughts on the *Spiegel* Interview," in Neske and Kettering, eds., *Martin Heidegger and National Socialism*, p. 67

26. *Ibid.*, p. 75.

27. Heidegger, "Die seinsgeschichtliche Bestimmung des Nihilismus," *Nietzsche*, 2, p. 395.

Bibliography of Works by W. H. Werkmeister

Compiled by Gwen A. Burda and Richard T. Hull

Note: Book reviews marked "*" indicate the review copy is in the Werkmeister Collection at Florida State University. Copies of all of Werkmeister's works listed below may be found in that Collection.

[W. H. Werkmeister born 10 August 1901, Asendorf, Germany.]

1919

Vorfrühling: Lieder eines Siebzehnjährigen. Leipzig: Bruno Volger Verlagsbuchhandlung, 1919. Pp. 53.

1920

[Graduated from a German gymnasium.]

1920-1923

[Student of international diplomacy, University of Münster, Germany, 1920-1923. Student, University of Frankfurt, Germany, Summer 1922.]

1924-1927

[Emigrated to the United States in April 1924. Brief periods of employment as a farm hand and as a clerk in a hardware store. Student, University of Nebraska, USA 1924-1927. Wrote a column for the Omaha Tribüne on Germans in Nebraska. Sold coffee and raincoats in the Russian German section of Lincoln. Held Harry Kirke Wolfe Memorial Fellowship, 1925-1927. During this period, Werkmeister was interested in the German settlers in the middle West, and partly earned his living writing their histories in a series of articles published in the Omaha Tribüne, a German language newspaper. 17 manuscripts of these articles, and a 4 chapter manuscript of a history that was commissioned but never published, are in the archives of the Nebraska

State Historical Society, Lincoln, Nebraska; copies are in the Werkmeister collection at Florida State University.]

1926

[Assistant Instructor, Department of Philosophy, University of Nebraska, 1926-1928.]

1927

"Driesch's Philosophy: an Exposition and a Critical Analysis." Ph.D. dissertation, University of Nebraska, 1927.

1928

[Instructor, Department of Philosophy, University of Nebraska, 1928-1931.]

1931

[Assistant Professor, Department of Philosophy, University of Nebraska, 1931-1940.]

1936

[Director *pro tempore* of the Institute for American Culture of the University of Berlin, 1936-1937. Lectured at the Universities of Bonn, Cologne, Giessen, Hamburg, Jena, Königsberg, Leipzig, Munich, and Münster.]

"The Second International Congress for the Unity of Science." *The Philosophical Review* 45 (1936): 593-600.

1937

"Philosophische Literatur in USA." *Blätter für deutsche Philosophie: Zeitschrift der Deutschen philosophischen Gesellschaft* 11 (1937): 177-183.

"Seven Theses of Logical Positivism Critically Examined." *The Philosophical Review* 46 (May 1937): 276-297.

"The Thirteenth Meeting of the German Philosophical Society." *The Philosophical Review* 46 (May 1937): 321-325.

"Seven Theses of Logical Positivism Critically Examined II." *The Philosophical Review* 46 (July 1937): 357-376.

1938

"The Meaning of 'Meaning' Re-Examined." *The Philosophical Review* 47 (May 1938): 245-266.

"Cultural Perspectives." *The Eleusis of Chi Omega* (Cincinnati, Ohio) 40 (May 1938): 179-182.

"Philosophie in USA." *Blätter für deutsche Philosophie: Zeitschrift der Deutschen philosophischen Gesellschaft* 12 (1938): 200-212.

"Scientific Method and the Presuppositions of Experiment." *The Personalist* 19 (Summer, July 1938): 255-263.

"Sete teses do positivismo logicó examinadas criticamenté." Translated by V. de Megalhãis Godinho. *Seara Nova* (1938-1939): 28-32, 51-55, 130-134, 174-176, 193-194. Translation of "Seven Theses of Logical Positivism Critically Examined" (see under 1937). Also published by *Seara Nova* as a separate pamphlet (Lisbon, 1939).

Reviews of Charles W. Morris, *Logical Positivism, Pragmatism, and Scientific Empiricism**, *Exposés de philosophie scientifique*, vol. 1 (Paris: Hermann & Cie, 1937); Hans Reichenbach, *Experience and Prediction** (Chicago: University of Chicago Press, 1938); and Jacques Maritain, *The Degrees of Knowledge**, trans. Bernard Wall (New York: Charles Scribner's Sons, 1938). *Ethics* 48 (July 1938): 549-554.

Reviews of Herbert Spiegelberg, *Gesetz und Sittengesetz* (Zurich: Max Niehans, 1935) and *Antirelativismus* (Zurich: Max Niehans, 1935). *Ethics* 48 (July 1938): 562-563.

Review of Nicolai Hartmann, *Möglichkeit und Wirklichkeit** (Berlin: Walter de Gruyter & Co., 1938). *Ethics* 49 (October 1938): 98-100.

1939

"Natural Languages as Cultural Indices." *Philosophy of Science* 6 (1939): 356-366.

"Sieben Leitsätze des logistischen Positivismus in kritischer Beleuchtung." Translated by Wilh. Krampf. *Philosophisches Jahrbuch im Auftrag der Görres-Gesellschaft* 55 (1939): 162-186, 365-388. [Ed. note: This was mistakenly published under the name C. W. Werkmeister.] Translation of "Seven Theses of Logical Positivism Critically Examined" (see under 1937).

Review of Otto Janssen, *Dasein und Wirklichkeit, eine Einführung in die Seinslehre** (Munich: Ernst Reinhardt, 1938). *Ethics* 49 (January 1939): 244-245.

Reviews of Gustav E. Muller, *Hegel über Offenbarung, Kirche und Philosophie* (Munich: Ernst Reinhardt, 1939), and Franz Schmidt, *Kleine Logik der Geisteswissenschaften* (Munich: Ernst Reinhardt, 1938). *Ethics* 49 (April 1939): 338.

Review of Willy Mueller, *Charakter und Moral: Eine Philosophie der Tugend und ihrer sozialen Werte auf der Grundlage einer absoluten Weltanschauung** (Munich: Reinhardt, 1939). *Ethics* 49 (July 1939): 494-495.

Review of Walter Ehrlich, *Das Verstehen* (Zurich and Leipzig: Rascher Verlag, 1938). *Ethics* 49 (July 1939): 504-505.

Review of John Dewey, *Logic, the Theory of Inquiry** (New York: Henry Holt & Co., 1938). *Ethics* 50 (October 1939): 98-102.

Review of James Bissett Pratt, *Naturalism** (New Haven: Yale University Press, 1939). *Ethics* 50 (October 1939): 102-105.

Review of Charles M. Perry, *Toward a Dimensional Realism* (Norman: University of Oklahoma Press, 1939). *Ethics* 50 (October 1939): 105-111.

1940

[Visiting Professor, Boston University, Summer. Associate Professor, Department of Philosophy, University of Nebraska, 1940-1947.]

A Philosophy of Science. New York: Harper, 1940. Pp. xii, 551. Paperback reprinted 1946 and 1965 by University of Nebraska Press. Reviewed by Paul Henle and Justus Buchler; see section below on Works about W. H. Werkmeister.

"Unified Science and Physicalistic Reductionism." *The Personalist* 21 (Summer, July 1940): 277-287.

Review of Paul Arthur Schilpp, ed., *The Philosophy of John Dewey**, The Library of Living Philosophers, vol. 1 (Evanston, Ill.: Northwestern University, 1939). *Ethics* 50 (April 1940): 353-359.

Review of Martin Klein, *Von der All-Einheit im Ich** (Munich: Ernst Reinhardt, 1939). *Ethics* 50 (April 1940): 370.

Review of Ernst Barthel, *Der Mensch und die ewigen Hintergründe* (Munich: Ernst Reinhardt, 1939). *Ethics* 50 (April 1940): 370-371.

Review of Joseph Ratner, ed., *Intelligence in the Modern World—John Dewey's Philosophy** (New York: Modern Library, 1939). *Ethics* 50 (April 1940): 375-376.

Review of Josef Maier, *On Hegel's Critique of Kant** (New York: Columbia University Press, 1939). *Ethics* 50 (July 1940): 484-485.

1941

"An Introduction to Heidegger's 'Existential Philosophy'." *Philosophy and Phenomenological Research* 2 (September 1941): 79-87.

Review of Paul Arthur Schilpp, ed., *The Philosophy of George Santayana**, The Library of Living Philosophers, vol. 2 (Evanston, Ill.: Northwestern University, 1940). *Ethics* 51 (April 1941): 361-365.

Review of Marvin Farber, ed., *Philosophical Essays in Memory of Edmund Husserl** (Cambridge, Mass.: Harvard University Press, 1940). *Ethics* 51 (April 1941) 366-368.

Review of Milton Karl Munitz, *The Moral Philosophy of Santayana** (New York: Columbia University Press, 1939). *Ethics* 51 (April 1941): 370-371.

1942-1946

[Period spent as civilian instructor in the pilot training program of the United States Air Force, University of Nebraska campus, Lincoln, Nebraska, 1942-1945. Subject: the theory of flight.]

[Chair, Department of Philosophy, University of Nebraska, 1945-1953.]

1947

[Professor, Department of Philosophy, University of Nebraska, 1947-1953.]

Review of Ralph Stayner Lillie, *General Biology and Philosophy of Organism* (Chicago: University of Chicago Press, 1945). *Philosophy and Phenomenological Research* 7 (June 1947): 654-659. (Lillie responded in a Discussion Note: see section below on Works about W. H. Werkmeister.)

1948

The Basis and Structure of Knowledge. New York: Harper, 1948. Pp. xi, 451. Reprinted in hardcover, Greenwood Press, 1968. Reviewed by Phillipp Frank, Ernest Nagel, and A. R. Turquette; see section below on Works about W. H. Werkmeister.

An Introduction to Critical Thinking: A Beginner's Text in Logic. Lincoln, Neb.: Johnsen Publishing Co., 1948. Pp. xx, 663. Reprinted five times through 1956; revised ed. 1957; 8th printing 1967.

1949

A History of Philosophical Ideas in America. New York: Ronald Press, 1949. Pp. xvi, 599. Reprinted in hardcover, Greenwood Press, 1981. Reviewed by Harold A. Larrabee, T. V. Smith, Rubin Gotesky; see section below on Works about W. H. Werkmeister.

"Cassirer's Advance Beyond Neo-Kantianism." In *The Philosophy of Ernst Cassirer,* The Library of Living Philosophers, vol. 6, ed. Paul A. Schilpp. Evanston, Ill.: Library of Living Philosophers, 1949. Pp. 757-798. Reprinted in hardcover, Greenwood Press, 1981.

"Science, Its Concepts and Laws." *The Journal of Philosophy* 46 (7 July 1949): 444-452.

1950

[Tully Cleon Knoles lecturer, College of the Pacific, May.]

[Guest Lecturer at Harvard University, 1950-1951.]

"An Epistemological Basis for Quantum Physics." Symposium on Quantum Mechanics, II. *Philosophy of Science* 17 (January 1950): 1-25.

Review of Marc Edmund Jones, *George Sylvester Morris* (Philadelphia: David McKay Company, 1948). *Philosophy and Phenomenological Research* 11 (December 1950): 287-289.

1951

"Normative Propositions and the Ideal of an Integrated and Closed System." *Philosophy of Science* 18 (April 1951): 124-131.

"On 'Describing a World'." *Philosophy and Phenomenological Research* 11 (March 1951): 303-325; extract in Spanish, 326.

"Some Aspects of Contemporary Personalism." *The Personalist* 32 (Autumn, October 1951): 349-357.

"Professor Margenau and the Problem of Physical Reality." *Philosophy of Science* 18 (July 1951): 183-192. Review article of Henry Margenau, *The Nature of Physical Reality** (New York: McGraw-Hill, 1950).

Review of Hans Reichenbach, *The Rise of Scientific Philosophy** (Berkeley and Los Angeles: University of California Press, 1951). *Isis* 42 (Part III, no. 129) (October 1951): 277-278.

1952

"The Problem of Physical Reality." *Philosophy of Science* 19 (July 1952): 214-224. Read on 15 March 1951 before the Philosophy Club of Harvard University.

"Problems of Value Theory." *Philosophy and Phenomenological Research* 12 (June 1952): 495-512; extract in Spanish, 512.

"Are There Two Kinds of Empirical Propositions?" *The Philosophical Forum* 10 (Spring 1952): 41-42.

Review of George Perrigo Conger, *Epitomization, A Study in Philosophy of the Sciences* (Minneapolis: Burgess Publishing Co., 1949). *Philosophy of Science* 19 (October 1952): 351-355. (Reply by Conger; see section below on Works about W. H. Werkmeister.)

1953

"Ethics and Value Theory." In *Proceedings of the XIth International Congress of Philosophy,* Brussels, 20-26 August 1953, vol. 10, Amsterdam: North-Holland Publishing Co., 1953, pp. 119-123.

Review of Otto Janssen, *Seinsordnung und Gehalt der Idealitäten; ein Beitrag zur Frage des Ideellen Seins** (Meisenheim/Glan: Westkultur-verlag Anton Hain, 1950). *Philosophy and Phenomenological Research* 13 (March 1953): 414-416.

Review of Ruth Nanda Anshen, ed., *Moral Principles of Action: Man's Ethical Imperative,* Science of Culture Series (New York: Harper and Brothers, 1952). *The Western Humanities Review* 7 (Spring 1953): 164-166.

Review of W. T. Jones, *A History of Western Philosophy* (New York: Harcourt, Brace & Co., 1952). *The Personalist* 34 (Summer, July 1953): 313-315.

Review of Wilfrid Sellars and John Hospers, eds., *Readings in Ethical Theory* (New York: Appleton-Century-Crofts, Inc., 1952). *Philosophy and Phenomenological Research* 13 (June 1953): 561-563.

1954

[Director, School of Philosophy, University of Southern California, 1954-1965.]

"Prolegomena to Value Theory." *Philosophy and Phenomenological Research* 14 (March 1954): 293-307; extract in Spanish, 308. ("The pages which follow should be considered a supplement to my article, 'Problems of Value Theory,' which was recently published in this journal." See vol. 12 (1952).)

"Some Philosophical Implications of the Life Sciences." *The Personalist* 35 (Spring, April 1954): 117-127.

1955

"An Empirical Approach to Value Theory." *The Personalist* 36 (Autumn, October 1955): 352-360.

"Il Problema della Realta' fisica." *Revista di filosofia* 46 (April 1955): 127-141. Translation of an address before the Harvard Philosophy Club, previously published in English in 1952.

Review of Radoslav A. Tsanoff, *The Great Philosophers** (New York: Harper & Bros., 1953). *The Personalist* 36 (Summer, July 1955): 298-299.

Review of Richard Bevan Braithwaite, *Scientific Explanation: A Study of the Functions of Theory, Probability and Law in Science** (Cambridge, Engl.: Cambridge University Press, 1953). *The Personalist* 36 (Summer, July 1955): 293-295.

Review of Minna Specht and Willi Eichler, eds., *Leonard Nelson, zum Gedächtnis** (Frankfurt: Verlag "Öffentliches Leben," 1953). *The Personalist* 36 (Summer, July 1955): 316-317.

1956

"Scientific Method." In *Collier's Encyclopedia*, vol. 20, ed. William D. Halsey and Bernard Johnston. New York: Macmillan Educational Co.,1956. Pp. 501-509. (Reprinted in every succeeding edition through 1994, with varying pagination.)

Review of C. C. L. Gregory and Anita Kohsen, *Physical and Psychical Research: An Analysis of Belief** (Reigate, Engl.: The Omega Press, 1954). *The Personalist* 37 (Spring, April 1956): 183-184.

Review of John J. Honigmann, *Culture and Personality* (New York: Harper & Bros., 1954). *The Personalist* 37 (Spring, April 1956): 199.

Review of Georgi Schischkoff, *Erschöpfte Kunst oder Kunstformalismus?* (Schlehdorf: Bronnen-Verlag, 1952). *The Personalist* 37 (Spring, April 1956): 215.

Review of S. H. Butcher, *Aristotle's Theory of Poetry and Fine Art* (New York: Dover Publications, 1955). *The Personalist* 37 (Summer, July 1956): 284.

Review of George Santayana, *The Sense of Beauty** (New York: Dover Publications, 1955). *The Personalist* 37 (Summer, July 1956): 286-287.

Review of Brand Blanshard, *The Impasse in Ethics and a Way Out* (Berkeley: University of California Press, 1955). *The Personalist* 37 (Summer, July 1956): 287.

Review of Ottokar Blaha, *Logische Wirklichkeitsstruktur und personaler Seinsgrund** (Braz: Verlag Stiasny, 1955). *The Personalist* 37 (Autumn, October 1956): 439.

Review of Paul Vogel, *Theodor Litt** (Berlin, Walter de Gruyter & Co., 1955). *The Personalist* 37 (Autumn, October 1956): 440.

1957

[Elected to Sigma Xi, National Science Honor Fraternity, at University of Southern California.]

An Introduction to Critical Thinking: A Beginner's Text in Logic, rev. ed. Lincoln, Neb.: Johnsen Publishing Co., 1957. Pp. [xx], 663. See under 1948.

"History and Human Destiny." *The Personalist* 38 (Spring, April 1957): 117-129.

Review of Pravasjivan Chaudhury, *Studies in Comparative Aesthetics* (Santiniketan, India: Visva-Bharati, 1953). *The Personalist* 38 (Spring, April 1957): 174-175.

Review of W. D. Lamont, *The Value Judgment** (New York: Philosophical Library, 1955). *The Personalist* 38 (Spring, April 1957): 175-176.

Review of A. Cornelius Benjamin, *Operationism** (Springfield: Charles C. Thomas, 1955). *The Personalist* 38 (Spring, April 1957): 180-181.

Review of William Earle, *Objectivity** (New York: Noonday Press, 1955). *The Personalist* 38 (Spring, April 1957): 181.

Reviews of Edward P. Cronan, *The Dignity of the Human Person** (New York: Philosophical Library, 1955): and Russell W. Davenport, *The Dignity of Man** (New York: Harper & Bros., 1955). *The Personalist* 38 (Spring, April 1957): 181-183.

Review of Wilhelm Keller, *Psychologie und Philosophie des Wollens* (München/Basel: Ernst Reinhardt Verlag, 1954). *The Personalist* 38 (Spring, April 1957): 207-208.

Review of Morris R. Cohen, *American Thought: A Critical Sketch**, ed. Felix S. Cohen (Glencoe: Free Press, 1954). *The Personalist* 38 (Summer, July 1957): 280-281.

Review of Vergilius Ferm, ed., *Encyclopedia of Morals** (New York: Philosophical Library, 1956). *The Personalist* 38 (Summer, July 1957): 328-330.

Review of Otto Tumlirz, *Anthropologische Psychologie* ([München/]Basel: Ernst Reinhardt Verlag, 1955). *The Personalist* 38 (Autumn, October 1957): 434-435.

Review of Ananda K. Coomaraswamy, *The Transformation of Nature in Art** (New York: Dover Publications, 1956). *The Personalist* 38 (Autumn, October 1957): 444.

1958

[Elected to Phi Kappa Phi. Editor, *The Personalist* 1958-1966.]

"The Symbolism of Myth." *The Personalist* 39 (Spring, April 1958): 117-126.

"Some Aspects of E. S. Brightman's Thesis in *Person and Reality** Re-examined," Symposium on Brightman, with Donald C. Williams and John Wild, *The Philosophical Forum* 16 (1958-59): 8-12.

Review of William Kluback, *Wilhelm Dilthey's Philosophy of History** (New York: Columbia University Press, 1956). *The Personalist* 39 (Winter, January 1958): 67-68.

Review of José Ferrater Mora, *Ortega y Gasset: An Outline of His Philosophy** (New Haven: Yale University Press, 1957). *The Personalist* 39 (Winter, January, 1958): 68.

Review of Sidney Hook, ed., *American Philosophers at Work** (New York: Criterion Books, 1956). *The Personalist* 39 (Winter, January 1958): 68-69.

Review of Henry P. David and Helmut von Bracken, eds., *Perspectives in Personality Theory** (New York, Basic Books, 1957). *The Personalist* 39 (Winter, January 1958): 72-73.

Review of Emmanuel Mounier, *The Character of Man** (New York: Harper & Bros., 1956). *The Personalist* 39 (Winter, January 1958): 73.

Review of DeWitt H. Parker, *The Philosophy of Value** (Ann Arbor: University of Michigan Press, 1957). *The Personalist* 39 (Winter, January 1958): 74.

Review of Carl H. Hamburg, *Symbol and Reality** (The Hague: Martinus Nijhoff, 1956). *The Personalist* 39 (Winter, January 1958): 74-75.

Review of Everett W. Hall, *Modern Science and Human Values** (Princeton, N.J.: Van Nostrand Company, Inc., 1956). *The Personalist* 39 (Winter, January 1958): 76-77.

Review of Sister Teresia Renata de Spiritu Sancto [Posselt], *Edith Stein: Eine grosse Frau unseres Jahrhunderts* (Freiburg: Herder-Bücherei, [1957]): *The Personalist* 39 (Winter, January 1958): 103-104.

Review of Max Hartmann, *Einführung in die allegemeine Biologie** (Berlin: Walter de Gruyter & Co., [1956]): *The Personalist* 39 (Winter, January 1958): 104.

Review of Nicolai Hartmann, *Kleinere Schriften** (2 vols.) (Berlin: Walter de Gruyter & Co., 1955-1957). *The Personalist* 39 (Winter, January 1958): 104-105.

Review of Milton C. Nahm, *The Artist as Creator* (Baltimore: Johns Hopkins Press, 1956). *The Personalist* 39 (Spring, April 1958): 172-173.

Review of Samuel Enoch Stumpf, *A Democratic Manifesto** (Nashville: Vanderbilt University Press, 1954). *The Personalist* 39 (Spring, April 1958): 193.

Review of Herbert W. Schneider, *Three Dimensions of Public Morality** (Bloomington, In., Indiana University Press, [1956]). *The Personalist* 39 (Spring, April 1958): 208-209.

Reviews of Susanne K. Langer, *Problems of Art** (New York: Charles Scribner's Sons, 1957), and Edward G. Ballard, *Art and Analysis* (The Hague: Martinus Nijhoff, 1957). *The Personalist* 39 (Summer, July 1958): 277-278.

Reviews of Ray Lepley, ed., *The Language of Value** (New York: Columbia University Press, 1957), and Jean Pucelle, *La source des valeurs* (Lyon: Emmanuel Vitte, 1957). *The Personalist* 39 (Summer, July 1958): 285-286.

Reviews of Samuel J. Warner, *The Urge to Mass Destruction** (New York: Grune and Stratton, 1957), and F. A. Lea, *The Tragic Philosopher: A Study of Friedrich Nietzsche** (New York: Philosophical Library, 1957). *The Personalist* 39 (Summer, July 1958): 293-295.

Review of Anna-Teresa Tymieniecka, *Essence et existence** (Paris: Aubier, Editions Montaigne, 1957). *The Personalist* 39 (Autumn, October 1958): 431-432.

1959

Bir değer teorisinin ana çizgileri: 6 konferans [translated by A. Turan Oflazoğlu] (Istanbul, 1959). Pp. 122. (On cover: Istanbul Üniversitesi Edebiyat Fakökultesi Yayinlari, 827.) Turkish version followed by English text with separate title page: *Outlines of a Value Theory: Six Lectures Delivered at the University of Istanbul.* Werkmeister was not able to deliver the lectures in person.

Editor. *Facets of the Renaissance: Essays by Wallace K. Ferguson*, Foreword by Tracy E. Strevey. Los Angeles: University of Southern California Press, 1959. Pp. [vii], 112. The Arensberg Lectures, 1st Series, comprising addresses by Garrett Mattingly, E. Harris Harbison, Myron P. Gilmore, and Paul O. Kristeller. Reprinted by: New York: Harper Torchbooks (1959); New York: Books for Library Press (1971); Assen and Amsterdam, The Netherlands: Van Gorcum (1976).

"Theory Construction and the Problem of Objectivity." In *Symposium on Sociological Theory*, ed. Llewellyn Gross. Evanston, Ill.: Row, Peterson, & Co., 1959. Pp. 483-508.

"Kant, Immanuel." In *Encyclopedia Americana,* 16 (1959): 304-306b. Reprinted in every successive edition through 1994, although with different pagination.

Review of James Ward Smith, *Theme for Reason** (Princeton, N.J.: Princeton University Press, 1957). *The Personalist* 40 (Winter, January 1959): 65.

Review of Noel B. Slater, *The Development and Meaning of Eddington's Fundamental Theory** (New York: Cambridge University Press, 1957). *The Personalist* 40 (Winter, January 1959): 72-73.

Review of Wolfgang Hermann Müller, *Die Philosophie Edmund Husserls** (Bonn: Bouvier & Co., [1956]), and Julius Kraft, *Von Husserl zu Heidegger** (revised edition) (Frankfort [am Main:] [Verlag] Offentliches Leben, [1957]). *The Personalist* 40 (Winter, January 1959): 101-102.

Review of Bart Landheer, *Pause for Transition** (The Hague: Martinus Nijhoff, 1957). *The Personalist* 40:1 (Winter, January 1959): 105-106.

Review of Paul Weiss, *Modes of Being** (Carbondale, Ill.: Southern Illinois University Press, 1958). *The Personalist* 40 (Spring, April 1959): 178-179.

Review of Charles W. Hendel, ed., *The Philosophy of Kant and Our Modern World** (New York: Liberal Arts Press, 1957). *The Personalist* 40 (Spring, April 1958): 180.

Reviews of Leonard Nelson, *System of Ethics**, trans. Norbert Guterman (New Haven: Yale University Press, 1956), and Alexander Sesonske, *Value and Obligation** (Berkeley: University of California Press, 1957). *The Personalist* 40 (Spring, April 1959): 182-184.

Review of Etienne Gilson, *Painting and Reality** (New York: Pantheon Books, 1957). *The Personalist* 40 (Spring, April 1959): 194-196.

Review of James L. Jarrett, *The Quest for Beauty* (Englewood Cliffs, N.J.: Prentice-Hall, 1957). *The Personalist* 40 (Spring, April 1959): 196.

Review of Edward Bullough, *Aesthetics*, ed. Elizabeth M. Wilkinson (Stanford, Cal.: Stanford University Press, 1957). *The Personalist* 40 (Spring, April 1959): 198.

Review of Ananda K. Coomaraswamy, *Christian and Oriental Philosophy of Art** (New York: Dover Publications, 1956). *The Personalist* 40 (Spring, April 1959): 199.

Review of Philip Wittenberg, ed., *The Lamont Case: History of a Congressional Investigation* (New York: Horizon Press, 1957). *The Personalist* 40 (Spring, April 1959): 212.

Review of Marjorie Grene, *Martin Heidegger* (New York: Hillary House, 1957). *The Personalist* 40 (Summer, July 1959): 294.

Review of Arthur Cohen, *Martin Buber** (New York: Hillary House, 1957). *The Personalist* 40 (Summer, July 1959): 294-295.

Review of Evander Bradley McGilvary, *Toward a Perspective Realism** (LaSalle, Ill.: Open Court Publishing Co., 1956). *The Personalist* 40 (Summer, July 1959): 295-296.

Review of Herbert Feigl, *et al.*, *Concepts, Theories, and the Mind-Body Problem** (Minneapolis: University of Minnesota Press, [1958]). *The Personalist* 40 (Summer, July 1959): 296-298.

Review of Frederick Mayer, *New Directions for the American University* (Washington, D. C.: Public Affairs Press, 1957). *The Personalist* 40 (Summer, July 1959): 323.

Review of Louis H. Sullivan, *The Autobiography of an Idea* (New York: Dover Publications, 1956). *The Personalist* 40 (Summer, July 1959): 324.

Review of Wilhelm Krampf, ed., *Hugo Dingler, Gedenkbuch zum 75. Geburtstag** (München: Eidos-Verlag, [1956]). *The Personalist* 40 (Summer, July 1959): 328.

Review of Richard and Gertrude Köbner, *Vom Schönen und seiner Warheit* (Berlin: Walter de Gruyter & Co., 1957). *The Personalist* 40 (Summer, July 1959): 328.

Review of Simon Moser, *Metaphysik einst und jetzt** (Berlin: Walter de Gruyter & Co., 1958). *The Personalist* 40 (Summer, July 1959): 329.

Review of Heinz-Rolf Lückert, *Konflikt-Psychologie* ([München:] Ernst Reinhardt Verlag, [1957]). *The Personalist* 40 (Summer, July 1959): 333-334

Review of Gerald F. Else, *Aristotle's Poetics: The Argument* (Cambridge, Mass.: Harvard University Press, [1957]). *The Personalist* 40 (Autumn, October 1959): 392.

Review of J. N. Findlay, *Hegel: A Re-Examination** (New York: Macmillan, 1958). *The Personalist* 40 (Autumn, October 1959): 393-394.

Review of Nathan Rosenstreich, *Between Past and Present** (New Haven: Yale University Press, 1958). *The Personalist* 40 (Autumn, October 1959): 400-401.

Review of D. W. Gotshalk, *The Promise of Modern Life** (Yellow Springs, OH: Antioch Press, 1958). *The Personalist* 40 (Autumn, October 1959): 402-403.

Reviews of Kurt Baier, *The Moral Point of View** (Ithaca, N.Y.: Cornell University Press, 1958), and Bernard Mayo, *Ethics and the Moral Life** (New York: St. Martin's Press, 1958). *The Personalist* 40 (Autumn, October 1959): 403-404.

Review of Archie J. Bahm, *What Makes Acts Right?* (Boston: Christopher Publishing House, 1958). *The Personalist* 40 (Autumn, October 1959): 406.

Review of Monroe C. Beardsley, *Aesthetics* (New York: Harcourt, Brace & Co., 1958). *The Personalist* 40 (Autumn, October 1959): 406-407.

Review of Gardner Murphy, *Human Potentialities** (New York: Basic Books, 1958). *The Personalist* 40 (Autumn, October 1959): 409-410.

Review of Joseph Mudry, *Philosophy of Atomic Physics* (New York: Philosophical Library, 1958). *The Personalist* 40 (Autumn, October 1959): 410.

Review of Werner Heisenberg, *The Physicist's Conception of Nature** (New York: Harcourt, Brace & Co., [1958]). *The Personalist* 40 (Autumn, October 1959): 410-411.

Review of Erwin Schrodinger, *Mind and Matter** (New York: Cambridge University Press, [1958]). *The Personalist* 40 (Autumn, October 1959): 411.

Review of Gerhard Häuptner, *Verhängnis und Geschichte** (Meisenheim [/Glan:] Verlag Anton Hain, [1956]. *The Personalist* 40 (Autumn, October 1959): 447-448.

Review of Anton Neuhäusler, *Ein Weg in die Relativitätstheorie** ([Meisenheim/Glan:] Verlag Anton Hain, [1957]). *The Personalist* 40 (Autumn, October 1959): 448.

Review of Gerhard Funke, *Gewohnheit* (Bonn: H. Bouvier und Co, [1958]). *The Personalist* 40 (Autumn, October 1959): 448.

1960

"The Meaning and Being of Values within the Framework of an Empirically Oriented Value Theory." In *Sinn und Sein: Ein philosophisches Symposion,* ed. Richard Wisser. Tübingen: Max Niemeyer, 1960. Pp. 549-557.

"Professor Dempf and the Problem of Value." In *Proceedings of the XIIth International Congress of Philosophy*, vol. 3, University of Padova, Italy (Florence: Sansoni, 1958-60). Pp. 451-457.

"Social Science and the Problem of Value." In *Scientism and Values,* ed. Helmut Schöck and James W. Wiggins. Princeton: Van Nos-trand, 1960. Pp. 1-21.

Review of Maxwell John Charlesworth, *Philosophy and Linguistic Analysis** (Pittsburgh: Duquesne University Press, [1959]). *The Personalist* 41 (Winter, January 1960): 72-73.

Review of Bertrand Russell, *The Problems of Philosophy* (New York: Oxford University Press, [1959]. *The Personalist* 41 (Winter, January 1960): 73.

Review of Loren Eisley, *The Immense Journey** (New York: Random House, [1957]). *The Personalist* 41 (Winter, January 1960): 92.

Review of Rudolf Schottländer, *Theorie des Vertrauens** (Berlin: Walter de Gruyter & Co., [1957]). *The Personalist* 41 (Winter, January 1960): 126.

Review of Gerhard Funke, ed., *Konkrete Vernunft** (Bonn: H. Bouvier u. Co., 1958). *The Personalist* 41 (Winter, January 1960): 126-127.

Review of Waldo Frank, *The Rediscovery of Man** (New York: George Braziller, 1958). *The Personalist* 41 (Spring, April 1960): 211-212.

Review of Arthur Schopenhauer, *The World as Will and Representation*, 2 vols., trans. E. F. J. Payne (Indian Hills, Colo.: Falcon's Wing Press, 1958). *The Personalist* 41 (Spring, April 1960): 212.

Review of Bertrand Russell, *The Will to Doubt** (New York: Philosophical Library, 1958). *The Personalist* 41 (Spring, April 1960): 213.

Review of Martin Heidegger, *An Introduction to Metaphysics**, trans. Ralph Manheim (New Haven: Yale University Press). *The Personalist* 41 (Spring, April 1960): 213.

Review of F. E. Sparshott, *An Enquiry into Goodness** (Chicago: University of Chicago Press, 1958). *The Personalist* 41 (Spring, April 1960): 213-214.

Review of P. W. Bridgman, *The Way Things Are** (Cambridge, Mass.: Harvard University Press, 1959). *The Personalist* 41 (Spring, April 1960): 216-217.

Review of Max Planck, *The New Science** (New York: Meridian Books, [1959]). *The Personalist* 41 (Spring 1960): 217.

Review of Mortimer J. Adler, *The Idea of Freedom** (Garden City, N.Y.: Doubleday & Co., 1958). *The Personalist* 41 (Spring, April 1960): 217-218.

Review of Suzanne K. Langer, *Reflections on Art* (Baltimore: Johns Hopkins Press, 1958). *The Personalist* 41 (Spring, April 1960): 220-221.

Review of Erich Neumann, *Art and the Creative Unconscious*, Bollingen Series 41 (New York: Pantheon Books, 1959). *The Personalist* 41 (Spring, April 1960): 221.

Review of Arnold Hauser, *The Philosophy of Art History* (New York: Alfred A. Knopf, 1959). *The Personalist* 41 (Spring, April 1960): 222-223.

Review of A. J. Bahm, *Philosophy of the Buddha* (New York: Harper and Brothers, [1958]). *The Personalist* 41 (Spring, April 1960): 229.

Review of Richard B. Sewall, *The Vision of Tragedy** (New Haven: Yale University Press, 1959). *The Personalist* 41 (Spring, April 1960): 238-239.

Review of Franz Grégoire, *Études Hégéliennes** (Louvain: University of Louvain Press, Éditions Nauwelaerts, 1958). *The Personalist* 41 (Spring, April 1960): 254.

Review of *Philosophes Roumains* (Bucharest: Éditions de l'Académia de la République Populaire Roumaine, 1958). *The Personalist* 41 (Spring, April 1960): 254-255.

Review of Nicolai Hartmann, *Kleinere Schriften** vol. 3 (Berlin: Walter de Gruyter & Co., 1958). *The Personalist* 41 (Spring, April 1960): 255.

Review of Katharina Kanthack, *Vom Sinn der Selbsterkenntnis** (Berlin: Walter de Gruyter & Co., [1958]). *The Personalist* 41 (Spring, April 1960): 256.

Review of Hans Welzel, *Die Naturrechtslehre Samuel Pufendorfs** (Berlin: Walter de Gruyter & Co., 1958). *The Personalist* 41 (Spring, April 1960): 256-257.

Review of Eugen Fink, *Sein, Wahrheit, Welt* (The Hague: Martinus Nijhoff, 1958). *The Personalist* 41 (Spring, April 1960): 257.

Review of Helmut Schöck, *USA: Motive und Strukturen** (Stuttgart: Deutsche Verlags-Anstalt, [1958]). *The Personalist* 41 (Spring, April 1960), 257-258.

Review of Robert Brackenbury, *Getting Down to Cases* (New York: G.P. Putnam's Sons, 1959). *The Personalist* 41 (Spring, April 1960): 268-269.

Review of Norman Malcolm, *Dreaming** (New York: Humanities Press, Inc., 1959). *The Personalist* 41 (Summer, July 1960): 375.

Review of L. L. Thurstone, *The Measurement of Values* (Chicago: University of Chicago Press, 1959). *The Personalist* 41 (Summer, July 1960): 376-377.

Review of Stanton A. Coblentz, *The Long Road to Humanity** (New York: Thomas Yoseloff, [1959]). *The Personalist* 41 (Summer, July 1960): 380.

Review of Paul Weiss, *Our Public Life** (Bloomington: Indiana University Press, 1959). *The Personalist* 41 (Summer, July 1960): 380-381.

Review of Sidney Hook, ed., *Psychoanalysis, Scientific Method, and Philosophy** (New York: New York University Press, 1959). *The Personalist* 41 (Summer, July 1960): 382-383.

Review of David L. Miller, *Modern Science and Human Freedom** (Austin: University of Texas Press, 1959). *The Personalist* 41 (Summer, July 1960): 385-386.

Review of J. L. McCary, ed., *Psychology of Personality** (New York: Grover Press, Inc., 1959). *The Personalist* 41 (Summer, July 1960): 386.

Review of Ottokar Blaha, *Das unmittelbare Wissen** (Vienna: Verlag Herder, 1959). *The Personalist* 41 (Summer, July 1960): 427.

Review of Otto Janssen, *Das Beziehungsgefüge der menschlichen Handlung und das Problem der Freiheit** ([München:] Ernst Reinhardt Verlag, 1958). *The Personalist* 41 (Summer, July 1960): 428.

Review of Joseph Wood Krutch, *Human Nature and the Human Condition** (New York: Random House, 1959). *The Personalist* 41 (Autumn, October 1960): 509-510.

Review of John Wild, *Human Freedom and Social Order* (Durham, N.C.: Duke University Press, 1959). *The Personalist* 41 (Autumn, October 1960): 510-511.

Review of *Hegel: Encyclopedia of Philosophy**, trans. Gustav Emil Mueller (New York: Philosophical Library, 1959). *The Personalist* 41 (Autumn, October 1960): 512.

Review of *Nietzsche: Unpublished Letters**, trans. and ed. by Kurt F. Leidecker (New York: Philosophical Library, 1959). *The Personalist* 41 (Autumn, October 1960): 512.

Review of Thomas Langan, *The Meaning of Heidegger** (New York: Columbia University Press, 1959). *The Personalist* 41 (Autumn, October 1960): 515.

Review of G. E. Moore, *Philosophical Papers** (New York: The Macmillan Company, 1959). *The Personalist* 41 (Autumn, October 1960): 520-521.

Review of Hazel E. Barnes, *The Literature of Possibility* (Lincoln, Neb.: University of Nebraska Press, 1959). *The Personalist* 41 (Autumn, October 1960): 523-524.

Review of Friedrich Schneider, *Die Hauptprobleme der Erkenntnistheorie** ([München/]Basel: Ernst Reinhardt Verlag, 1959). *The Personalist* 41 (Autumn, October 1960): 558.

Review of Erwin D. Conham, ed., *Man's Great Future* (New York: Longmans, Green and Company, 1959). *The Personalist* 41 (Autumn, October 1960): 559-560.

Review of Jacques Maritain, *The Responsibility of the Artist* (New York: Charles Scribner's Sons, 1960). *The Personalist* 41 (Autumn, October 1960): 568.

Review of Mario Lins, *Foundations of Soft Determinism**, trans. George Reed (Rio de Janeiro[: Livraria Freitas Bastos], 1959. *The Personalist* 41 (Autumn, October 1960): 570.

1961

Theories of Ethics: A Study in Moral Obligation. Lincoln, Neb.: Johnsen Publishing Co., 1961. Pp. 445.

Review of Oliver A. Johnson, *Rightness and Goodness** (The Hague: Martinus Nijhoff, 1959). *The Personalist* 42 (Winter, January 1961): 104-105.

Review of Lewis White Beck, *A Commentary on Kant's Critique of Practical Reason** (Chicago: University of Chicago Press, 1960). *The Personalist* 42 (Winter, January 1961): 92-93.

Review of Paul Arthur Schilpp, ed., *Kant's Pre-Critical Ethics**, 2nd ed. (Evanston, Ill: Northwestern University Press, 1960). *The Personalist* 42 (Winter, January 1961): 93.

Review of Raymond B. Blakney, ed. and trans., *An Immanuel Kant Reader** (New York: Harper and Brothers, 1960). *The Personalist* 42 (Winter, January 1961): 93.

Review of Wanda Orynski, *Hegel Highlights** (New York: Philosophical Library, 1960). *The Personalist* 42 (Winter, January 1961): 93-94.

Review of Immanuel Kant, *Religion within the Limits of Reason Alone**, trans. Theodore M. Greene and Hoyt H. Hudson (New York: Harper Torchbooks, 1960). *The Personalist* 42 (Winter, January 1961): 94.

Review of Gustav E. Müller, *Hegel: Denkgeschichte eines Lebendigen** (Bern: Francke Verlag, 1959). *The Personalist* 42 (Winter, January 1961): 94.

Review of Raymond Jaffe, *The Pragmatic Conception of Justice** (Berkeley: University of California Press, 1960). *The Personalist* 42 (Winter, January 1961): 96.

Review of H. L. van Breda and J. Taminiaux, *Edmund Husserl*, 1859-1959* (The Hague: Martinus Nijhoff, 1959). *The Personalist* 42 (Winter, January 1961): 97.

Review of S. Radhakrishnan, trans., *The Brahma Sūtra: The Philosophy of Spiritual Life** (New York: Harper & Brothers, 1960). *The Personalist* 42 (Winter, January 1961): 101.

Review of A. C. Ewing, *Second Thoughts in Moral Philosophy** (New York: Macmillan Company, 1959). *The Personalist* 42 (Winter, January 1961): 103-104.

Review of F. S. C. Northrop, *Complexity of Legal and Ethical Experience** (Boston: Little, Brown and Co., 1959). *The Personalist* 42 (Winter, January 1961): 105.

Review of Austin Farrer, *The Freedom of the Will** (New York: Charles Scribner's Sons, 1960). *The Personalist* 42 (Winter, January 1961): 105-106.

Review of Leo Tolstoy, *What Is Art?* (New York: Liberal Arts Press, 1960). *The Personalist* 42 (Winter, January 1961): 111.

Review of Adolf Katzenellenbogen, *The Sculptural Programs of Chartres Cathedral* (Baltimore: Johns Hopkins Press, 1959). *The Personalist* 42 (Winter, January 1961): 112.

Review of Jerome G. Manis and Samuel I. Clark, eds., *Man and Society* (new York: Macmillan Company, 1960). *The Personalist* 42 (Winter, January 1961): 139.

Review of Leopold von Wiese, *Soziologie: Geschichte und Hauptprobleme*, 6th ed. ([Berlin/Leipzig: Walter de Gruyter & Co., 1926] [Berlin:] Sammlung Göschen, 1960). *The Personalist* 42 (Winter, January 1961): 141.

Review of Kurt F. Reinhardt, *The Existentialist Revolt* [New York: Ungar Pub. Co.] Atlantic Paperbacks, 1960). *The Personalist* 42 (Spring, April 1961): 245.

Review of W. H. Walsh, *Philosophy of History**, 3rd ed. (New York: Harper Torchbooks, 1960). *The Personalist* 42 (Spring, April 1961): 246-247.

Review of Ethel M. Albert and Clyde Kluckhohn, *A Selected Bibliography on Values, Ethics And Esthetics** (Glencoe, Ill.: The Free Press, 1959). *The Personalist* 42 (Spring, April 1961): 248.

Review of Felix S. Cohen, *Ethical Systems and Legal Ideals** (Ithaca, N. Y.: Cornell University Press, 1959). *The Personalist* 42 (Spring, April 1961): 248.

Review of Gerhard Lehmann, *Geschichte der Philosophie* (Berlin: Göschen, 1960). *The Personalist* 42 (Spring, April 1961): 280.

Review of Alfred Schütz, *Der sinnhafte Aufbau der Sozialen Welt**, 2nd ed. (Vienna: Springer-Verlag, 1960). *The Personalist* 42 (Spring, April 1961): 280.

Review of Jakob Hommes, *Zwiespältiges Dasein: Die existentiale Ontologie von Hegel bis Heidegger* (Freiburg: Verlag Herder, 1960 [sic][1953]). *The Personalist* 42 (Spring, April 1961): 281.

Review of Hans Wagner, *Philosophie und Reflexion** ([München/]Basel: Ernst Reinhardt Verlag, 1959). *The Personalist* 42 (Spring, April 1961): 282-283.

Review of Hwang-Tsong, *The Last Principle** (Taiwan: [ ], 1958). *The Personalist* 42 (Spring, April 1961): 283.

Review of Reginald O. Kapp, *Towards a Unified Cosmology** (New York: Basic Books, 1960). *The Personalist* 42 (Spring, April 1961): 286-287.

Review of Immanuel Kant, *Education**, trans. Annette Churton (Ann Arbor, Mich.: University of Michigan, 1960). *The Personalist* 42 (Summer, July 1961): 398.

Review of Tulane Studies in Philosophy, v. 9, *Studies in Hegel* (New Orleans, La.: Tulane University, 1960). *The Personalist* 42 (no 3) (Summer, July 1961): 398.

Review of Martin Heidegger, *Essays in Metaphysics**, trans Kurt F. Leidecker (New York: Philosophical Library, 1960). *The Personalist* 42 (Summer, July 1961): 399-400.

Review of Everett W. Hall, *Philosophical Systems: A Categorial Analysis** (Chicago: University of Chicago Press, 1960). *The Personalist* 42 (Summer, July 1961): 403-404.

Review of E. M. Adams, *Ethical Naturalism and the Modern World-View** (Chapel Hill, N. C.: University of North Carolina Press, 1960). *The Personalist* 42 (Summer, July 1961): 404-405.

Review of Herbert W. Schneider, *Morals for Mankind** (Columbia, Mo.: University of Missouri Press, 1960). *The Personalist* 42 (Summer, July 1961): 408.

Review of D. D. Raphael, *The Paradox of Tragedy* (Bloomington, Ind.: University of Indiana Press, 1960). *The Personalist* 42 (Summer, July 1961): 422.

Review of Charles E. Böwe and Roy F. Nichols, eds., *Both Human and Humane** (Philadelphia: University of Pennsylvania Press, 1960). *The Personalist* 42 (Summer, July 1961): 447.

Review of Cecil J. Schneer, *The Search for Order* (New York: Harper & Brothers, 1960). *The Personalist* 42 (Summer, July 1961): 458-459.

1962

Editor. Fulton H. Anderson, *Francis Bacon: His Career and His Thought.* Los Angeles: University of Southern California Press (distributed by University Publishers, New York), 1962. The Arensberg Lectures, 2d Series.

Editor. *The Forest of Yggdrasill: The Autobiography of Ralph Tyler Flewelling.* Introduction by Wilbur Long. Los Angeles: University of Southern California Press (distributed by University Publishers, New York), 1962. Pp. 179.

"Scientism and the Problem of Man." In *Philosophy and Culture—East and West: East-West Philosophy in Practical Perspective*, ed. Charles A. Moore. Proceedings of the Third East-West Philosophers' Conference, Honolulu, 1959. Honolulu: University of Hawaii Press, 1962. Pp. 135-155.

"Beyond the Call of Duty." In *Essays in Philosophy Presented to T.M.P. Mahadevan on His Fiftieth Birthday*, ed. C. T. K. Chari. Madras: Ganesh & Co., 1962; Hollywood, Cal.: Vendanta Society of Southern California, 1963. Pp. 132-138.

Review of Stephen C. Pepper, *Ethics** (New York: Appleton-Century-Crofts, Inc., 1960). *The Personalist* 43 (Winter, January 1962): 101-103.

Review of James E. Royce, S. J., *Man and His Nature* (New York: McGraw-Hill Book Company, 1961). *The Personalist* 43 (Winter, January 1962): 105.

Review of Irving Louis Horowitz, *Philosophy, Science and the Society of Knowledge* (Springfield, Ill.: Charles C. Thomas, 1961). *The Personalist* 43 (Winter, January 1962): 105-106.

Review of Bertram Morris, *Philosophical Aspects of Culture** (Yellow Springs, Oh.: The Antioch Press, 1961).*The Personalist* 43 (Winter, January 1962): 106.

Reviews of Giovanni Gentile, *Genesis and Structure of Society**, trans. H. S. Harris (Urbana, Ill.: University of Illinois Press, 1960), and H. S. Harris, *The Social Philosophy of Giovanni Gentile** (Urbana, Ill.: University of Illinois Press, 1960). *The Personalist* 43 (Winter, January 1962): 107.

Review of Joseph Chiari, *Realism and Imagination* (London: Barrie and Rockliff, 1960). *The Personalist* 43 (Winter, January 1962): 136-137.

Review of Nicolai Hartmann, *Die Philosophie des Deutschen Idealismus** (Berlin: Walter de Gruyter & Co., 1960). *The Personalist* 43 (Winter, January 1962): 138.

Review of Gunther Eigler, *Metaphysiche Voraussetzungen in Husserls Zeitanalysen** (Meisenheim am Glan: Verlag Anton Hain, 1961). *The Personalist* 43 (Winter, January 1962): 138-139.

Review of Michael Landmann, *Der Mensch als Schöpfer und Geschöpf der Kultur** (München\ Basel: Ernst Reinhardt Verlag, 1961). *The Personalist* 43 (no.1) (Winter, January 1962): 139.

Review of Norman Cousins. *In Place of Folly* (New York: Harper and Brothers, 1961). *The Personalist* 43 (Winter, January 1962): 151.

Review of Jules de Gaultier, *From Kant to Nietzsche*, trans Gerald M. Spring (New York: Philosophical Library, 1961). *The Personalist* 43 (Spring, April 1962): 256-257.

Review of Brand Blanshard, *Reason and Goodness** (New York: The Macmillan Company, 1961). *The Personalist* 43 (Spring, April 1962): 261-262.

Review of Marcus George Singer, *Generalization in Ethics** (New York: Alfred A. Knopf, 1961). *The Personalist* 43 (Spring, April 1962): 262-263.

Review of Baldwin V. Schwarz, ed., *The Human Person and the World of Values** (New York: Fordham University Press, 1960). *The Personalist* 43 (Spring, April 1962): 263-264.

Review of Everett W. Hall, *Our Knowledge of Fact and Value** (Chapel Hill, N.C.: University of North Carolina Press, 1961). *The Personalist* 43 (Spring, April 1962): 264-265.

Review of John Wilson, *Reason and Morals** (Cambridge, Engl.: Cambridge University Press, 1961). *The Personalist* 43 (Spring, April 1962): 265.

Review of Arthur O. Lovejoy, *The Reason, the Understanding, and Time** (Baltimore: The Johns Hopkins Press, 1961). *The Personalist* 43 (Spring, April 1962): 268.

Review of Robert N. Beck, *Perspectives in Philosophy* (New York: Holt, Reinhart and Winston, 1961). *The Personalist* 43 (Spring, April 1962): 270.

Review of Josef Schmucker, *Die Ursprünge der Ethik Kants** (Meisenheim: Verlag Anton Hain, 1961). *The Personalist* 43 (Spring, April 1962): 303-304.

Review of Bella K. Milmed, *Kant and Current Philosophical Issues** (New York: New York University Press, 1961). *The Personalist* 43 (Spring, April 1962): 404.

Review of Edmund Husserl, *Cartesian Meditations**, trans. Dorion Cairns (The Hague: Martinus Nijhoff, 1960). *The Personalist* 43 (Spring, April 1962): 405-406.

Review of Vincent Vycinas, *Earth and Gods. An Introduction to the Philosophy of Martin Heidegger** (The Hague: Martinus Nijhoff, 1961). *The Personalist* 43 (Spring, April 1962): 406.

Review of Angelo A. De Gennaro, *The Philosophy of Benedetto Croce: An Introduction* (New York: Philosophical Library, 1961). *The Personalist* 53 (Summer, July 1962), 406-407.

Review of Domingo Carvallo, *Die ontische Struktur** (Stuttgart: Verlag Neske, 1961). *The Personalist* 43 (Summer, July 1962): 408.

Review of Donald N. Barrett, ed., *Values in America** (Notre Dame, Ind.: University of Notre Dame Press, 1961). *The Personalist* 43 (Summer, July 1962): 408.

Review of D. M. Armstrong, *Perception and the Physical World** (New York: The Humanities Press, 1961). *The Personalist* 43 (Summer, July 1962): 409.

Review of Douglas E. Lawson, *Wisdom and Education* (Carbondale, Ill.: Southern Illinois University Press, [1961]). *The Personalist* 43 (Summer, July 1962): 411.

Review of Albert Schweitzer, *Pilgrimage to Humanity* (New York: Philosophical Library, Inc., 1961). *The Personalist* 43 (Summer, July 1962): 412.

Review of Vivian Charles Walsh, *Scarcity and Evil** ([Englewood Cliffs, N.J.: Prentice-Hall] A Spectrum Book, 1961). *The Personalist* 43 (Summer, July 1962): 412-413.

Review of Robert C. Tucker, *Philosophy and Myth in Karl Marx* ([Cambridge, Engl.:] Cambridge University Press, 1962 (*sic*) [1961]). *The Personalist* 43 (Summer, July 1962): 413.

Review of J. M. Bocheński and T. J. Blakeley, eds., *Studies in Soviet Thought** (Dordrecht, Holland: D. Reidel Publishing Company, 1961). *The Personalist* 43 (Summer, July 1962): 414.

Review of Giorgio de Santillana, *The Origins of Scientific Thought** ([Chicago: University of Chicago Press], A Mentor Book, 1961). *The Personalist* 43 (Summer, July 1962): 441.

Review of K. William Kapp, *Toward a Science of Man in Society** (The Hague: Martinus Nijhoff, 1961). *The Personalist* 43 (Summer, July 1962): 442-443.

Review of Max Black, ed., *The Social Theories of Talcott Parsons** (Englewood Cliffs, N.J.: Prentice-Hall, Inc., 1961). *The Personalist* 43 (Summer, July 1962): 443.

Review of Martin Heidegger, *Kant and the Problem of Metaphysics**, trans. James S. Churchill (Bloomington, Ind.: Indiana University Press, 1962). *The Personalist* 43 (Summer, July 1962): 551.

Review of Paul W. Taylor, *Normative Discourse* (Englewood Cliffs, N.J.: Prentice-Hall, Inc., 1961). *The Personalist* 43 (Autumn, October 1962): 554.

Review of Anne and Harry Paolucci, eds., *Hegel on Tragedy* (New York: Doubleday & Company, 1962). *The Personalist* 43 (Autumn, October 1962): 570.

Review of Paul Diel, *Psychologie de la Motivation* (Paris: Presses Universitaires de France, 1962). *The Personalist* 43 (Autumn, October 1962): 588-589.

Review of Joseph de Vries, *La Pensée et l'Être: Une Épistémologie* (Louvain-Paris: Éditions Nauwelaerts, 1962). *The Personalist* 43 (Autumn, October 1962): 589.

Review of Gilles Deleuze, *Nietzsche et la Philosophie** (Paris: Presses Universitaires de France, 1962). *The Personalist* 43 (Autumn, October 1962): 589-590.

Review of Ivan Gobry, *La Personne** (Paris: Presses Universitaires de France, 1961). *The Personalist* 43 (Autumn, October 1962): 590.

Review of Johannes Linschoten, *Auf dem Wege zu einer phänomenologischen Psychologie* (Berlin: Walter de Gruyter & Co., Berlin, 1961). *The Personalist* 43 (Autumn, October 1962): 590-591.

Review of Frederic Harold Young, *La Filosofía Contemporanéa en los Estados Unidos de América del Norte 1900-1950*, trans. Florentino M. Torner (Mexico: Ediciones Cuadernos Americanos, 1961). *The Personalist* 43 (Autumn, October 1962): 591.

Review of Gerhard Adler, *The Living Symbol: A Case Study in the Process of Individuation*, Bollingen Series, vol. 63 (New York: Pantheon Books, Inc., 1961). *The Personalist* 43 (Autumn, October 1962): 594-595.

Review of John C. Bennett, ed., *Nuclear Weapons and the Conflict of Conscience* (New York: Charles Scribner's Sons, 1962). *The Personalist* 43 (Autumn, October 1962): 598.

1963

Editor, *Facets of the Renaissance: Essays by Wallace K. Ferguson*, rev. ed. New York: Harper Torchbooks, 1963. Pp. [v,] 130. See under 1959.

"Propaganda Devices." In *Exposition and the English Language: Introductory Studies,* ed. James L. Sanderson and Walter K. Gordon. New York: Appleton-Century-Crofts, 1963, reprinted 1969. Pp. 362-377. Reprint of Chap. 4, secs. 4 and 5, *Introduction to Critical Thinking,* 1948.

Review of Henry David Aiken, *Reason and Conduct** (New York: Alfred A. Knopf, 1962). *The Personalist* 44 (Winter, January 1963): 111.

Review of J. N. Findlay, *Values and Intentions** (New York: The Macmillan Company, 1961). *The Personalist* 44 (Winter, January 1963): 111.

Review of David Pole, *Conditions of Rational Inquiry** (London, Engl.: University of London, The Athlone Press, 1961). *The Personalist* 44 (Winter, January 1963): 116-117.

Review of Charles Guignebert, *Ancient, Medieval, and Modern Christianity* (New Hyde Park, N.Y.: University Books, Inc., 1961. *The Personalist* 44 (Winter, January 1963): 129.

Review of Martin Heidegger, *Being and Time**, trans. John Macquarrie and Edward Robinson (New York: Harper & Brothers, 1962). *The Personalist* 44 (Spring, April 1963): 244.

Review of Calvin O. Schrag, *Existence and Freedom* (Evanston, Ill.: Northwestern University Press, 1961). *The Personalist* 44 (Spring, April 1963): 245.

Review of John Macmurray, *Persons in Relation* (New York: Harper & Brothers, 1961). *The Personalist* 44 (Spring, April 1963): 245-246. [Ed. note: Werkmeister published a slightly different review of this work in this journal, 44 (Autumn, October 1963).]

Review of Arthur O. Lovejoy, *Reflections on Human Nature** (Baltimore, Md.: The Johns Hopkins Press, 1961). *The Personalist* 44 (Spring, April 1963): 246.

Review of Louis J. Halle, *Men and Nations** (Princeton, N.J.: Princeton University Press, 1962). *The Personalist* 44 (Spring, April 1963): 247.

Review of Robert T. Harris, *Social Ethics** (Philadelphia and New York: J. B. Lippincot Company, 1962). *The Personalist* 44 (Spring, April 1963): 247.

Review of Rosalie B. Gerber, *The Responsibilities of Man** (Washington, D. C.: Public Affairs Press, 1962). *The Personalist* 44 (Spring, April 1963): 248.

Review of Carl Wellman, *The Language of Ethics** (Cambridge, Mass.: Harvard University Press, 1961). *The Personalist* 44 (Spring, April 1963): 248-249.

Review of Sir W. David Ross, *Foundations of Ethics** (Oxford, Engl.: Oxford University Press, 1960). *The Personalist* 44 (Spring, April 1963): 249.

Review of Pieter Geyl, *Encounters in History** ([Cleveland:] Meridian Books, 1961). *The Personalist* 44 (Spring, April 1963): 249.

Review of Arthur Pap, *An Introduction to the Philosophy of Science** (New York: The Free Press of Glencoe, 1962). *The Personalist* 44 (Spring, April 1963): 259.

Review of Herbert Feigl and Grover Maxwell, eds., *Scientific Explanation, Space and Time**, Minnesota Studies in the Philosophy of Science vol. 3 (Minneapolis: University of Minnesota Press, 1962). *The Personalist* 44 (Spring, April 1963): 259-260.

Review of P. Henry Van Laer, *Philosophy of Science**, part 2. (Pittsburgh: Duquesne University Press, 1962). *The Personalist* 44 (Summer, July 1963): 261.

Review of Moody E. Prior, *Science and the Humanities** (Evanston, Ill.: Northwestern University Press, 1962). *The Personalist* 44 (Autumn, October 1963): 280-281.

Review of Katherina Kanthack, *Nicolai Hartmann und das Ende der Ontologie** (Berlin: Walter de Gruyter & Co., 1962). *The Personalist* 44 (Autumn, October 1963): 281-282.

Review of Baldwin V. Schwarz, ed., *The Human Person and the World of Values** (New York: Fordham University Press, 1960). *The Personalist* 44 (Autumn, October 1963): 395. [Ed. note: Werkmeister published a somewhat different review of this work in this journal, 43 (Spring 1963).]

Review of Georg Henrick von Wright, *The Varieties of Goodness** (New York: The Humanities Press, Inc., 1963). *The Personalist* 44 (Autumn, October 1963): 539.

Review of Peter A. Bertocci and Richard M. Millard, *Personality and the Good* (New York: David McKay Company, Inc., 1963). *The Personalist* 44 (Autumn, October 1963): 539-540.

Review of P. T. Raju, *Indian Idealism and Modern Challenges** (Chandigarh: Panjap (sic; Panjab) University Publication Bureau, 1961). *The Personalist* 44 (Autumn, October 1963): 540-541.

Review of Samuel L. Hart, *Ethics** (New York: Philosophical Library, Inc., 1963). *The Personalist* 44 (Autumn, October 1963): 541.

Review of John MacMurray [sic], *Persons in Relation** (New York: Harper & Brothers, 1961). *The Personalist* 44 (Autumn, October 1963): 545-546. [Ed. note: Werkmeister published a slightly different review of this work in 44 (Spring 1963).]

Review of Sidney Hook, ed., *Philosophy and History** (New York: New York University Press, 1963). *The Personalist* 44 (Autumn, October 1963): 549-550.

Review of Louis Gottschalk, ed., *Generalization in the Writing of History**, by the Social Science Research Council (U.S.), Committee on Historical Analysis (Chicago: The University of Chicago Press, 1963). *The Personalist* 44 (Autumn, October 1963): 550-551.

Review of Alfred Stern, *Philosophy of History and the Problem of Values** ('s-Gravenhage [The Hague], The Netherlands: Mouton and Company, 1962). *The Personalist* 44 (no 4) (Autumn, October 1963): 551-52.

Review of W. T. Jones, *The Romantic Syndrome** (The Hague: Martinus Nijhoff, 1961). *The Personalist* 44 (Autumn, October 1963): 553.

Review of Karl R. Popper, *Conjectures and Refutations** (New York: Basic Books, 1962). *The Personalist* 44 (Autumn, October 1963): 553-554.

Review of W. H. Watson, *Understanding Physics Today** (Cambridge, Engl.: Cambridge University press, 1963). *The Personalist* 44 (Autumn, October 1963): 554-555.

Review of Loren Eisley, *Francis Bacon and the Modern Dilemma* (Lincoln, Neb.: University of Nebraska Press, 1962). *The Personalist* 44 (Autumn, October 1963): 555.

Review of Thomas Neville Bonner, *American Doctors and German Universities* (Lincoln, Neb.: University of Nebraska Press, 1963). *The Personalist* 44 (Autumn, October 1963): 577-578.

1964

[President of The American Philosophical Association, Pacific Division, 1964-1965.]

"Value Theory and the Problem of Moral Obligation." *The Personalist* 45 (Summer, July 1964): 354-361. Based on a paper first presented at the Inter-American Congress of Philosophy at Buenos Aires, Argentina. 1959. Reprinted in *Exploring Philosophy,* ed. Peter A. French. Cambridge, Mass.: Schenkman, 1970. Pp. 51-56. Revised edition, 1972.

Review of Norwood Russell Hanson, *The Concept of the Positron** (New York: Cambridge University Press, 1963). *The Personalist* 45 (Winter, January 1964): 116-117.

Review of Risieri Frondisi (*sic*), *What Is Value?** trans. Solomon Lipp (LaSalle, Ill.: Open Court, 1963). *The Personalist* 45 (Winter, January 1964): 119.

Review of J. N. Findlay, *Language, Mind and Value** (New York: Humanities Press, 1963). *The Personalist* 45 (Winter, January 1964): 119-120.

Review of J. von Rintelen, *Beyond Existentialism** (New York: The Humanities Press, 1962). *The Personalist* 45 (Winter, January 1964): 120.

Review of Z. A. Jordan, *Philosophy and Ideology** (Dordrecht, Holland: D. Reidel Publishing Company, 1963). *The Personalist* 45 (Winter, January 1964): 121.

Review of Friedrich Grossart, *Gefühl und Strebung** ([München/]Basel: Ernst Reinhardt Verlag, 1961). *The Personalist* 45 (Winter, January 1964): 149.

Review of Johan Frederik Bjelke, *Zur Begründung der Werterkenntnis** (Oslo/Bergen: Scandinavian University Books, Universitetsforlaget, 1962). *The Personalist* 45 (Winter, January 1964): 152. [Ed. note: Werkmeister published another Review of this book in German in *The Journal of the History of Philosophy* 4 (January 1966).]

Review of Henry B. Veatch, *Rational Man** (Bloomington: Indiana University Press, 1962). *The Personalist*, 45 (Spring, April 1964): 265.

Review of Brand Blanshard, *Reason and Analysis** (LaSalle, Ill.: Open Court Publishing Company, 1962). *The Personalist* 45 (Spring, April 1964): 265-266.

Review of William H. Hay, Marcus G. Singer, and Arthur E. Murphy, eds., *Reason and the Common Good** (Englewood Cliffs, N. J.: Prentice-Hall, Inc., 1963). *The Personalist* 45 (Spring, April 1964): 266.

Review of Hector-Neri Castaneda [sic; Castañeda] and George Nakhnikian, *Morality and the Language of Conduct** (Detroit: Wayne State University Press, 1963). *The Personalist* 45 (Spring, April 1964): 266-267.

Review of Shepard B. Clough, *Basic Values of Western Civilization** (New York: Columbia University Press, 1961). *The Personalist* 45 (Spring, April 1964): 267.

Review of Rudolph H. Weingartner, *Experience and Culture: The Philosophy of Georg Simmel** (Middletown, Conn.: Wesleyan University Press, 1962). *The Personalist* 45 (Spring, April 1964): 268.

Review of William P. McEwen, *The Problems of Social-Scientific Knowledge** (Totowa, N.J.: The Bedminster Press, 1963). *The Personalist* 45 (Spring, April 1964): 268-269.

Review of Grace E. Cairns, *Philosophies of History** (New York: Philosophical Library, 1962). *The Personalist* 45 (Spring, April 1964): 269-270.

Review of Radoslav A. Tsanoff, *Worlds to Know** (New York: The Humanities Press, 1962). *The Personalist* 45 (Spring, April 1964): 270-271.

Review of Johan H. Greidanus, *Fundamental Physical Theory and the Concept of Consciousness** (New York: Pergamon Press, 1961). *The Personalist* 45 (Spring, April 1964): 273.

Review of D. W. Gotshalk, *Patterns of Good and Evil** (Urbana, Ill.: University of Illinois Press, 1963). *The Personalist* 45 (Summer, July 1964): 421.

Review of Max [sic] W. Wartosfky [sic], *Boston Studies in the Philosophy of Science** (Dordrecht, Holland: D. Reidel Publishing Company, 1963). *The Personalist* 45 (Summer, July 1964): 426-427.

Review of J. J. C. Smart, *Philosophy and Scientific Realism** (New York: Humanities Press, Inc., 1964). *The Personalist* 45 (Summer, July 1964): 427.

Review of Charles Hartshorne, *The Logic of Perfection** (LaSalle, Ill.: Open Court Publishing Company, 1962). *The Personalist* 45 (Autumn, October 1964): 557.

Review of Frederic[k] C. Dommeyer and the San Jose State College Associates in Philosophy, *In Quest of Value** (San Francisco: Chandler Publishing Company, 1964). *The Personalist* 45 (Autumn, October 1964): 557-558.

Review of Nathan Rotenstreich, *Spirit and Man: An Essay on Being and Value** (The Hague: Martinus Nijhoff, 1963). *The Personalist* 45 (Autumn, October 1964): 558.

Review of Roman Ingarden, *Time and Modes of Being* (Springfield, Ill.: Charles C. Thomas, 1964). *The Personalist* 45 (Autumn, October 1964): 560-561.

Review of Anatol von Spakovsky, *Freedom, Determinism, Indeterminism** (The Hague: Martinus Nijhoff, 1963). *The Personalist* 45 (Autumn, October 1964): 561.

Review of Ernan McMullin, ed., *The Concept of Matter** (Notre Dame, Ind.: University of Notre Dame Press, 1963). *The Personalist* 45 (Autumn, October 1964): 561.

Review of Erich Kahler, *The Meaning of History** (New York: George Braziller, 1964). *The Personalist* 45 (Autumn, October 1964): 561-562.

Review of Morris Lazerowitz, *Studies in Metaphilosophy** (New York: Humanities Press, Inc., 1964). *The Personalist*, 45 (Autumn, October 1964): 562-563.

Review of David Hawkins, *The Language of Nature: An Essay in the Philosophy of Science** (San Francisco: W. H. Freeman and Company, 1964). *The Personalist* 45 (Autumn, October 1964): 564.

Review of Daniel Lerner, ed., *Parts and Wholes** (New York: The Free Press of Glencoe, 1963). *The Personalist* 45 (Autumn, October 1964): 564-565.

Reviews of Richard Taylor, *Metaphysics**, Foundations of Philosophy Series (Englewood Cliffs, N.J.: Prentice-Hall, Inc., 1963): and William H. Dray, *Philosophy of History**, Foundations of Philosophy Series (Englewood Cliffs, N.J.: Prentice-Hall, Inc., 1964). *The Personalist* 45 (Autumn, October 1964): 566-567.

Review of Philip Wheelwright and Peter Fuss, eds., *Five Philosophers: Aristotle, René Descartes, David Hume, Immanuel Kant, William James** (New York: The Odyssey Press, 1963). *The Personalist* 45 (Autumn, October 1964): 567.

Review of Daisuke Veda, *Zen and Science: A Treatise on Causality and Freedom* (Tokyo: Risosh Ltd., 1963). *The Personalist* 45 (Autumn, October 1964): 573.

1965

"Reflections on the Possibilities of Metaphysics." *Proceedings and Addresses of the American Philosophical Association, 1964-65* 38 (October 1965): 37-48. (Presidential Address delivered before the thirty-eighth annual meeting of the Pacific Division at the University of Washington, Seattle, 5 September 1964.)

"The Role of the Philosopher Today." *University of Southern California Alumni Review* (December-January, 1964-1965,): 12-13.

"Neo-Kantianism." In *Encyclopedia Americana*, 20 (1965): 96.

"Process and Reality." In *Encyclopedia Americana*, 22 (1965): 628-629.

"Alfred North Whitehead." In *Encyclopedia Americana* 28 (1965): 628-629.

Review of William J. Richardson, S. J., *Heidegger: Through Phenomenology to Thought** (The Hague: Martinus Nijhoff, 1963). *The Personalist* 46 (Winter, January 1965): 109-110.

Review of Edward Pols, *The Recognition of Reason* (Carbondale, Ill.: Southern Illinois University Press, 1963). *The Personalist* 46 (Winter, January 1965): 110.

Review of *An Index to Book Reviews in the Humanities*, vol. 4, 1963 (Detroit: Phillip Thomson, 1964). *The Personalist* 46 (Winter, January 1965): 138.

Review of S. Rawidowicz, *Ludwig Feuerbachs Philosophie: Ursprung und Schicksal**, 2nd printing (Berlin: Walter de Gruyter & Co., 1964). *The Personalist* 46 (Winter, January 1965): 149.

Review of Hermann Drüe, *Edmund Husserls System der phänomenologischen Psychologie** (Berlin: Walter de Gruyter & Co., 1963). *The Personalist* 46 (Winter, January 1965): 149-150.

Review of Frederick Patka, *Value and Existence** (New York: Philosophical Library, 1964). *The Personalist* 46 (Summer, July 1965): 389.

Review of Karl Löwith, *From Hegel to Nietzsche**, trans. David E. Green (New York: Holt, Rinehart and Winston, 1964). *The Personalist* 46 (Summer, July 1965): 391-392.

Review of R. D. Laing and D. G. Cooper, *Reason and Violence: A Decade of Sartre's Philosophy, 1950-1960** (New York: Humanities Press, 1964). *The Personalist* 46 (Summer, July 1965): 392.

Review of Hajime Nakamura, *Ways of Thinking of Eastern Peoples,* ed. Philip P. Wiener (Honolulu, Hawaii: East-West Center Press, 1964). *The Personalist* 46 (Summer, July 1965): 394.

Review of Stephan Strasser, *Phänomenologie und Erfahrungswissenschaft vom Menschen**, Phänomenologisch-psychologische Forschungen, Band 5 (Berlin: Walter de Gruyter & Co., 1964). *The Personalist* 46 (Summer, July 1965): 426.

1966

[Retired from the University of Southern California; accepted professorship at Florida State University.]

"C. I. Lewis: The Man and His Philosophy." *The Personalist* 47 (Fall, October 1966): 475-483.

"Notes to an Interpretation of Berkeley: Kant, Berkeley and James Beattie, and a Berkeley Parallel." In *New Studies in Berkeley's Philosophy*, ed. Warren E. Steinkraus. New York: Holt, Rinehart and Winston, 1966. Pp. 163-72.

"Cassirers Verhältnis zur neukantischen Philosophie." In *Ernst Cassirer,* ed. Paul A. Schilpp. Mainz: W. Kohlhammer Verlag, 1966. Pp. 532-65. German translation of 1949 edition Library of Living Philosophers.

Review of Johan Frederik Bjelke, *Zur Begründung der Werterkenntnis* (Oslo/Bergen: Universitetsforlaget, 1962). *Journal of the History of Philosophy* 4 (January 1966): 89-90. [Ed. note: Werkmeister also published another Review of this book in English in another journal in 1964.]

Review of Jacob Löwenberg, *Hegel's Phenomenology: Dialogues of the Life of Mind** (La Salle, IL: The Open Court Publishing Company, 1965). *The Personalist* 47 (Winter, January 1966): 126.

Review of Walter Kaufmann, *Hegel** (Garden City, N. Y.: Doubleday and Company, Inc., 1965). *The Personalist* 47 (Winter, January 1966): 127.

Review of R. J. Hollingdale, *Nietzsche: The Man and His Philosophy** (Baton Rouge: Louisiana State University Press, 1965). *The Personalist* 47 (Winter, January 1966): 129.

Review of Francisco Romero, *Theory of Man**, trans. William F. Cooper (Berkeley and Los Angeles: University of California Press, 1964). *The Personalist* 47 (Winter, January 1966): 129.

Review of Josef Pieper, *The Four Cardinal Virtues** (New York: Harcourt, Brace & World, Inc., 1965). *The Personalist* 47 (Winter, January 1966): 130.

Review of Joseph Margolis, *The Language of Art and Art Criticism* (Detroit: Wayne State University Press, 1965). *The Personalist* 47 (Winter, January 1966): 131.

Review of Albert Hofstadter, *Truth and Art* (New York: Columbia University Press, 1965). *The Personalist* 47 (Winter, January 1966): 131-132.

Review of Martin G. Plattel, *Social Philosophy**, trans. Henry J. Koren (Pittsburgh: Duquesne University Press, 1965). *The Personalist* 47 (Winter, January 1966): 132.

Review of Kurt Schilling, *Weltgeschichte der Philosophie* (Berlin: Duncker & Humboldt, 1964). *Journal of the History of Philosophy* 4 (April 1966): 161.

Review of Morton White, *Foundations of Historical Knowledge** (New York: Harper & Row, 1965). *The Personalist* 47 (Spring, April 1966): 264-265.

Review of Edward C. Moore and Richard S. Robin, eds., *Studies in the Philosophy of Charles Sanders Peirce**, 2nd series (Amherst: University of Massachusetts Press, 1964). *The Personalist* 47 (Summer, July 1966): 415. [Ed. note: Werkmeister published a mostly different review of this work in this journal, 47 (Fall, October 1966).]

Review of Everett Hall, *Categorial Analysis**,. ed. E. M. Adams (Chapel Hill, N.C.: University of North Carolina Press, 1964). *The Personalist* 47 (Summer, July 1966): 415-416.

Review of Paul Weiss, *The God We Seek* (Carbondale, Ill.: Southern Illinois University Press, 1964). *The Personalist* 47 (Summer, July 1966): 417-418.

Review of Arthur E. Murphy, *Theory of Practical Reason** (La Salle, Ill.: Open Court, 1965). *The Personalist* 47 (Summer, July 1966): 423-424.

Review of Arthur C. Danto, *Analytical Philosophy of History** (Cambridge, Engl.: Cambridge University Press, 1965). *The Personalist* 47 (Summer, July 1966): 424.

Review of Konstantin Kolenda, *The Freedom of Reason** (San Antonio, Texas: Principia Press, 1964). *The Personalist* 47 (Summer, July 1966): 424-425.

Review of J. Bronowski, *The Identity of Man** (Garden City, N. Y.: The Natural History Press, 1965). *The Personalist* 47 (Summer, July 1966): 425.

Review of Jean-Paul Sartre, *Situations**, trans. Benita Eisler (New York: George Braziller, 1965). *The Personalist* 47 (Summer, July 1966): 425-426.

Review of Gottfried Martin, *Allgemeine Metaphysik** (Berlin: Walter de Gruyter & Co., 1965). *The Personalist* 47 (Summer, July 1966): 453.

Review of Ingeborg Wirth, *Realismus und Apriorismus in Nicolai Hartmanns Erkenntnistheorie** (Berlin: Walter de Gruyter & Co., 1965). *The Personalist* 47 (Summer, July 1966): 450.

Review of Martin Buber, *The Knowledge of Man**, ed. Maurice Friedman (New York: Harper & Row, 1965). *The Personalist* 47 (Fall, October 1966): 548.

Review of John R. Platt, ed., *New Views of the Nature of Man** (Chicago: The University of Chicago Press, 1965). *The Personalist* 47 (Fall, October 1966): 549.

Review of W. T. Jones, *The Sciences and the Humanities** (Berkeley and Los Angeles: University of California Press, 1965). *The Personalist* 47 (Fall, October 1966): 549-550.

Review of D. W. Gotshalk, *Human Aims in Modern Perspective* (Yellow Springs, Ohio: The Antioch Press, 1966). *The Personalist* 47 (Fall, October 1966): 550-551

Review of L. M. Loring, *Two Kinds of Values** (New York: The Humanities Press, 1966). *The Personalist* 47 (Fall, October 1966): 551.

Review of Stuart Hampshire, *Freedom of the Individual** (New York: Harper & Row, 1965). *The Personalist* 47 (Fall, October 1966): 551-552.

Review of Richard T. DeGeorge, ed., *Ethics and Society** (Garden City, N.Y.: Doubleday & Company, Inc., 1966). *The Personalist* 47 (Fall, October 1966): 552.

Review of Elder Olsen, ed., *Aristotle's "Poetics" and English Literature* (Chicago: University of Chicago Press, 1965). *The Personalist* 47 (Fall, October 1966): 553.

Reviews of George P. Klubertanz, S.J., *Habits and Virtues* (New York: Appleton Century-Crofts, 1965), and St. Thomas Aquinas, *Treatise on the Virtues*, trans John A. Österle (Englewood Cliffs, N.J.: Prentice-Hall, Inc., 1966). *The Personalist* 47 (Fall, October 1966): 553.

Review of Lewis White Beck, *Studies in the Philosophy of Kant** (Indianapolis: The Bobbs-Merrill Company, Inc., 1965). *The Personalist* 47 (Fall, October 1966): 558.

Review of Edward C. Moore and Richard S. Robin, eds., *Studies in the Philosophy of Charles Sanders Peirce*, 2nd series (Amherst: University of Massachusetts Press, 1964). *The Personalist* 47 (Fall, October 1966): 559. [Ed. note: Werkmeister published a mostly different review of this work in this journal, 47 (July 1966).]

Review of Martin Heidegger, *Discourse on Thinking**, trans. John M. Anderson and E. Hans Freund (New York: Harper & Row, 1966). *The Personalist* 47 (Fall, October 1966): 559-560.

Review of Donald C. Williams, *Principles of Empirical Realism** (Springfield, Ill.: Charles C. Thomas Publishers, 1966). *The Personalist* 47 (Fall, October 1966): 560-561.

Review of Paul K. Feyerabend and Grover Maxwell, eds., *Mind, Matter, and Method** (Minneapolis: University of Minnesota Press, 1966). *The Personalist* 47 (Fall, October 1966): 561-562.

Review of Samuel Enoch Stumpf, *Morality and the Law** (Nashville: Vanderbilt University Press, 1966). *The Personalist* 47 (Fall, October 1966): 562-563.

Review of Abraham Kaplan, *The Conduct of Inquiry** (San Francisco: Chandler Publishing Co., 1964). *The Personalist*, 47 (Fall, October 1966): 563-564.

Reviews of William H. Dray, ed., *Philosophical Analysis and History** (New York: Harper & Row, 1966); Stuart Hampshire, ed., *Philosophy of Mind** (New York: Harper & Row, 1966); and Bernard Berofsky, ed., *Free Will and Determinism** (New York: Harper & Row, 1966). *The Personalist* 47 (Fall, October 1966): 564.

Review of George L. Kline, ed., *European Philosophy Today** ([Chicago:] Quadrangle Books, 1965). *The Personalist* 47 (Fall, October 1966): 565.

Review of Joyce O. Hertzler, *A Sociology of Language** (New York: Random House, 1965). *The Personalist* 47 (Fall, October 1966): 565-566.

Review of Merle E. Brown, *Neo-Idealistic Aesthetics: Croce - Gentile - Collingwood** (Detroit: Wayne State University Press, 1966). *The Personalist* 47 (Fall, October 1966): 566.

Review of Geddes MacGregor, *God Beyond Doubt** (Philadelphia & New York: J. B. Lippincot Company, 1966). *The Personalist* 47 (Fall, October 1966): 574-575.

Review of Heinz Heimsöth, *Transzendentale Dialektik** (Berlin: Walter de Gruyter & Co., 1966). *The Personalist* 47 (Fall, October 1966): 575-576.

Review of Lothar Schäfer, *Kant's (sic) Metaphysik der Natur** (Berlin: Walter de Gruyter & Co., 1966). *The Personalist* 47 (Fall, October 1966): 576-577.

Review of Eugen Fink, *Studien zur Phänomenologie 1930-1939** (The Hague: Martinus Nijhoff, 1966). *The Personalist* 47 (Fall, October 1966): 577.

Review of Hans Reiner, *Gut und Böse** (Freiburg: L. Bielefelds Verlag, 1965). *The Personalist* 47 (Fall, October 1966): 577-578.

Review of Nancy Sullivan, *The History of the World as Pictures* (Columbia, Mo.: University of Missouri Press, 1965). *The Personalist* 47 (Fall, October 1966): 579.

Review of Archie J. Bahm, ed., *Directory of American Philosophers* (Albuquerque, New Mexico, 1966). *The Personalist* 47 (Fall, October 1966): 580.

1967

Facets of the Renaissance, ed. W. H. Werkmeister. New York: Recording for the Blind, Inc., 1967. Magnetic tape recording. See under 1959.

Man and His Values. Lincoln, Neb.: University of Nebraska Press, 1967. Pp. [xii], 239. (Reviewed by Stephen C. Pepper. See section below on Works about W. H. Werkmeister.)

"Grundzüge der menschlichen Existenz." (in German) In *Menschliche Existenz und moderne Welt,* vol. 2, ed. Richard Schwartz. Berlin: Walter de Gruyter, 1967. Pp. 150-156.

"Driesch, Hans Adolf Eduard." In *Encyclopedia of Philosophy,* vol. 2, ed. Paul Edwards (New York: Macmillan, 1967). Pp. 418-20.

"Flewelling, Ralph Tyler." In *Enciclopedia Filosofica,* Vol. 2. Firenze, 1967. Cols. 1440-1441.

Review of Oliver A. Johnson, *Moral Knowledge* (The Hague: Martinus Nijhoff, 1966).*The Personalist* 48 (Spring, April 1967): 242-243.

Review of Klaus Hartmann, *Sartres Sozialphilosophie** (Berlin: Walter de Gruyter & Co., 1966). *The Personalist* 48 (Spring, April 1967): 247.

Review of Karl J. Weintraub, *Visions of Culture** (Chicago, University of Chicago Press, 1966). *The Personalist* 48 (Spring, April 1967): 248-249.

Review of E. J. Faulkner, ed., *Man's Quest for Security* (Lincoln, Neb.: University of Nebraska Press, 1966). *The Personalist* 48 (Spring, April 1967): 250.

Review of Stephan Körner, *Experience and Theory** (New York: The Humanities Press, 1966). *The Personalist* 48 (Spring, April 1967): 250-251.

Review of Raymond Williams, *Modern Tragedy** (Stanford, Cal.: Stanford University Press, 1966). *The Personalist* 48 (Spring, April 1967): 260.

Review of Jerome Ashmore, *Santayana, Art, and Aesthetics* (Cleveland, Oh.: Western Reserve University Press, 1966). *The Personalist* 48 (Spring, April 1967): 260-261.

Review of J. A. Appleyard, S. J., *Coleridge's Philosophy of Literature* (Cambridge, Mass: Harvard University Press, 1965). *The Personalist* 48 (Spring, April 1967): 266-267.

Review of Charles I. Clicksberg, *Modern Literature and the Death of God* (The Hague: Martinus Nijhoff, 1966). *The Personalist* 48 (Spring, April 1967): 269.

Review of E. A. Burtt. *In Search of Philosophic Understanding** (New York: The New American Library, 1965). *The Personalist* 48 (Spring, April 1967): 271-272.

Review of W. H. Capitan and D. D. Merrill, eds., *Metaphysics and Explanation* [Pittsburgh:] University of Pittsburgh Press, [1966]). *The Personalist* 48 (Spring, April 1967): 272-273.

Review of George C. Kerner, *The Revolution in Ethic[al] Theory** (New York: Oxford University Press, 1966). *The Personalist* 48 (Summer, July 1967): 405-406.

Review of William R. Mueller, *The Prophetic Voice in Modern Fiction* (Garden City, N.Y.: A Doubleday Anchor Book, 1966). *The Personalist*, 48 (Summer, July 1967): 432.

Review of Frederick C. Dommeyer, ed., *Current Philosophical Issues: Essays in Honor of Curt John Ducasse** (Springfield, Ill.: Charles C. Thomas, 1966). *The Personalist* 48 (Autumn, October 1967): 593.

Review of Akademie der Wissenschaften, Göttingen, *Kants Vorlesungen. Vol. 1: Vorlesungen über Logik;* Erste Hälfte, (Berlin: Walter de Gruyter & Col, 1966). *The Personalist* 48 (Autumn, October 1967): 596-597.

1968

"Dr. Datta and the Comprehensiveness and Practicality of Philosophy." In *World Perspectives in Philosophy, Religion and Culture: Essays Presented to Professor Dhirendra Mohan Datta*, ed. Ram Jee Singh. Patna: Bharati Bhawan, [1968]. Pp. 446-452.

"Husserl and Hegel." In *Akten des XIV. Internationalen Kongresses für Philosophie.* Vienna: Herder, 1968. Pp. 553-558.

"The Status of the Person in Western Ethics." In *The Status of the Individual in East and West*, ed. Charles A. Moore with the assistance of Aldyth V. Morris. Proceedings of the Fourth East-West Philosophers' Conference, Honolulu, 1964. Honolulu: University of Hawaii Press, 1968. Pp. 317-329.

Review of Iso Kern, *Husserl und Kant: Eine Untersuchung über Husserls Verhältnis zu Kant und zum Neukantianismus** (The Hague: Martinus Nijhoff, 1964). *Journal of the History of Philosophy* 6 (January 1968): 97-98.

Review of Roderick M. Chisholm, *Theory of Knowledge** (Englewood Cliffs, N.J.: Prentice-Hall, Inc., 1966). *The Personalist* 49 (Spring 1968): 266.

Review of Marvin Farber, *Phenomenology and Existence: Toward a Philosophy within Nature** (New York: Harper Torchbooks, 1967). *The Personalist* 49 (Spring, April 1968): 270.

Review of Martin Foss, *Death, Sacrifice, and Tragedy** (Lincoln, Neb.: University of Nebraska Press, 1966). *The Personalist* 49 (Spring 1968): 271.

Review of Justus Buchler, *Metaphysics of Natural Complexes** (New York: Columbia University Press, 1966). *The Personalist* 49 (Summer, July 1968): 400-401.

Review of Donald Atwell Zoll, *The Twentieth-Century Mind** ([Baton Rouge, La.:] Louisiana State University Press, 1967). *The Personalist* 49 (Summer, July 1968): 408-409.

Review of Rober[t] G. Colodny, ed., *Beyond the Edge of Certainty** (Englewood Cliffs, N.J.: Prentice-Hall, Inc., 1966). *The Personalist* 49 (Summer 1968): 410-411.

Review of Stanley L. Jaki, *The Relevance of Physics** (Chicago: University of Chicago Press, 1966). *The Personalist* 49 (Summer, July 1968): 411-412.

Review of Nathan Rotenstreich, *On the Human Subject: Studies in the Phenomenology of Ethics and Politics** (Springfield, Mass. [sic][Ill.]: Charles C. Thomas, 1966). *Journal of the History of Philosophy* 6 (October 1968): 413-414.

1969

An Introduction to Critical Thinking, rev. ed., 8th printing. Lincoln, Neb.: University of Nebraska Press, 1967. Pp. [xii], 663. See under 1957.

"A Value Perspective on Our Changing Society." In *Value Attitudes in a Changing Society*, ed. J. R. Sasnett. Pasadena, Cal.: The Religion in Education Foundation, 1969. Pp. 10-24.

Review of Ottokar Blaha, *Die Ontologie Kants**, Salzburger Studien zur Philosophie, 7 (Salzburg: Verlag Anton Pustet, 1967). *Journal of the History of Philosophy* 7 (January 1969): 97-98.

Review of Lauchlin D. MacDonald, *John Grote: A Critical Estimate of His Writings** (The Hague: Martinus Nijhoff, 1966). *Journal of the History of Philosophy* 7 (April 1969): 217-218.

1970

Historical Spectrum of Value Theories. Vol. 1: German-Language Group. Lincoln, Neb.: Johnsen Publishing Co., 1970. Pp. [xxvii], 453. (Reviewed by George Stack, Alfred Stern, Stephen C. Pepper, Konstantin Kolenda, Dallas Willard, Alex C. Michalos; see section below on Works about W. H. Werkmeister.)

A History of Philosophical Ideas in America. Des Moines, Iowa Commission for the Blind, 1970. Magnetic tape recording, and Braille edition. See under 1949.

"Hegel's Phenomenology of Mind as a Development of Kant's Basic Ontology." In *Hegel and the Philosophy of Religion: The Wofford Symposium* [1970], ed. Darrel E. Christensen. The Hague: Nijhoff, 1970. Pp. 93-110; "Reply to Commentators." pp. 121-24.

"Husserl and Hegel." *Seishin-Kagaku* [Science of Mind] (Tokyo) 9 (1972): 90-95. See also Yoshio Sezai, "On Dr. W.H. Werkmeister's Theory of Value." *Seishin-Kagaku* 8 (1971): 94-106. Texts in Japanese.

"Is Truth a Value?" *Southwestern Journal of Philosophy* 1 (Fall 1970): 45-49.

1971

"Hegel and Heidegger." In *New Studies in Hegel's Philosophy,* ed. Warren E. Steinkraus. New York: Holt, Rinehart and Winston, 1971. Pp. 142-55.

"Heidegger and the Poets." *The Personalist* 52 (Winter 1971): 5-22.

"The Universalistic Evolutionism of Charles Sanders Peirce." *Southern Journal of Philosophy* 9 (Fall 1971): 327-333.

"Process and Reality." In *Encyclopedia Americana,* 22 (1971): 628-629.

Review of Gian N. G. Orsini, *Coleridge and German Idealism** (Carbondale, Ill.: Southern Illinois University Press, 1969). *Journal of the History of Philosophy* 9 (January 1971): 104-110.

Review of Gerhard Lehmann, *Beiträge zur Geschichte und Interpretation der Philosophie Kants** (Berlin: Walter de Gruyter & Co., 1969). *Journal of the History of Philosophy* 9 (July 1971): 385-392.

Review of Frederick Gustav Weiss, *Hegel's Critique of Aristotle's Philosophy of Mind** (The Hague: Martinus Nijhoff, 1969). *Journal of the History of Philosophy* 9 (October 1971): pp. 525-526.

1972

"A Value-Perspective on Human Existence." In *Value and Valuation: Axiological Studies in Honor of Robert S. Hartman*, ed. John William Davis. Knoxville, Tenn.: University of Tennessee Press, 1972. Pp. 63-70. Reissued on computer diskette, George Parrish and John Austin, eds., Muskegon, Mich.: Research Concepts, [ ].

Review of Helmut Holzhey, *Kants Erfahrungsbegriff: Quellengeschichtliche und bedeutungsanalytische Untersuchungen** (Basel/Stuttgart: Schwabe & Co. Verlag, 1970). *Journal of the History of Philosophy* 10 (January 1972): 99-101.

Review of Alexander Altmann, *Moses Mendelssohns Frühschriften zur Metaphysik** (Tübingen: J. C. B. Mohr, 1969). *Journal of the History of Philosophy* 10 (July 1972): 363-366.

Review of Jean-Jacques Anstett, ed., *Philosophie der Geschichte*, vol. 9 of *Friedrich Schlegel, Kritische Ausgabe seiner Werke** (Paderborn: Verlag Ferdinand Schöningh, 1971). *Journal of the History of Philosophy* 10 (October 1972): 482-483.

1973

Historical Spectrum of Value Theories, Vol. 2: Anglo-American Group. Lincoln, Neb.: Johnsen Publishing Co., 1973. Pp. [xxiii], 370. (Reviewed by Konstantin Kolenda; see section below on Works about W. H. Werkmeister.)

"Analytic and Synthetic Concepts According to Kant's *LOGIK*." *Southwestern Journal of Philosophy,* 4 (Summer 1973): 25-28. (Review by Gabriele Fritsch; see section below on Works about W. H. Werkmeister.)

Review of Seymour W. Itzkoff, *Ernst Cassirer: Scientific Knowledge and the Concept of Man** (Notre Dame, Ind.: University of Notre Dame Press, 1971). *Journal of the History of Philosophy* 11 (January 1973): 139-142.

Reviews of Franz Gabriel Nauen, *Revolution, Idealism, and Human Freedom** (The Hague: Martinus Nijhoff, 1971) and H. S. Harris, *Hegel's Development* (Oxford: The Clarendon Press, 1972). *Journal of the History of Philosophy* 11 (July 1973): 416-417.

Review of Paul Janssen, *Geschichte und Lebenswelt: Ein Beitrag zur Diskussion von Husserls Spätwerk** (The Hague: Martinus Nijhoff, 1970). *Journal of the History of Philosophy* 11 (July 1973): 427-429.

Reviews of Lewis White Beck, ed., *Proceedings of the Third International Kant Congress** (New York: The Humanities Press, 1972), and Sadik J. Al-Azm, *The Origins of Kant's Arguments in the Antinomies* (Oxford: The Clarendon Press, 1972). *Journal of the History of Philosophy* 11 (October 1973): 561.

Review of Ewald Bucher, Eric F. J. Payne, and Karl O. Kurth, eds., *Von der Aktualität Schopenhauers**, vol. 53 of *Schopenhauer-Jahrbuch für 1972* (Frankfurt Am Main: Verlag Waldemar Kramer, 1972). *Journal of the History of Philosophy*, 11 (October 1973): 562-563.

1974

"The World I Live In." In *Mid-Twentieth Century American Philosophy: Personal Statements*, ed. Peter A. Bertocci. New York: Humanities Press, 1974. Pp. 227-39.

"Explanation, Correlation and Causal Relations." *Journal of Advertising* 3 (1974): 21-22.

Reviews of Quentin Lauer, S.J., *Hegel's Idea of Philosophy** (New York: Fordham University Press, 1971), Malcolm Clark, *Logic and System** (The Hague: Martinus Nijhoff, 1971), Dominique Dubarle and André Doz, *Logique et Dialectique* (Paris: Librarie Larousse, 1972), and Jacques d'Hondt, *De Hegel à Marx** (Paris: Presses Universitaires de France, 1972). *Journal of the History of Philosophy* 12 (January 1974): 125-128.

Review of Peter Fuss and Henry Shapiro, eds. and trans., *Nietzsche: A Self-Portrait from his Letters** Cambridge, Mass.: Harvard University Press, 1971). *Journal of the History of Philosophy* 12 (January 1974): 129.

Review of Max Scheler, *Ressentiment**, trans. William Holdheim, ed. by Lewis A. Coser (New York: Schocken Books, 1972). *Journal of the History of Philosophy* 12 (January 1974): 132.

Reviews of Frederick P. Van De Pitte, *Kant as Philosophical Anthropologist** (The Hague: Martinus Nijhoff, 1971), Hardy E. Jones, *Kant's Principle of Personality** (Madison, Wisc.: The University of Wisconsin Press, 1971), Olivier Reboul, *Kant et le Problème du Mal** (Montréal: Les Presses de L'Université de Montréal, [1971]), Theodore E. Uehling, Jr., *The Notion of Form in Kant's Critique of Aesthetic Judgment** (The Hague: Mouton, 1971), and Otto Schöndörfer, ed., *Immanuel Kant: Briefwechsel** (Hamburg: Felix Meiner, 1972). *Journal of the History of Philosophy* 12 (July 1974): 405-410.

Review of Ingeborg Schüssler, *Die Auseinandersetzung von Idealismus und Realismus in Fichtes Wissenschaftslehre** (Frankfurt am Main: Vittorio Klostermann, 1972). *Journal of the History of Philosophy* 12 (October 1974): 537.

1975

Editor. *Reflections on Kant's Philosophy*. Gainesville, Fla.: University Presses of Florida, 1975. Pp. [ix], 181. (Reviewed by Alexander von Schönborn; see section below on Works about W. H. Werkmeister.)

"Kant's Philosophy and Modern Physics." In *Reflections on Kant's Philosophy*, above, pp. 109-133.

"Kant's Philosophy and Modern Science." *Kant-Studien* 66 (Heft 1) (1975): 35-57. Japanese translation by Yoshio Sezai published in *Seishin-Kagaku* (*Science of Mind*) 16(1979): pp. 79-93.

"Changes in Kant's Metaphysical Conception of Man." *Idealistic Studies* 5 (May 1975): 97-107. (Reviewed by C. Burgher; see section below on Works about W. H. Werkmeister.)

"Kant's Conception of 'The Highest Form of Transcendental Philosophy'." *Southwestern Journal of Philosophy* 6 (Fall 1975): 19-27.

Review of Keith Ward, *The Development of Kant's View of Ethics** (New York: Humanities Press, 1972). *Journal of the History of Philosophy* 13 (January 1975): 113-15.

Review of P. A. E. Hutchings, *Kant [on] Absolute Value** (Detroit: Wayne University Press, 1972). *Journal of the History of Philosophy* 13 (April 1975): 261-262.

Review of Silvestro Marcucci, *Aspetti Epistemologici della Finalità in Kant** (Firenze: Felice Le Monnier, 1972). *Journal of the History of Philosophy* 13 (July 1975): 415-416.

Review of Sergio Givone, *La storia della filosofia secondo Kant** (Milano: U. Mursica & Co., 1972). *Journal of the History of Philosophy* 13 (October 1975): 535-536.

Review of Fritz Joachim von Rintelen, *Values in European Thought* (Pamplona, Spain: Ediciones Universidad de Havarra, 1972). *Journal of the History of Philosophy* 13 (October 1975): 546.

1976

Editor. *Facets of Plato's Philosophy: The Robert D. Miller Memorial Symposium. Phronesis,* Supplementary Volume 2. Assen, Netherlands: Van Gorcum, 1976. Pp. [xii]-102. (Reviewed by John M. Rist, Robert Hahn, Jeffrey Tlumak, Anthony Preus; see section below, Works on W. H. Werkmeister.)

"Reflections on Our Times." In *The Abdication of Philosophy: Philosophy and the Public Good: Essays in Honor of Paul A. Schilpp*, ed. Eugene Freeman. LaSalle, Ill.: Open Court, 1976. Pp. 243-49.

"The Function and Limits of Moral Authority." In *Authority*, ed. R. Baine Harris. University, Ala.: University of Alabama Press, 1976. Pp. 94-100.

1977

"The Critique of Pure Reason and Physics." *Kant-Studien* 68 (Heft 1) (1977): 33-45.

"A Value-Theoretical Approach to Literature." *The Journal of Value Inquiry,* 11 (Summer 1977): 117-25. Reprinted in *A Quarter Century of Value Inquiry: Presidential Addresses of the American Society for Value Inquiry*, ed. Richard T. Hull (Amsterdam and Atlanta: Rodopi, 1994): pp 81-89.

"Kant's Refutation of Idealism." *The Southern Journal of Philosophy,* 15 (Winter 1977): 551-565. (Reviewed by C. Burgher; see section below on Works about W. H. Werkmeister.)

Review of Charles M. Sherover, *Heidegger, Kant, and Time* (Bloomington, Ind.: Indiana University Press, 1971). *Journal of the History of Philosophy* 15 (January 1977): 119-123.

1979

Kant's Silent Decade. Tallahassee, Fla.: Florida State University Press, 1979. Pp. 148. (Reviewed by Eric Sandburg; see section below on Works about W. H. Werkmeister.)

"From Kant to Nietzsche: The Ontology of Martin Heidegger." *The Personalist* 60 (October 1979): 397-401.

"A Philosophical Perspective." *The Southern Journal of Philosophy* 17 (Summer 1979): 263-272.

1980

Kant: The Architectonic and Development of His Philosophy. LaSalle, Ill.: Open Court, 1980. Pp. [viii], 250. (Reviewed by Robert Pippin, Jeffrey Tlumak, Frederick P. Van de Pitte, Darrel E. Christensen, M. Glouberman, Robert R. Williams; see section below on Works about W. H. Werkmeister.)

1981

"The Complementarity of Phenomena and Things in Themselves." *Synthese* 47 (May 1981): 301-311.

"The Critique of Pure Reason in Perspective." In *Akten des 5. Internationalen Kant-Kongresses, Mainz 4.-8. April 1981*, vol. 2, ed. Gerhard Funke (Bonn: Herbert Gundmann, 1981). Pp. 185-199.

"Kant, Nicolai Hartmann, and the Great Chain of Being." In *The Great Chain of Being and Italian Phenomenology*, ed. Angela Ales Bello (Analecta Husserliana, vol. 11) (Dordrecht: Reidel, 1981): pp. 69-97. Reviewed by Manfred Kugelstadt; see section below on Works about W. H. Werkmeister.

1982

"Eine philosophische Perspektive." In *Überlieferung und Aufgabe: Festschrift für Erich Heintel sum 70. Geburstag*, ed. Herta Nagl-Docekal (Vienna: Wilhelm Braumuller, 1982): pp. 23-32.

"What Did Kant Say and What Has He Been Made to Say?" *Kant-Studien* 73 (Heft 2) (1982): 119-129; reprinted in *Interpreting Kant*, ed. Moltke S. Gram (Iowa City: University of Iowa Press, 1982, 133-145).

Review of Gordon G. Brittan, Jr., *Kant's Theory of Science** (Princeton: Princeton University Press, 1978). *Journal of the History of Philosophy* 20 (April 1982): 206-209.

1983

"Gerald Prauss, Kant und das Problem der Dinge an Sich." In *Contemporary German Philosophy*, vol. 2, ed. Darrel E. Christensen, *et al.* (University Park, Penn.: The Pennsylvania State University Press, 1983): pp. 221-234.

Review of Mary-Barbara Zeldin, *Freedom and the Critical Undertaking: Essays on Kant's Later "Critiques"** (Ann Arbor, Mich.: University Microfilms International, 1980). *Journal of the History of Philosophy* 21 (January 1983): 107-109.

1984

"Introduction: Reflections on Hartmann's Value Theory." In *Searchlight on Values: Nicolai Hartman's Twentieth-Century Value Platonism*, by Eva Hauel Cadwallader (Lanham, Md.: University Press of America, 1984). Pp. xi-xxv.

1987

Letter, in "Pages from the History of The Association," *Proceedings and Addresses of The American Philosophical Association* 60 (January 1987): 500-501.

Review of Ernst Cassirer, *Symbol, Technik, Sprache,** ed by John Michael Krois and Ernst Wolfgang Orth. Vol. 372 of Philosophische Bibliothek (Hamburg: Felix Meiner Verlag, 1985). *Philosophy and Rhetoric* 20 (1987): 205-207.

1989

Review of John Michael Krois, *Cassirer: Symbolic Forms and History** (New Haven: Yale University Press, 1987). *Journal of the History of Philosophy* 27 (July 1989): 493-494.

1990

Nicolai Hartman's New Ontology. Tallahassee, Fla.: Florida State University Press, 1990. Pp.[xvii], 252.

1993

"The Two Theses of Kant's Opus Postumum." In *Kant and Critique: New Essays in Honor of W. H. Werkmeister*, Synthese Library, no. 227, ed. Russell M. Dancy (Dordrecht and Boston: Kluwer Academic Publishers, 1993), pp. 169-187.

[Werkmeister passed away on 24 November 1993 in Tallahassee, Florida.]

Posthumous Publications

1994

"Autobiographical Sketch." In *A Quarter Century of Value Inquiry: Presidential Addresses of the American Society for Value Inquiry*, ed. Richard T. Hull (Amsterdam and Atlanta, Ga.: Rodopi, 1994), 78-80 (with photo).

1996

Martin Heidegger on the Way, ed. Richard T. Hull. Amsterdam and Atlanta, Ga.: Rodopi, 1995. Pp. xlvii + 193 (index). [Ed. note: Contains a complete Bibliography of W. H. Werkmeister's published philosophical works to date.]

"Nicolai Hartmann's View of the Comic," ed. by Richard T. Hull, *Journal of Value Inquiry* 30 (1996).

Bibliography of Works about

W. H. Werkmeister

Compiled by Richard T. Hull and Gwen A. Burda

J[ustus] B[uchler]. Review of W. H. Werkmeister, *A Philosophy of Science. The Journal of Philosophy* 372 (24 October 1940), 614-615. See Bibliography of Works by W. H. Werkmeister, 1940.

Paul Henle. Review of W. H. Werkmeister, *A Philosophy of Science. Ethics* 52 (January 1941). 239-240. See Bibliography of Works by W. H. Werkmeister, 1940.

Ralph S. Lillie. "Philosophy of Organism: A Rejoinder to Professor Werkmeister." *Philosophy and Phenomenological Research* 8 (June 1948), 706-711. See Bibliography of Works by W. H. Werkmeister, 1947.

A. R. Turquette. Review of W. H. Werkmeister, *The Basis and Structure of Knowledge. Ethics* 59 (October 1948), 72-73. See Bibliography of Works by W. H. Werkmeister, 1948.

Ernest Nagel. Review of W. H. Werkmeister, *The Basis and Structure of Knowledge. The Journal of Philosophy* 452) (21 October 1948), 605-607. See Bibliography of Works by W. H. Werkmeister, 1948.

T. V. Smith. Review of W. H. Werkmeister, *A History of Philosophical Ideas in America. Ethics* 60 (January 1950), 153. See Bibliography of Works by W. H. Werkmeister, 1949.

Rubin Gotesky. Review of W. H. Werkmeister, *A History of Philosophic Ideas in America. The Annals of the American Academy of Political and Social Science* 267 (January 1950), 248-249. See Bibliography of Works by W. H. Werkmeister, 1949.

Aubury Castell. "Philosophy." In *The New International Year Book for 1949*, ed. by Henry E. Vizetelly. New York: Funk & Wagnalls, 1950. Pp. 424-426.

Phillip Frank. Review of W. H. Werkmeister, *The Basis and Structure of Knowledge. Isis* 42 (Part 1, no. 127) (April 1951), 68-9. See Bibliography of Works by W. H. Werkmeister, 1948.

Geroge P. Conger. "Comments on a Review by Werkmeister." *Philosophy of Science* 20 (July 1953): 226. See Bibliography of Works by W. H. Werkmeister, 1952.

Stephen C. Pepper. Review article on W. H. Werkmeister, *Man and his Values. The Journal of Value Inquiry* 3 (Summer 1969), 147-150. See Bibliography of Works by W. H. Werkmeister, 1967.

Yoshio Sezai. "On Dr. W. H. Werkmeister's Theory of Value." *Seishin-Kagaku* (*Science of Mind*) 8 (1971), 94-106. (Japanese text.)

Darrel E. Christensen. "Preface. The Wofford Symposium: Its Purpose, Genesis, and Theme." In *Hegel and the Philosophy of Religion*, The Wofford Symposium, ed. by Darrel E. Christensen (The Hague: Martinus Nijhoff, 1970), vii-xiii.

Murray Greene. "Comment on W. H. Werkmeister, Hegel's Phenomenology as a Development of Kant's Basic Ontology." In *Hegel and the Philosophy of Religion*, The Wofford Symposium, ed. by Darrel E. Christensen (The Hague, Netherlands: Martinus Nijhoff, 1970), 111-115. See Bibliography of Works by W. H. Werkmeister, 1970.

George Schrader. "Comment on W. H. Werkmeister, Hegel's Phenomenology of Mind as a Reflection of Kant's Basic Ontology." In *Hegel and the Philosophy of Religion*, The Wofford Symposium, ed. by Darrel E. Christensen (The Hague, Netherlands: Martinus Nijhoff, 1970), 116-120. See Bibliography of Works by W. H. Werkmeister, 1970.

Alfred Stern. Review of W. H. Werkmeister, *Historical Spectrum of Value Theories*, vol. 1. *International Journal for Philosophy of Religion* 3 (Spring 1972), 51-54. See Bibliography of Works by W. H. Werkmeister, 1970.

Stephen C. Pepper. Review of W. H. Werkmeister, *Historical Spectrum of Value Theories*, vol. 1. *Journal of the History of Philosophy* 10 (April 1972), 237-239. See Bibliography of Works by W. H. Werkmeister, 1970.

Dallas Willard. Review of W. H. Werkmeister, *Historical Spectrum of Value Theories*, vol. 1. *The Personalist* 53 (Autumn 1972), 454-456. See Bibliography of Works by W. H. Werkmeister, 1970.

Konstantin Kolenda. Review of W. H. Werkmeister, *Historical Spectrum of Value Theories*, vol. 1. *Southwestern Journal of Philosophy* 3 (Fall 1972), 150-154. See Bibliography of Works by W. H. Werkmeister, 1970.

Alex C. Michalos. Review of W. H. Werkmeister, *Historical Spectrum of Value Theories*, vol. 1. *Theory and Decision* 3 (June 1973), 388-389. See Bibliography of Works by W. H. Werkmeister, 1970.

A[ntonio] S. C[ua]. Review of W. H. Werkmeister, *Historical Spectrum of Value Theories*, vols. 1 and 2. *The Review of Metaphysics* 27 (June 1974), 819-820. See Bibliography of Works by W. H. Werkmeister, 1970 and 1973.

George J. Stack. Review of W. H. Werkmeister, *Historical Spectrum of Value Theories*, vol. 1. *The Journal of Value Inquiry* 8 (Winter 1974), 317-319. See Bibliography of Works by W. H. Werkmeister, 1970.

Konstantin Kolenda. Review of W. H. Werkmeister, *Historical Spectrum of Value Theories*, Vol. 2. *Southwestern Journal of Philosophy* 6 (Winter 1975), 169-171. See Bibliography of Works by W. H. Werkmeister, 1973.

G[abriele] F[ritsch]. Review of W. H. Werkmeister, "Analysis [sic] and Synthetic Concepts According to Kant's Logik [sic]." *Kant-Studien* 67 (Heft 2) (1976), 276. See Bibliography of Works by W. H. Werkmeister, 1973.

Alfred Stern. Problemas Filosoficos de la Ciencia. (Universidad de Puerto Rico: editorial universitaria, 1976), 51, 89-90. References to "Kant's Philosophy and Modern Physics," *Philosophy of Science*, and "An Epistemological Basis for Quantum Physics," all by Werkmeister (see Bibliography of Works by W. H. Werkmeister, 1975, 1940, 1950, resp.)

Alexander von Schönborn. Review of W. H. Werkmeister, ed., *Reflections on Kant's Philosophy. Southwestern Journal of Philosophy* 8 (Winter 1977), 171-173. See Bibliography of Works by W. H. Werkmeister, 1975.

John M. Rist. Review of W. H. Werkmeister, ed., *Facets of Plato's Philosophy. The Classical World* 71 (March 1978), 397-398. See Bibliography of Works by W. H. Werkmeister, 1976.

C. B[urgher]. Review of W. H. Werkmeister, "Changes in Kant's Metaphysical Conception of Man." *Kant-Studien* 70 (Heft 1) (1979), 110. See Bibliography of Works by W. H. Werkmeister, 1975.

Robert Hahn. Review of W. H. Werkmeister, ed., *Facets of Plato's Philosophy. Journal of the History of Philosophy* 19 (April 1981), 242-245. See Bibliography of Works by W. H. Werkmeister, 1976.

Editorial Committee, Department of Philosophy, Florida State University, E. F. Kaelin, chairman, eds., *Man and Value: Essays in Honor of William H. Werkmeister* (Tallahassee, Fla.: University Presses of Florida, 1981).

E. F. Kaelin. "Preface." *Ibid*, vii-ix.

Wayne McEvilly. "The Teacher Remembered." *Ibid.*, 3.

Charles H. Patterson. "Scholar, Administrator, Colleague and Friend." *Ibid.*, 4-10.

E. F. Kaelin. "The Enduring Person." *Ibid.*, 11-21.

R[obert] B. P[ippin]. Review of W. H. Werkmeister, *Kant. The Architectonic and Development of His Philosophy. The Review of Metaphysics* 34 (June 1981), 813-814. See Bibliography of Works by W. H. Werkmeister, 1980.

D[onald] J. Z[eyl]. Review of W. H. Werkmeister, ed., *Facets of Plato's Philosophy. The Review of Metaphysics* 35 (December 1981), 417-419. See Bibliography of Works by W. H. Werkmeister, 1976.

Jeffrey Tlumak. Review of W. H. Werkmeister, *Kant: The Architectonic and Development of His Philosophy*, and J. N. Findlay, *Kant and the Transcendental Object —A Hermeneutic Study. Teaching Philosophy* 5 (July 1982), 251-254. See Bibliography of Works by W. H. Werkmeister, 1980.

Frederick P. Van de Pitte. Review of William H. Werkmeister, *Kant: The Architectonic and Development of His Philosophy. International Studies in Philosophy* 15 (1983), 121-123. See Bibliography of Works by W. H. Werkmeister, 1980.

Anthony Preus. Review of W. H. Werkmeister, ed., *Facets of Plato's Philosophy. International Studies in Philosophy* 15 (1983), 123-124. See Bibliography of Works by W. H. Werkmeister, 1976.

C. B[urgher]. Review of W. H. Werkmeister, "Kant's Refutation of Idealism." *Kant-Studien* 74 (Heft 2) (1983), 258. See Bibliography of Works by W. H. Werkmeister, 1977.

Eric C. Sandberg. Review of W. H. Werkmeister, *Kant's Silent Decade. Kant-Studien* 77 (Heft 2) (1986), 252-253. See Bibliography of Works by W. H. Werkmeister, 1979.

Darrel E. Christensen. "Kant and Hegel," review article of works on Kant and Hegel including W. H. Werkmeister, *Kant: The Architectonic and Development of His Philosophy. The Review of Metaphysics* 40 (December 1986), 339-363. See Bibliography of Works by W. H. Werkmeister, 1980.

Yoshio Sezai. "The Enduring Person—Dr. W. H. Werkmeister." *Seishin Kagaku (The Science of Mind)* 23 (1986),

M. Glouberman. Review of Lewis White Beck, *Essays on Kant and Hume*; W. H. Werkmeister, *Kant: The Architectonic and Development of His Philosophy*, and Robert B. Pippin, *Kant's Theory of Form. Philosophia* 17 (January 1987), 87-95. See Bibliography of Works by W. H. Werkmeister, 1980.

M[anfred] K[ugelstadt]. Review (in German) of W. H. Werkmeister, "Kant, Nicolai Hartmann, and the Great Chain of Being." *Kant-Studien* 78 (Heft 1) (1987), 130. See Bibliography of Works by W. H. Werkmeister, 1981.

Robert R. Williams. Review of W. H. Werkmeister, *Kant: The Architectonic and Development of His Philosophy. Religious Studies Review* 13 (July 1987), 235. See Bibliography of Works by W. H. Werkmeister, 1980.

R. M. Dancy, ed. *Kant and Critique: New Essays in Honor of William Henry Werkmeister* (Synthese Library, vol. 223). Amsterdam, The Netherlands: Kluwer, 1993.

E. F. Kaelin. "Guest Foreword" in Richard T. Hull, ed., William H. Werkmeister, *Martin Heidegger on the Way.* Amsterdam and Atlanta: Rodopi, 1995: pp. xv-xxviii.

Other Articles and Notices

"German Day Fete Viewed by 4,000," Omaha World-Herald (16 September 1929). "It was voted at this (business) session (of the third annual convention and festival of the Nebraska Federation of German-American Societies) that the federation will finance the publication of a history of the Germans in Nebraska that has been compiled by Dr. W. H. Werkmeister, of the foreign languages department at Nebraska university."

"No Surprise Expressed at N. U. on Nazi Move," *Omaha Sunday World-Herald* (7 March 1936).

"Uni Professor to Visit Berlin," *Omaha World-Herald* (25 April 1936).

"Nebraska Instructor Sees Sudenten Autonomy—and War," Omaha World-Herald (16 September 1938).

"Prof. Werkmeister marries Student," *Omaha World-Herald* (14 August 1940).

"Harper to Publish Book by U. N. Prof," *Omaha World-Herald* (10 July 1943).

Article in the Nebraska University *Bulletin Board* (24 November 1947), reporting on Werkmeister attending a meeting of philosophers of the Mountain and Plains Area to organize a division of The American Philosophical Association to be known "probably as the Mountain-Plains Division. Dr. Werkmeister read a paper entitled 'The Status—Past, Present, and Future—of Philosophy at the University of Nebraska.' He also served as chairman of the organization meeting."

"Werkmeister Book 'Major Contribution.'" [Review of *A History of Philosophical Ideas in America*.] Lincoln Sunday *Journal and Star*, 18 June 1950. Article reporting that the New International Year Book, 1950 edition, has said in part: "A growing number of books are being written in the U.S. on one phase or another of philosophical thought. The most learned and ambitious of these volumes for 1949 is W. H. Werkmeister's 'History of Philosophical Ideas in America.' For the period since the Civil War, Werkmeister's book provides a detailed and technical account. And it has the distinction of doing more than any other book to make intelligible the career of metaphysical idealism in this country."

"National Philosophy Honors to U of N's Dr. Werkmeister," *Omaha World-Herald* (18 July 1950).

"Werkmeister Gets Post at Southern Cal," *Omaha World-Herald* (14 April 1953).

"To a Larger Field," *Lincoln Daily Star*(?) (? 1953). "Dr. Werkmeister . . . is a kindly man, quiet and inclined to be reserved, but in the field of study to which he has devoted his life his enthusiasm for the gifted mind never fails to find response in the ranks of the serious-minded student. His departure is a loss to the faculty."

"History and Human Destiny," *The Aryan Path* 28 (August 1957), 344. Article on Werkmeister's paper by the same title. See Bibliography of Works by W. H. Werkmeister, 1957.

"Queen Frederick in Southern California," *University of Southern California Mirror News* (24 November 1958). Article reporting a long conversation between Werkmeister and Queen Frederika of Sweden.

Article on Fourth East-West Conference, *Honolulu Advertiser* (1 August 1964). Photo.

Ann Salisbury, "Professor of Philosophy Honored by Students," *Nebraska Trojan* (16 February 1966). The graduate students in the Graduate School of Philosophy, reacting to an article in *Time*, which accused "modern-day philosophers of 'philosophizing about philosophy rather than life, and of having bitterly segregated philosophy departments,'" wrote a letter of protest, maintaining that the "accusations" do not hold true for the USC Philosophy Department. The letter was signed by all the students and submitted to Werkmeister in person. The letter reads, "The recent *Time* essay has once again reminded us of our indebtedness to you. Accordingly, we graduate students would like to express thanks for your unique contribution to philosophy at USC and to philosophy at large. Most of us came to USC to do philosophy with you, attracted not only by your personal achievements, but also by the character of the School you have shaped. The *Time* essay describes philosophy as having forgotten the important questions which once guided its quest. This certainly does not describe philosophy at our school, where the whole range of thought is covered by a faculty of varied and complementary interests." The article goes on to say that one of Werkmeister's goals was to build a school which "could survive in competition with UCLA." It then quotes Werkmeister: "Six years ago we had only three philosophy graduate students. Now we have 40. There has not only been an increase in number, but we now have three Woodrow Wilson Fellows, two Danforth Fellows, and one student doing post-doctoral work." The article concludes: "Graduate students attribute the success of the department to 'Dr. Werkmeister's immense store of knowledge, his ability to penetrate deeply into the subject at hand, and his concern for the well-being of the student.'"

"Philosophy With a Smile: Dr. William Werkmeister," *St. Petersburg Times* (21 June 1972). Article on Werkmeister on the occasion of his official retirement, reporting on an extended interview with him. He talks of retirement as being only "an extended sabbatical for research purposes." He has "one dominant philosophical trait—a calculated [re]servation against pessimism." Only history "will reveal whether our current value changes are good or bad." There are, he admits, "definite parallels with American society and the crumbling decadence of ancient Rome." But there are also encouraging signs, the interest of young people in values. "I was born with rose-colored glasses and I still wear them" he concludes; "I have hope." Well, he adds, "I think after my writing slows down I may get a horse. I have always wanted a horse. It's very relaxing to me just to ride a horse."

"William H. Werkmeister: Right-Sized Philosopher," *FSU Bulletin of Research in Review* 2 (May 1977). Reprinted in Nebraska Alumna 74 (May/June 1978).

Milton Rockmore, "Perfection: Sounds Good, but Can It Hurt?" *Chicago Tribune* (12 November 1977), Sec 1, p. 12. Quotation from Werkmeister: "In mathematics and the technological industries, perfection is essential. However, in human contact, tolerance enables us to live with perfection. While we should set high standards, we should refrain from dogmatically insisting on implementation. Experience teaches us to forgive ourselves, like we must others, for not always living up to the ultimate. Imposed perfection is fanaticism and all fanaticism is detrimental, whether it is a father forcing it on a Little-Leaguer or an institution on its employees. We're told our societal standards are less "perfect" today than they used to be. We're in a transition period of tremendous proportions. The world has been through this before and historically these ethical declines result in an upswing along the way."

"FSU Confers Honorary Degree on Dr. William Werkmeister," *FSU Faculty/Staff Bulletin*, 117 (17-24 April 1978), 1.

Obituary, "William Henry Werkmeister," *Tallahassee Democrat*, (25 November 1993).

About the Author

William Henry Werkmeister was born on 10 August 1901 in Asendorf, Germany. He emigrated to the United States in April 1924, enrolling the following autumn at the University of Nebraska for graduate studies. He stayed on there after completing his doctoral dissertation in 1927, rising eventually to the rank of Professor.

Werkmeister is author of thirteen books (counting this posthumously published one), editor of five others, has published 75 articles and chapters and over 450 book reviews in a career that spanned nearly 70 years, and has been honored twice with *Festschriften*. He has served as editor of *The Personalist*. He was a founder of the Mountain-Plains Philosophical Association, chaired the Department of Philosophy at the University of Nebraska and directed the School of Philosophy at the University of Southern California. He served as President of the Pacific Division of The American Philosophical Association in 1963-1964, and as President of the American Society for Value Inquiry in 1974-1975.

Werkmeister spent the last 28 years of his professional life at the University of Florida at Tallahassee. He passed away on 24 November 1993, and is survived by his wife, Dr. Lucyle Thomas Werkmeister, and a son and daughter. Acting on a plan they conceived together, Lucyle T. Werkmeister has created the William H. and Lucyle T. Werkmeister Eminent Scholar Chair in Philosophy at Florida State University, to be endowed from her estate and occupied by prominent visiting scholars devoted to value inquiry. His personal library, and copies of all his published works, have been donated to the Florida State University, and the bibliography of his work contained in this volume offers something of a guide to its vast range. A part of his service to Florida State University was to replicate in their collection the library used by Immanuel Kant.

Werkmeister served American Philosophy by helping foster interest in such prominent German philosophers as Immanuel Kant, Nicolai Hartmann, and now Martin Heidegger. He also has been a major figure in axiology, and has chronicled the impact of German Idealism on nineteenth and early twentieth-century American Philosophy. His texts in Critical Thinking and Philosophy of Science helped educate a generation of American Philosophers.

Werkmeister was known for his inspirational teaching and nurturing of young philosophers. Eva Hauel Cadwallader, author of *Searchlight on Values: Nicolai Hartmann's Twentieth-Century Value Platonism*, illustrates this affirming character: in a letter to the editor of this volume, she writes, "Werky's encouragement was close to life-sustaining at this crucial point in my career. His comments were so valuable for restructuring the dissertation into a book that readers of the book manuscript usually did not realize it had ever been a dissertation. Werky continued after this to help me professionally in various ways for about twenty years . . . . The words 'a gentleman and a scholar' still come to mind whenever I remember him." It was Werkmeister who recruited Cadwallader to the Presidency of the American Society for Value Inquiry.

An autobiographical sketch by Werkmeister is included in *A Quarter Century of Value Inquiry*, published in 1994 by Rodopi as a volume in Value Inquiry Book Series.

About the Editor

Richard Thompson Hull has taught philosophy at the State University of New York at Buffalo since 1967. His primary and secondary education was completed in the Oklahoma City public schools. His undergraduate work commenced at Park College, Parkville, Missouri, and was completed at Austin College, Sherman, Texas, where he met and married Elaine Mangelsdorf Hull, of Houston, Texas, who is now Professor and Area Head of Behavioral Neuroscience in the Psychology Department, also at State University of New York at Buffalo. He received the PhD in 1971 from the Department of Philosophy at Indiana University, Bloomington, Indiana, with a dissertation on *The Role of the Principle of Acquaintance in Contemporary Disputes over the Relation of Mental, Perceptual, and Physical*, directed by Milton T. Fisk.

A long dormant interest in medicine was rekindled when he was asked to develop a course in Social and Ethical Values in Medicine, and much of his published work since the late 1970s has been on topics in the philosophy of medicine and the health care professions. He served as President of the American Society for Value Inquiry in 1979-80. In 1990 he published *Ethical Issues in the New Reproductive Technologies* with Wadsworth Publishing Company. In 1994 his first book in Value Inquiry Book Series (VIBS), *A Quarter Century of Value Inquiry: Presidential Addresses of the American Society for Value Inquiry*, was published by Rodopi. He is now editor of two special series in VIBS: Histories and Addresses of Philosophical Societies (HAPS) and Werkmeister Studies (WS).

In 1994 he received the SUNY Chancellor's Award for Excellence in Teaching, in recognition of exemplary teaching and significant contribution to institutional quality in instruction. In 1995 he was promoted to Professor.

During a trip to Tallahassee, Florida, on business for VIBS in early 1994, Hull was entrusted with casting into living textual form a set of notes left by his late colleague in value inquiry, William H. Werkmeister. Since Hull was already an editor of VIBS and greatly appreciated Werkmeister's scholarship, he accepted the commission.

An autobiographical sketch by Hull is included in *A Quarter Century of Value Inquiry* volume published in 1994 by Rodopi.

INDEX

Compiled by Richard T. Hull

VIBS

The **Value Inquiry Book Series** is co-sponsored by:

American Society for Value Inquiry
Association for Personalist Studies
Association for Process Philosophy of Education
Center for East European Dialogue and Development,
Rochester Institute of Technology
Centre for Cultural Research, Aarhus University
College of Education and Allied Professions,
Bowling Green State University
Concerned Philosophers for Peace
Conference of Philosophical Societies
Conference on Value Inquiry
International Academy of Philosophy of the Principality of Liechtenstein
International Society for Universalism
International Society for Value Inquiry
Natural Law Society
Philosophical Society of Finland
Philosophy Seminar, University of Mainz
R.S. Hartman Institute for Formal and Applied Axiology
Society for Iberian and Latin-American Thought
Society for the Philosophic Study of Genocide and the Holocaust.

Titles Published

1. Noel Balzer, **The Human Being as a Logical Thinker.**

2. Archie J. Bahm, **Axiology: The Science of Values.**

3. H. P. P. (Hennie) Lötter, **Justice for an Unjust Society.**

4. H. G. Callaway, **Context for Meaning and Analysis: A Critical Study in the Philosophy of Language.**

5. Benjamin S. Llamzon, **A Humane Case for Moral Intuition.**

6. James R. Watson, **Between Auschwitz and Tradition: Postmodern Reflections on the Task of Thinking.** A volume in **Holocaust and Genocide Studies.**

7. Robert S. Hartman, **Freedom to Live: The Robert Hartman Story,** edited by Arthur R. Ellis. A volume in **Hartman Institute Axiology Studies.**

8. Archie J. Bahm, **Ethics: The Science of Oughtness.**

9. George David Miller, **An Idiosyncratic Ethics; Or, the Lauramachean Ethics.**

10. Joseph P. DeMarco, **A Coherence Theory in Ethics.**

11. Frank G. Forrest, **Valuemetrics: The Science of Personal and Professional Ethics.** A volume in **Hartman Institute Axiology Studies.**

12. William Gerber, **The Meaning of Life: Insights of the World's Great Thinkers.**

13. Richard T. Hull, Editor, **A Quarter Century of Value Inquiry: Presidential Addresses of the American Society for Value Inquiry.** A volume in **Histories and Addresses of Philosophical Societies.**

14. William Gerber, **Nuggets of Wisdom from Great Jewish Thinkers: From Biblical Times to the Present.**

15. Sidney Axinn, **The Logic of Hope: Extensions of Kant's View of Religion.**

16. Messay Kebede, **Meaning and Development.**

17. Amihud Gilead, **The Platonic Odyssey: A Philosophical-Literary Inquiry into the *Phaedo*.**

18. Necip Fikri Alican, **Mill's Principle of Utility: A Defense of John Stuart Mill's Notorious Proof.** A volume in **Universal Justice.**

19. Michael H. Mitias, Editor, **Philosophy and Architecture.**

20. Roger T. Simonds, **Rational Individualism: The Perennial Philosophy of Legal Interpretation.** A volume in **Natural Law Studies.**

21. William Pencak, **The Conflict of Law and Justice in the Icelandic Sagas.**

22. Samuel M. Natale and Brian M. Rothschild, Editors, **Values, Work, Education: The Meanings of Work.**

23. N. Georgopoulos and Michael Heim, Editors, **Being Human in the Ultimate: Studies in the Thought of John M. Anderson.**

24. Robert Wesson and Patricia A. Williams, Editors, **Evolution and Human Values.**

25. Wim J. van der Steen, **Facts, Values, and Methodology: A New Approach to Ethics.**

26. Avi Sagi and Daniel Statman, **Religion and Morality.**

27. Albert William Levi, **The High Road of Humanity: The Seven Ethical Ages of Western Man**, edited by Donald Phillip Verene and Molly Black Verene.

28. Samuel M. Natale and Brian M. Rothschild, Editors, **Work Values: Education, Organization, and Religious Concerns.**

29. Laurence F. Bove and Laura Duhan Kaplan, Editors, **From the Eye of the Storm: Regional Conflicts and the Philosophy of Peace.** A volume in **Philosophy of Peace.**

30. Robin Attfield, **Value, Obligation, and Meta-Ethics.**

31. William Gerber, **The Deepest Questions You Can Ask About God: As Answered by the World's Great Thinkers.**

32. Daniel Statman, **Moral Dilemmas.**

33. Rem B. Edwards, Editor, **Formal Axiology and Its Critics.** A volume in **Hartman Institute Axiology Studies.**

34. George David Miller and Conrad P. Pritscher, **On Education and Values: In Praise of Pariahs and Nomads.** A volume in **Philosophy of Education.**

35. Paul S. Penner, **Altruistic Behavior: An Inquiry into Motivation.**

36. Corbin Fowler, **Morality for Moderns.**

37. Giambattista Vico, **The Art of Rhetoric** (*Institutiones Oratoriae,* 1711-1741), from the definitive Latin text and notes, Italian commentary and introduction by Giuliano Crifò, translated and edited by Giorgio A. Pinton and Arthur W. Shippee. A volume in **Values in Italian Philosophy.**

38. W. H. Werkmeister, **Martin Heidegger on the Way,** edited by Richard T. Hull. A volume in **Werkmeister Studies.**